Health and the Sociology of Emotions

Sociology of Health and Illness Monograph Series

Edited by Jonathan Gabe
Department of Social Policy and Social Sciences
Royal Holloway
University of London

Current and forthcoming titles:

Medicine, Health and Risk
Edited by Jonathan Gabe

Heath and the Sociology of Emotions
Edited by Veronica James and Jonathan Gabe

The Sociology of Medical Science
Edited by Mary Ann Elston

The Sociology of Health Inequalities
Edited by Mel Bartley, David Blane and George Davey Smith

Health and the Sociology of Emotions

Edited by Veronica James and Jonathan Gabe

Blackwell Publishers/Editorial Board

Copyright © Blackwell Publishers Ltd/Editorial Board 1996

ISBN 0-631-20351-6

First published in 1996

Blackwell Publishers Ltd
108 Cowley Road, Oxford OX4 1JF, UK
and
238 Main Street,
Cambridge, MA 02142, USA

British Library Cataloguing in Publication Data

A CIP catalogue record for this book is available from the British Library

Library of Congress Cataloging-in-Publication Data

applied for

Printed in Great Britain by Page Bros, Norwich, Norfolk.
This book is printed on acid-free paper.

Acknowledgements

We would like to thank all those involved in supporting the production of this monograph at its various stages. Our partners, Rob Watling and Liz Gabe have given crucial background support. In addition we would like to thank Marie Hayes for her willing secretarial support throughout and Sarah Smith for stepping in when necessary. Anthea Holme worked swiftly and incisively as a copy-editor for which we are most grateful. We also appreciate the support of the staff at Blackwell's who have been responsive and helpful and Mike Bury for commenting on the introduction. The production of a monograph such as this depends on the expertise and scholarship of the anonymous referees who read and commented on chapters on two or three occasions. We are greatly indebted to them for the assistance they gave to the contributors and ourselves.

Contents

Contents

Connecting Emotions and Health

Veronica James and Jonathan Gabe

Introduction

E.M. Forster's (1956) phrase 'only connect' is the basis for the title of this introduction.[1] It is an invitation to consider the benefits of linking the sociological sub fields of emotions and health. Such benefits are not taken for granted, however, and we intend to use this introductory chapter to assess the merits of making such connections. In this way we hope to address the concerns of critical colleagues who continue to ask 'so what?' both about the sociology of emotions and connections between health, illness and emotions.

The advantages of linking the sociologies of emotions and health have already been recognised. Freund, for example, has argued that the person, body and society are combined through somatic, cultural and social relational connections – a combination that seems relevant to issues of health and illness. He also notes that, by their very nature, notions of embodiment make what counts as 'empirical precision' necessarily problematic (personal communication, 1996). Similarly, David Franks has claimed that 'the real contribution of sociology to the question "what emotions are" is in detailing how the intersubjective, hypothetical symbolic process enters into them *but only* as enablers' (1991: 21, his emphasis).

As we explore the possibilities and the limits of these connections we are aware that this involves identifying the methodological consequences of theoretical claims. In particular, we question the implications for the sociology of emotions as it becomes associated with the more established field of health and illness. In this way, connecting the sociology of emotions with health and illness may be a way of obtaining novel insights from new and re-examined data. Ontological questions about whether there are 'realities' in emotions and in health and illness could lead to a breadth of theoretical, methodological and empirical perspectives redolent of those elsewhere in sociology. Common-sense connections that might feel like a 'reality' are easy to make, but subjecting them to academic scrutiny is a different matter. Just to take one personal example, one of the editors made a connection between emotions and health at the end of a day's work in a hospice. She was absolutely exhausted, but the question arose as to why, when the bulk of the time had been spent talking to people, albeit people who were dying and their attentive and, later that day, bereaved relatives (James 1984)? Hardly a physically demanding task, so where did the physical effects come from and how was it that, despite the excruciating experiences of life and death, there was a sense of order? These sorts of personal and social observations are real enough, but there is a need to understand what makes them so and to identify the academic tools which could be used to ask appropriate questions and gather appropriate data.

The introduction falls into three sections, each of which traces connections between sociology, health and emotions. In the first the development, potential and constraints of this relatively new sub-discipline are discussed. In the second section some of the moral and ethical concerns that have been expressed are rehearsed and linked to debates about relevance, at a time of growing international polarity in morbidity, mortality and health funding. In the final section the structure of the book is outlined, together with the questions which contributors to this volume were asked to address, and the authors' contributions are summarized.

Development, potential and constraints

Health and the sociology of emotions bring together three sets of interests each of which is associated with diverse histories – sociology, medical sociology and emotions. Part of the energy of new sub-disciplines is the fresh constellation of diverse approaches which have the potential to address questions from all of them, as well as generating new ones. Sociology's status varies in different sub-disciplines and in different countries. As a result the academic study of emotions, joined with health and illness, is likely to enjoy a range of approaches depending on the component elements and how they are accepted within sociological communities. In this first section, we consider the development of the sociology of emotions, and the sociology of health and illness and consider opportunities for their joint development.

Sociology of emotions

At the 1989 inaugural meeting of the *British Sociological Association*'s (*BSA*) Sociology of Emotions Interest Group, in Birmingham, England, developments in the sociology of emotions from North America hardly registered. However, there was a vehement debate over whether a sociology of emotions would necessarily transgress and thereby exploit feelings. A plea that studies of emotions should allow the emotions to remain 'real' and unaltered was contrasted with a view that the academic process manipulates, reifies, predicts and distorts. Passion was both part of the subject matter and an outcome of this subject matter.

There remain wide differences in how the sociology of emotions is perceived. Oakley, writing from Britain in 1990, claimed a 'lack of any sociology of feeling and emotions', noting that 'because mainstream knowledge considers them unimportant (it) has consequently developed no methodology for studying them' (1990:216). Meanwhile, in the same year in the United States, Kemper's (1990) *Research Agendas in the Sociology of Emotions* traced the start of the sociology of emotions in that country back fifteen years to the 'watershed year' of 1975. In that year Hochschild published an article on emotions in a feminist journal, Scheff organised the first session on emotions at the American Sociological Association, and Collins theorised a central place for emotions in his book *Conflict Sociology*. The gap between Oakley and Kemper tells something of the continental differences, but intriguingly, in 1992, Wouters, writing from Holland, claimed that there are so many approaches and agendas that the 'attempt at "bringing emotions back in" seems to stumble over its very success' (1992:248). These contradictory comments imply that views on the sociology of emotions range from a shadow of no substance, suggesting its lack of penetration into mainstream sociology agendas, to an established means of addressing basic human concerns. The statements also imply differences in the cultural capital of the countries concerned and the sociological communities within them. Despite these differences we can offer three examples which illustrate how the study of emotions can be connected with mainstream sociology and how it is developing.

The *first* example shows the ways in which the study of emotions draws on humanities as well as sciences. Since emotions have been the subject of scrutiny for thousands of years, it is worth reflecting on how we have learned about them. It is likely that academic treatises have played a lesser part than lay experience, combined with the sense and symbolism explored in great and popular works of literature, art and music from Shakespeare to Goya to the Beatles. As we look at the incorporation of emotions into sociology we can rethink what Dilthey drew on in his version of human studies. In his view social science could adapt the humanities' goal of evoking the general and use it together with science's aspiration to provide systematic studies of the particular. Through this combination, in human studies, we may elicit factual as well as symbolic truth. The point Dilthey was making was that human studies are concerned both with individuals and with cultural and social systems (Hammersley 1992:17). It is interesting, then, to see Scheff – one of those who contributed to the 1975 'watershed' in the United States – writing with Mahlendorf, a specialist in German Studies (Scheff and Mahlendorf 1988), and examining the particulars of emotions through Goethe's novel *Werther*. Scheff and Mahlendorf claim that what is so often missing from verbatim records of emotions is the 'inner experience', *pace* Craib (1995), where even psychoanalytic sessions only tap a small part of such emotions. In order to obtain more comprehensive data Scheff and Mahlendorf draw on art and artists. They analyse an incident from *Werther* and suggest how testable propositions about the development of false consciousness can be created. The success of their enterprise is mixed but we mention it here to suggest that there is much in our emotional worlds which may need to be accessed by more imaginative methods and sources along with traditional social science methods.

The question of the subjectivity-objectivity dualism offers a *second* example. It is an interest shared by those involved in science as well as social science inquiry. Code (1993) uses a feminist analysis to argue that epistemology, in its traditional sense, depends on defining 'normal' in such a way as to exclude most people. She states:

> Ideals of rationality and objectivity . . . have been constructed through processes of excluding the attributes and experiences commonly associated with femaleness and underclass social status: emotion, connection, practicality, sensitivity, and idiosyncracy (1993:21)

She continues:

> . . . it is deceptive and dangerous to ignore questions about subjectivity in the name of objectivity and value-neutrality' (1993:27).

Together with other feminists (Harding 1991, Alcoff and Potter 1993), Code addresses epistemological bias and attempts to develop ways of working actively with subjectivities while grounding them in empirical knowledge. This issue of subjectivity is central to an understanding of emotions which attempts to move beyond a crude duality with objectivity.

Heller (1990), coming from a more literary and historical sociology perspective, attempts to establish whether we are 'living in a world of emotional impoverishment'. She argues that 'subjectivity is the condition of differentiation of emotions and of the cultivation of emotional sensibility' (1990:87) and stakes her 'bet' on the reappearance of not just emotional culture, but the appearance of several emotional cultures. Franks (1991) also addresses the issue of subjectivity/objectivity, in his paper 'Subjectivity and objectivity in constructing emotions as real'. He outlines the ways in which emotions can be associated with the diverse meanings of the terms subjective and objective, and uses these terms as a way of understanding emotions, whilst also highlighting the ways in which subjectivity and objectivity presuppose each other. Franks appreciatively quotes De Souza who suggests that emotions ground the very possibility of rationality – a debate which feeds into feminist critiques of the inappropriateness of emotionality-rationality as a dualism (James 1989).

The *third* example illustrates the passage of time in the sociology of emotions. Social constructionism, a jewel in the sociological repertoire since Berger and Luckman's *Social Construction of Reality* in 1966, has been a focus for debate. In the United States, Kemper's 1981 paper 'Social constructionist and positivist approaches to the sociology of emotions' gave rise to sparky responses from Hochschild (1983) and Hunsaker (1983). Over ten years later, in Britain, Craib (1995) published a commentary on the theme of social constructionism in the study of emotions in sociology. This too generated lively retorts (Duncombe and Marsden 1996, Williams and Bendelow 1996). However, the subject matter of the two debates was quite different. In the first it was Kemper's championing of the bio-physiological in emotions that offered the core subject matter. The second debate centred on Craib's critique of the sociology of emotions from a psychoanalytic perspective. He characterized this sociological work as colonising, and running the risk of crudely narrowing the understanding of emotions. During the period between the two debates sociological interest in the body showed that we miss crucial insights if we study fields with too narrow a conception of the social and its influences (Turner 1984, 1992, Crossley 1995). As biological issues become more integral to sociological understanding, so too, in the sociology of emotions, they become linked with debates about the person, body and society.

Whether emotions are amenable to sociological study in the same way that other parts of human life are is an important matter for debate. At its best the sociology of the emotions may be able to make connections between the observable and the unobservable, challenge the juxtaposition of emotional and rational, and create a space for fruitful theoretical and methodological agendas which engage in fundamental issues of social science. Yet the extent to which science, social science and humanities contribute to refining assertions and truths associated with emotions, and the extent to which these findings can be associated with knowledge, certainty, predictability and control remains to be seen.

Sociology of health and illness

If the sociology of emotions can be partially characterised by its association with subjectivities, the development of sociology of health and illness comes from a quite different tradition. As one writer with a strong attachment to a public health view has observed:

> When analysing the factors influencing the development of medical sociology, one usually discussed the role of changing morbidity and mortality patterns, extensive advancements in medical knowledge and the development of explanatory capabilities in sociology (Ostrowska 1996:100).

Whilst those interested in health and those interested in emotions share a concern about their contribution to the sociological enterprise, the hard issues of morbidity and mortality associated with the public health dimensions of medical sociology are in striking contrast to the miasma of examining sentiment, feelings and emotions.

Jefferys' (1996) resumé of forty years of involvement in medical sociology, since its small beginnings in the early post-war years, deliberately emphasises its socio-political aspects. Nevertheless she starts with a review of changing fertility and mortality statistics, new social mores, epidemiological evidence of problems of old age and the growing prominence of mental health concerns. Lived experience of illness and disability underlie this analysis which identifies cost, longer survival, growing health service expectations and family and kin responsibilities as the context within which medical sociology grew. Jefferys points out that Parsons' (1951) work on the social-control functions of health was slow to cross to Europe. When it came it collided with neo-Marxist ideas, the growth of feminism, and symbolic interactionism (see also Gabe *et al.* (1991). The mix of ideas generated interest in health from social theorists as well as meeting a pragmatism caused by a growing concern over the future of the welfare state. However, Jefferys contrasts medical sociology as it was established with and by physicians where it was enabled to move forward (United States), with the struggle for recognition encountered in areas where it was primarily sociologically led (*eg* Britain).

Since the late 1970s medical sociology has been redefined as the sociology of health and illness and is now more broadly conceived than ever. The incorporation of lay perspectives on health and illness and emphasis on social diversity have meant that greater account is now taken of health beliefs, as well as such matters as household production and reproduction of health and issues of race, gender and class inequality (Stacey 1988, 1991, Thomas 1995). The contribution of sociological theory to health and illness has also grown through Foucauldian perspectives and theorisation around the body and embodiment. Further ideas come from studies of health care professions, the health needs of user groups and newly developed research methods such as action research (Turner 1992, Witz 1992, Hart and Bond 1995, Wilson 1995).

At the same time that sociological perspectives on health and illness have grown in breadth, 'medicine' has expanded, not only through more holistic approaches to the individual (Arney and Bergen 1983), but also as epidemiology, public health and primary care services co-opt many sociological insights into their practice and training (Armstrong 1987). As professions allied to medicine have moved into higher education, particularly in countries such as Australia, Britain and the United States, the carework associated with such occupations offers fertile ground for examining and co-opting the sociology of emotions. Such occupations bring with them access and insight into health problems not only in specific communities but also in institutional worlds, with all the emotional connotations alluded to by Goffman (1968). As occupational groups in higher education they also massively increase the numbers taught about the sociology of health and illness. Thus sociology of health and illness, and potentially emotions, is taught in an applied form to those who, to use Jefferys' term, are 'conventionally . . . endowed with the power of status and position' (1996:95).' Recognition of the multiple faces of sociology of health and illness, ranging from theory building and social engineering through to working within a public health paradigm, enables Jefferys to argue that there was and is no orthodoxy. As a result, not only is the sociology *of* medicine eclectic, but it continues to co-exist alongside a more pragmatic sociology *in* medicine.

Health and the sociology of emotions

Health is a state of complete physical, mental and social wellbeing (WHO 1958).

Arguably, analyses of health should be concerned with the issues of individual potential that are incorporated into the *World Health Organisation's* definition of health – much criticised for being unrealistic. It is also about more than that, being associated with institutions and ideologies as the changes in Eastern Europe make obvious (Ostrowska 1996). Connecting the sociology of emotions to the field of sociology of health and illness thus opens up the possibility of addressing a wide range of issues from emotions in organisations (Fineman 1993) to individual accounts (James 1993). The opportunities may heighten expectations that the sub-disciplines will contribute to the development of both sociology and health studies. The extent to which health and emotions becomes sociologically influential will depend, in part, on how it is perceived and acted on in traditional sociology departments and used in mainstream sociological thinking. An alternative interpretation is that health and emotions will take on a particular meaning amongst practitioners involved in a variety of forms of health services research. The sociology of health and of emotions may grow through the development of mutual interests across different groups.

The challenge involved in such an enterprise, like any new area, is an odd mix of recognising the enormous range of established work whilst not being so corralled by sociological history that the opportunity provided by a new focus is weighed down by the past. Thus those with interests in health and emotions are faced with the potential and constraints of 'new' areas of study. At the early *BSA* meetings on emotions those struggling with the new territory and initially experiencing a freshness of vision were eventually confronted with more established agendas. There were reminders that a range of thinkers and schools had already had much to say on the subject. It is worth remembering Marx on alienation; Spencer's (1897) chapter 'Subjective difficulties – emotional' in the *Study of Sociology*; Parsons' characterisation of expressive and instrumental roles; and Freud's (1935) claim that psychoanalysis could be used to understand society. In addition there is the more recent work of critical theorists, interactionists, ethnomethodologists, phenomenologists and feminists.

As sociological priorities have increasingly taken account of pluralities and diversities, so there have been international shifts in the funding and organisation of research on health and illness. While some have begun the process of linking health and emotions they have tended to do so without clarifying the parameters and limitations of their approach (Finch and Groves 1983, James 1993, Hockey 1993). In this context it was valuable that Freund (1990) identified a particular task for the sociology of health and emotions. Emphasising the centrality of the body, he suggested that sociologists should show how 'this active, expressive and experiencing body relates to historically shaped, socially organised systems of human activity' (1990:456). The value of this agenda was its association of massive structural effects with the complexity of embodiment. Many chapters in this book continue that task in a variety of ways. Simon Williams and Gillian Bendelow (chapter one), Margot Lyon (chapter two) and Deborah Lupton (chapter seven) all explore the macro effect of micro issues and the micro effects of macro issues, as do Patricia Baker, William Yoels and Jeffrey Clair (chapter eight) although not from a perspective of embodiment. What is also interesting is that Geraldine Lee Treweek (chapter five) and Sally Ruane (chapter six), while both addressing issues of social construction, also identify, almost in passing, the biophysiological states which trigger particular actions. Perhaps it is the chapters on methodology by Andrew Finlay (chapter three) and Elizabeth Young and Ray Lee (chapter four) that least directly adhere to Freund's agenda. Thus, while the agenda is a useful starting point, it does raise the issue of whether the claim to a single 'task', however complex, is likely to succeed in an area which, as Jefferys pointed out, has no orthodoxy and which, for better or worse, is often funded to influence policy and practice.

Morality, ethics and relevance

Researching vulnerable populations is fundamental to much of the work of the sociology of health and illness and makes an interesting juxtaposition with the view that the subjectivities of emotions deserve careful attention. The international socio-economic dimensions of health assessment, delivery and practices combined with the academic drive for knowledge and 'truth', suggest that any research associated with health and emotions cannot escape being bound up with issues of morality (in its broadest social sense), ethics (in terms of 'good practice') and relevance. Whilst these are all deeply inter-related, for the purposes of clarity we discuss them under separate sub-headings.

Morality

Part of the passion of the initial debates in the sociology of emotions in Britain was about a basic perception of emotions as different from other realities, an intimate part of people to be protected from intrusion but also so deeply rooted in humanness as to be pre-linguistic (Kristeva 1982). Culturally dominated moralities have long been associated with health and emotions – the appropriateness of how to grieve, how to love – and involve bringing them together in 'dying of a broken heart'. Sontag (1979, 1990) has alerted us to the moralities associated with cancer and HIV/AIDS and how such morality spreads through powerful metaphors, while Samuel Butler's 'Erewhon' (1967) offers a novel insight into a world where illness is managed by punishment, and crime with sympathetic support and treatment.

Since we also know that knowledge about ourselves, unlike knowledge of the physical universe, changes something about our self understanding and relationships with others, there are grounds for the fear that the knowledge we generate will be used to manipulate and manage us (Polkinghorne 1989:8). Perhaps the more intimate a subject is, the more the knowledge is associated with subjectivities, the greater the fear of abuse. In these terms health and emotions combine two areas invoking personal sensitivities and experiences. This raises the question of whether there is something about joining emotions and health which should provoke particular forms of concern. This might involve thinking through whether research about emotions can be used to manipulate and control. The traditional response to this concern, as argued by Polkinghorne, is that:

> . . . we can use knowledge of ourselves that does indeed account for our complexity and for our essential qualities to overcome manipulation. This knowledge can also be used to enable us to make decisions that will improve our ability to live together harmoniously on our small planet (1989:8).

This, of course, does little to ameliorate fears of the ways in which knowledge may be harnessed by people in positions of power to shape and control. Arney and Bergen (1983) and Armstrong (1987) have been amongst those who have identified the ways in which medicine has co-opted psychosocial issues to extend the terrain and depth of medical influence. Similarly the authors of one of the chapters in this monograph, Baker et al, quote the quality-of-life guru, Spitzer (1987), who writes that:

> . . . indices can be designed so that clinicians can score the quality of life or health status after observing or examining a patient even without eliciting information from the patient about how he or she feels at a given point in time (1987:470).

Nevertheless, fear of the exploitation of emotions through academic study presents a rather over-deterministic association between research and social change in suggesting either that manipulation is the only use to which such knowledge is put or that even where it is used it is altogether negative. Greater openness in discussions about dying in recent years have been deemed to be positive by many, enabling people with cancer as well as professionals to state their case more effectively (Dickenson and Johnson 1993). However, such a counter point should not deny the seriousness of the potential for moral control and manipulation. Academic study is necessarily associated with programmes which strive for objectivity and neutrality as the core of their values. There are echoes of this debate in Kemper (1990) who identifies the tension between managing and accounting for emotions. Managing emotions is seen as dominant in sociological research because it is compatible with an anti-positivist stance. The academic process through which data are collected and analysed also dictates who disseminates it, to whom and how, and therefore the ways in which it is used. This leaves open whether, and in what ways, such studies of emotion may contribute to new moralities of emotion (*see* Lyon, Finlay, Ruane and Lee Treweek).

Ethics and Methodologies
There is, of course, a link between moral concerns and professional codes of ethics which shape and are shaped by the methods and methodologies chosen to expand work on emotions and health. Ethical guidelines, for example those developed by the *BSA*, insist that the vulnerable are not exploited. The need to avoid gender, race and class stereotypes in research on emotions also needs to be emphasised. Yet, in attempting to guard against this, misguided forms of paternalistic and maternalistic protectionism may lead to the ignoring of central but sensitive issues. For example, at the *Stone Symposium on Symbolic Interactionism* held in Nottingham, England, in July 1996, Frey and Adelman (1996) were questioned about their study of an AIDS residence. In particular, there was concern about the potentially exploitive nature of a video they had produced which involved participants (or are they subjects?) discussing the way in which death, a regular feature of the household, was managed by those still alive and living in the residency. The debate about potential exploitation appeared to be associated with concerns about exposing the residents to public identification and scrutiny.

Political issues concerning the appropriateness of particular methodologies and methods for health and emotions are pronounced. Negotiation of access, presentation of findings, self-reflection, intersubjectivity, power relations between research participants, researchers and students, all require examination, alongside the subjectivities which are so fundamental to the sociology of emotions. At the same time, avoiding moralities which stifle new ideas and cripple appropriate innovation has to be part of the negotiated outcome.

Concerned about transgression of feelings, Craib (1995) sparked the debate referred to above, and explored by Finlay in this volume. Writing as a sociologist and a psychotherapist used to moving between two worlds which 'know practically nothing of each other', Craib makes a general observation that 'when sociologists comment on emotions, they do so with the same sensitivity and understanding that psychoanalists display when commenting on society – which is . . . none at all' (1995:151). However, his main critique is reserved for two papers by Jackson (1993), and Duncombe and Masden (1993) which were published in an earlier issue of *Sociology*. His concern is particularly with a social constructionist view of emotions which employs concepts such as work, power and equality despite their questionable applicability to emotions. He notes that even after years of psychotherapeutic training it remains difficult to distinguish between one's own and others' emotions, and therefore that the quality of data from interviews and observations is likely to be limited. His conclusion is that sociologists need to be aware that they are studying emotions at a relatively superficial, abstract level. If we accept this position, which not all sociologists do (*see* Williams and Bendelow 1996, Duncombe 1996), even those who take particular care to account for subjectivities are likely to be damned by the limits of their knowledge and expertise. In this context the nature of reflection in first person accounts, for example in the chapter by Young and Lee, may be subjected to criticism that even authors reporting on their own feelings do not take adequate account of the emotions generated.

Relevance

In her chapter entitled 'Are we living in a world of emotional impoverishment?', Heller (1990:84) reminds us that in the eighteenth and nineteenth centuries certain groups amongst the bourgeoisie of England and France developed a culture of emotional refinement and self cultivation. She notes the separation from others that this refined culture engendered, its esotericism and introspection. Clearly any area of study engenders its own interests, differentiated language and usually the ritual of a conference. The sociology of health and illness has always worked with reminders that health is associated with day to day problems which require resolution of apparently simple matters of water and sanitation on a massive scale (WHO 1995). By default, connecting health and emotions has to meet the challenge of esotericism and relevance.

One author who has written about relevance is Hammersley (1992). His analysis concerns ethnography, but the principles he raises are more broadly applicable. He argues that social science has no value if its findings are not relevant to people outside the research community. Hammersley identifies a series of factors by which relevance may be judged, such as the importance of the topic, the contribution to literature and improvement in practice. He notes that the last of these is very different to the first two since it is likely to involve prescriptive rules. He does not advocate a return to Aristotle's separation of theory and practice, although he recognises the value of Aristotle's conception of practice as involving judgement and knowledge derived from experience. Accepting this, he sees limited influence of research over practice, but urges us to explore how social research might be made more relevant to practitioners.

Left implicit in Hammersley's account is the issue of research as a sensitising device. Clearly, research both responds to and influences social change. Yet it would appear from the history of the sociology of emotions described above that early developments in the US and UK occurred without reference to each other and still somehow captured a social mood or interest. Reading the chapters in this volume, many of which are associated with lay and professional practices in various ways, it appears that the literature on emotions both contributes to and is responsive to the post-war developments toward a more holistic understanding of health delivery. At the same time, this literature (including several chapters in this monograph) has an important sensitising function which has a bearing on methodological and theoretical as well as practice issues. This function offers a counterpoint to direct, 'applied', or outcome oriented versions of relevance.

Development of thematic questions, sections and contributions.

To enhance the coherence of the chapters as a collection, the editors asked the authors to locate their chapter in current debates in the sociology of emotions. They were also invited to identify the contribution their chapter would make to the sociology of emotions as applied to health or examine how it extended the conception of the sociology of emotions. The intention was that through these themes, collectively, their contributions would help move the subject of health and the sociology of emotions forward. It was this point which led to the selection of sub-themes into which the chapters are categorised – theory, methodology, social constructionism and social change.

To some extent the identification of sub-themes is artificial. This is partly because all the chapters can be read in more than one way and could be re-ordered into other sections. In addition, while theory and methodology seem relatively self-explanatory when considering the development of a sub-discipline, identifying social constructionism and social change out of all the possible sociological permutations available may be less obvious. As a theme associated with the production and reproduction of society 'change' could be argued to complement theory and methodology as a sociological standard. This might be given additional impetus as the impending millenium makes us reflect on the past as well as the future. Accepting change as a norm of sociological enquiry leaves social constructionism as the only theme unaccounted for. Yet social constructionism, particularly within the context of post-structural critiques, offers a significant means of examining power and status while re-theorising subjectivity (Henriques, *et al.* 1984). If recognising the importance of the subject is part of the examination of the production and reproduction of structures, it contributes to the study of health and the sociology of emotions by posing 'the question of the subject: who is this structure for?' (Easthope 1988:30–1). This type of question highlights the range of political agendas which underlie many of the chapters – Lyon on *Prozac*, Finlay on 'wanted' and 'unwanted' teenage pregnancy and Baker *et al.* on emotional expression during medical encounters, as well as Lee Treweek on residential care assistants and Ruane on 'maternal-baby unbonding' prior to adoption. In our view these 'political agendas' feed into, but are also affected by many of the questions about methodology, ethics and relevance which can be related to health and emotions. For these reasons, the section on social constructionism is included as a balance to what may be a growing orthodoxy in the sociology of emotions in which focusing on the individual can obscure debates on 'micro versus macro' (Kemper 1990). By including social constructionism we are taking an overt position which recognises both the politics of health and the political issues raised in studying the sociology of emotions.

Having selected the sub-headings, contributors were asked to address not only the general questions mentioned above, but some more specific to their sub-area. Chapters were chosen for their complementarity to each other as well as to the overall collection. This resulted in similar key issues being addressed in different ways within the sub-section.

In the following discussion, the questions in the sub-areas are identified, and related to the relevant chapters. In outlining the main argument from each chapter, we also mention the ways in which they have something to contribute to other sub-areas.

Theoretical issues
The papers in this section were selected to offer a theoretical framework by addressing the questions:

a) what opportunities does the sociology of emotions open up in terms of theoretical analysis of health and illness and what are the gaps that can thus be filled?
b) how does a sociology of emotions explore issues of embodiment as applied to health and best theorise biological and social connections?

In addressing these questions, both Williams and Bendelow (chapter one) and Lyon (chapter two) contribute to the debate on 'what is emotion'.

Williams and Bendelow offer a review, with associated case studies. The breadth of their literature review, drawing in 'old masters' as well as current thinkers, is an illustration of our earlier point about the opportunities for, and need to establish the legitimacy of, a new sub-discipline. Thus Williams and Bendelow take the separation of reason from emotion as their point of departure, associating it with a series of dualisms – mind and body, nature and culture, biology and society in scientific medicine – going on to argue for an 'embodied' approach which transcends these dualistic legacies. They seek to illustrate the relevance of emotions to the sociology of health and illness through three areas: the phenomenological experience of illness, pain and suffering; the relationship between social structure and health; and the growth of holistic therapies. They argue that 'emotion' is the crucial 'missing link' in sociology, providing the chance to fashion 'a non-dualist ontology of the mindful body'. In terms of micro-macro relations, for them the fundamentally *embodied* nature of human emotions means that these emotions are uncontainable within any one explanation, be it biological, cultural, or social.

Lyon's approach both complements and contrasts with this view. She carries out a detailed examination of the development of *Prozac*, looking at the way it is used to transform the subject (self) into an object (ideal self) in the name of treating 'depression'. Drawing on C. Wright Mills' argument that the modern world needs to understand personal problems from the perspective of their connections with the social and historical context in which they emerge, she suggests that this is as true of medical problems as social ones. She argues that the *Prozac* debate is framed in terms of the biological versus psycho-social origins of depression and like Williams and Bendelow, indicates that the 'biological' needs to be brought into the realm of social explanation. Also like Williams and Bendelow, she argues for emotion as a linking mechanism, because it is simultaneously physical and socio-psychological, which in turn expands our understanding of health and illness. However, whereas Williams and Bendelow argue that greater attention to emotions would offer a more human face to the increasingly technologised nature of late modern medicine, Lyon concludes that the tendency toward a more profound medicalisation of social life can be supervened by the social emotion approach she outlines. In making these statements about the 'benefits' of their particular positions, Williams and Bendelow, and Lyon, are making statements about the relevance of studying health and emotions, but also contributing to the debate about 'relevance' to whom?

Methodology

The theme of 'reflection' to which Finlay (chapter three) and Young and Lee (chapter four) respond is implicit in the guideline questions for the methodology section, namely:

   a) is there anything about the sociology of emotions as related to
health that takes us forward methodologically in relation to broader
sociological concerns?

   b) what is the nature of the relationship between the researcher and
the researched when studying the sociology of emotions associated with
health?

Finlay uses his chapter to re-examine data collected by a team of
researchers of which he was one, undertaking a health services research
project on teenage pregnancy. Having become aware of the sociology of
emotions after the research was completed he realised the need to focus
on the impact of a code of romantic love on young peoples' sexual and
contraceptive behaviours. In his chapter he addresses both of the questions for the section. He notes the moral-technical discourses of his and
his colleagues' research and questions whether they privileged the rational
and cognitive over the emotional as they developed their interview schedules by re-iterating policy terms like 'planned' and 'unplanned' pregnancy.
He considers whether they were party to inadvertently shoring up the
debate on morality which underpins policy on teenage pregnancy, especially in Ireland. Rejecting this position he suggests the framework
employed, like the results, was more symptomatic of a transformation of
intimacy. By using the literature on romantic love, Finlay is not only able
to critique the work he and his colleagues carried out, but also move the
argument on to suggest that the problem may no longer be that emotions
are neglected so much as apprehended in a reductive way. In his view, the
sociological tendency to neglect or subsume emotions is particularly damaging in the case of research on reproductive behaviour, not only because
it involves the neglect of love but also fear, concupiscence, envy and loneliness. He suggests that the youthful respondents came 'to regard their sex
lives as a haven of spontaneous, authentic feeling in an increasingly rationalistic and instrumental world', but that the feelings associated with this
are as relevant to adults as to young people. In raising these points, he
challenges what he refers to as the 'complacent assumption that qualitative methods are appropriate to the study of emotions' because, from his
experience and that of his colleagues, serious problems remain even with a
qualitative approach. He takes seriously the point mentioned earlier in the
introduction that the academic method may distort feelings, and quotes
Craib's (1995) warning about forms of social constructionism which give
priority to cognition. According to Craib '. . . the danger . . . is that emotions will be reduced to ideas: they will have no autonomy from the
rational world with which they co-exist' (1995:153).

   Reflection follows a different methodological path for Young as she
reflects after a series of incidents, with her co-author Lee, about her feelings
on carrying out depth interviews with dying women as a means of examining the basis on which first person fieldwork accounts are generated.

Building on Dingwall's critique that fieldwork descriptions are anecdotal and lacking a comparative theoretical base, the authors use Hochschild's concepts of 'emotion work' and 'feeling rules' to inform their analysis. They argue that the emotion work that is done in research is best seen as an attempt to manage implicit feeling rules. In doing this they emphasise how feeling rules vary with different methodological perspectives. They also note that dissonance is not only inevitable but offers potentially valuable insights into the competing tensions of involvement, comfort and identification. A key message of their chapter is a reiteration of the point that it is not enough to say how different fieldwork can be; the roots of the difficulty must also be explored. In this way, as with Finlay, reflexivity is used to identify nuances associated with different methodologies.

Interestingly, both chapters contribute to the question about relationships between the research and researched. Finlay's response highlights the dangers of ignoring or subsuming respondents' emotions, whereas Young and Lee show that the question the editors posed was too narrowly conceived as it failed to take account of the researcher and his or her own feelings in relation to particular methodologies.

In addition to the points identified for attention in this section, two further issues emerged during the drafting of the chapters – research as an ongoing process, and the linguistic challenge of first person reflexivity on joint projects. Both Finlay's chapter and that of Young and Lee illustrate that research is a process in which categorisation and interpretation affect data collection before, during and after the event. It can also involve drawing on other academic networks after data collection to extend the process and critique both methods and methodology. Their part in what were joint enterprises with others in turn led to difficulties in referring to 'I' and 'we' in any systematic manner. Both chapters were returned by referees and editors with a request to be clearer about what was jointly produced, what was an individual contribution and what were the relations between those involved. This was not because any of the authors failed to give due acknowledgement, but because there are inherent difficulties in differentiating between an individual's own analysis and those resulting from the collective enterprise. This is an interesting example of 'the non-unitary subject' alluded to above in the discussions of post-structuralism.

Social constructionism
In sociological standards, such as Berger and Luckman's (1966) *Social Construction of Reality*, biology gets no mention. It is a measure of the way in which sociology has progressed, including the contribution of the sociology of emotions to health, that in the chapters by both Lee Treweek (chapter five) and Ruane (chapter six), we can observe biology is used by particular occupational groups (care assistants and nurses/social workers) to explain specific actions. It is these occupations' interpretation of these

biological developments which gives the impetus for action. Such connections were not identified in the guideline questions which were:

a) what does the sociology of emotions as applied to health and illness contribute to debates on social constructionism?

b) what is the nature of the connection between emotions and social reproduction?

Lee Treweek questions the negativity associated with emotional labour in some sociological literature, suggesting instead that emotional labour is empowering, not least for the low-paid female, care-workers in the residential home in which she carried out her participant observation. Adapting categories developed by Helen Evers in her study of long-stay geriatric wards, Lee Treweek refers to residents as 'the lovelies', 'the disliked' and the 'confused', and claims that care workers use emotion work to structure their labour and organise those they care for. Making reference to Foucault's notion of pastoral care, she notes the power that care-workers are able to exert, thereby refuting the implications of earlier work on the sociology of emotions that emotional skills are necessarily commodities used by management against the best interests of the workers. Lee Treweek's account suggests that, for the women workers, emotion is a key frame of reference and cultural resource from which to derive methods of ordering others. Yet it is the 'biological' which leads the care-assistants to designate confused residents as 'NHM' (nursing home material). The social context within which this occurs is that as long as the confused exhibited amiable character traits, and were susceptible to the staff's emotion work through 'cajoling, cuddling and kind words', they could remain in the home. In the staff's view, the accumulation of unmanageable symptoms heralded the need for an NHM to move to the more intensively supported environment of a nursing home. Lee Treweek argues that while the staff claimed that NHM had 'lost it' or 'gone', from her observations the primary difference between them and other residents was one of control, not of the symptoms themselves. In this analysis Lee Treweek implicity recognises the subjectivities of those involved. Yet she remains persuaded by the force of the social factors (as compared to symptoms) which appeared to construct the framework through which residents deemed to have moved beyond control by emotional means. The consequence of this staff analysis was, literally, to increase the institutionalisation of the management of emotions by facilitating the resident's move to a nursing home.

Ruane addresses the issue of emotion and its place in social reproduction through its antithesis – an analysis of mother-baby unbonding. Examining the ways in which this process involves more than the management of emotion, Ruane, like Lee Treweek, uses Hochschild's influential work on emotions, as a framework for her analysis. What is of particular interest is Ruane's observation that the staff's interpretation of bonding is automatic but is only a part of what has to be managed. Ruane suggests the concept of bonding used by the professionals involves more than biology because part of the un-bonding involves blocking the process by which the woman comes to be socially defined as a mother. Thus, it is not merely biological, but social and cultural influences at work as well. These require not only the management of 'instinctive' or 'hormonal' triggers, but also the management of social and self definition. In addition, Ruane notes the significance of professional differentiation, with nurses and midwives conceptualising the unbonding as a termination rite, and social workers appealing to long-term mental health (grief and bereavement) in identifying a rite of initiation. It is notable that so far this selective resume of Ruane's chapter is removed, detached. Yet her chapter is a palimpsest of emotion, attempting neither to over nor underestimate its significance. One social worker compared loss through adoption to death:

> They (the nurses) said: 'That girls doesn't want to part from her baby; she's being crying all morning.' And I say: 'Yes, she's been crying. How would you feel if you had experienced a bereavement or death?'

The similarities between Lee Treweek and Ruane lie not merely in their joint concern with worlds of women as they cross domestic and institutional boundaries, but also in their observations of how identities are made and remade. Lee Treweek and Ruane contribute to the literature on the management of emotion rather than that on accounting for emotion referred to earlier (see Kemper on p. 10). In doing so they also contribute to our understanding of the ways in which different occupational groups shape the lives of those with whom they are associated and how a mix of caring and decision making are employed for what is intended to be a 'best' outcome for the user.

Social change
The two chapters in this section complement each other in so far as they both draw conclusions about what is required of doctors. In chapter seven Lupton develops an analysis of 'trust in the medical encounter' from a lay perspective. Her chapter is based on sixty interviews with lay people recruited through a variety of social networks and limited snowball sampling. The interviewees' comments were subjected to a 'post-structuralist phenomenological approach' which recognised the participants' accounts as 'situated narratives'. In contrast, the next chapter by Baker, Yoels and Clair use their recordings of thirty-nine encounters between new clinic patients and their doctor to concentrate on how doctors and patients expressed themselves. The transcripts were subsequently coded by a system which combined elements of discourse analysis with an adaptation of the interaction exchange system. This allowed the conversations to be examined as

complementary pairs of utterances by doctors and patients. Both chapters should be read within the context of the guideline questions:

a) what do social changes tell us about emotions and their place in the power relations of health care settings?

b) has organisational change brought about 'new' emotions or emphasised 'old' emotions, making health systems or practice inherently different?

Lupton's starting point is the proposition that in the two decades since the mid-1970's, the dominance of the medical profession has been diminished by its loss of prestige and patients' trust. Instead of a clear shift towards consumers taking control which such a proposition suggests Lupton argues that the medical encounter is characterised by profound ambivalence as people move between wanting to maintain control and assertiveness, and wanting to relinquish control to their doctor. In this analysis, the social change which academic commentators claimed had occurred was not nearly as profound as suggested because these commentators had failed to acknowledge the emotional ties that bind people, particularly when they are vulnerable and anxious. This recognition of the limits of individuality and consumerism is a significant observation. It contributes both to the sociology of emotions and to sociology more generally as it draws our attention to the importance of method and analysis. Lupton's observations remind us that the method must be appropriate to the minutiae of emotions which cause such ambivalence and that the analysis must not over-simplify for the sake of clarity where there is tension.

Baker *et al* also develop their analysis from traditional power and status differentials between doctors and nurses. They suggest that during the twentieth century medicine has increasingly moved from the 'more intimate setting of the hearth and bedside to the more impersonal, bureaucratic world of clinics, large-scale hospitals, and health maintenance organisations'. They note that while Hochschild claims a general shift from work based on producing goods to occupations involving emotion work, hospital-based American medicine appears to be an exception to this closer association with emotion work. In their view medicine is an illustration of a shift from a person-centred perspective to a technical activity, in which only procedures are paid for by health-care insurers. The value of their observations are several-fold. They offer a quantitative analysis which identifies doctors' emotional expressions during encounters as brief and positive, whereas those of patients are more anxiety-laden. The methods of data collection and analysis contrast with others in this book, and contribute to the methodological debates raised earlier in this introduction about the reification of emotions. Further, their identification of procedure-led medicine dominated by health insurers while deliberately limiting emotional expressiveness, offers a model against which health services in other countries may be judged. While their interpretation of a patient-centred past may be open to challenge on structural grounds of class, race and gender, in making this observation they encourage us to think again.

Both Lupton and Baker *et al.* contribute to sociological debate about power and status as it relates to emotions. Interestingly, their contribution to the literature on social change is to challenge what appear to them to be over-dramatic claims about the degree of movement. Lupton's argument is that trust cannot simply be abandoned and Baker *et al.* note the tension between what patients want and what health insurers will pay for. Both papers have relevance for the professionals described, but also serve as a caution against over-simplification in interpreting what is going on in medical encounters. In essence, both require that the detail of medical encounters is looked at more closely to see what is happening and whether sociological theories of change, change in emotions and change in organisations are supported by evidence from health and the sociology of emotions.

Conclusion: Making connections

In writing this introduction we have attempted to answer some of the 'so what?' questions by suggesting where health and the sociology of emotions may contribute to sociological thinking. The questions we generated can be used in a number of ways. They may be used as a measure of where this particular collection is grounded, as a 'state of the art' comment. The monograph goes some way to illustrate what the sociology of emotions has to offer, historically and analytically to health and vice-versa, at this time in its development. Perhaps more interactively, readers may suggest what would have been better editorial questions for us to have asked and why they would have been better.

We make no grand claims for sociological progress when emotions and health are combined and in our view the question 'so what' should persist. Nevertheless, we hope that during this introduction we have identified some of the benefits of making such connections. These can be summarised as follows:

a) there is an opportunity to re-think the connections between humanities, social science and science and their associated epistemological and methodological positions;

b) whilst offering ample opportunity for generalisation, connecting health and emotions also encourages the generation of specific insights;

c) the issue of subjectivities is ever present and connecting health and emotions highlights relations not merely between individual and society, but also between person, body and society. At the same time international statistics on patterns of health and morbidity are a constant reminder of the need for relevance;

d) finally, connecting health and emotions encourages reflexivity, not merely in the methodological sense, important though that is, but also in terms of a social consciousness of the micro and macro elements of health in our social world.

In forging a new sub-discipline there may be a tendency to be inward looking. Yet psychologists, anthropologists and philosophers are also actively working in the field (Harré 1986, Harré and Parrott 1996, Solomon 1993, Shweder and LeVine 1984). Sociologists are faced with the challenge of how far to establish health and emotions as part of a single sociological discipline, and how far to work toward inter-disciplinarity and potential cross-fertilisation. These dilemmas remain to unfold. Yet reminders of the potential of combining studies of human feeling and health are all around, in our lay experience and captured daily by journalists. Embarrassment, fear and patience are part of most health encounters and current sociological debates about the 'reality' of these feelings are significant. Nevertheless it is worth remembering that sociology does not hold a monopoly on the understanding of realities or of the experience of feeling.

Note

1. We are grateful to Sian Maslin Prothero for drawing our attention to this phrase by E.M. Forster.

References

Alcoff, L. and Potter, E. (eds) (1993) *Feminist Epistemologies*. London: Routledge.

Armstrong, D. (1987) Theoretical tensions in biopsychosocial medicine, *Social Science and Medicine*, 25, 1213–18.

Arney, W. and Bergen, B. (1983) The anomaly, the chronic patient and the play of medical power, *Sociology of Health and Illness*, 5, 1–24.

Berger, P. and Luckman, T. (1966) *The Social Construction of Reality*. Harmondsworth: Penguin.

Butler, S. (1967) *Erewhon*. New York: Airmont.

Code, I. (1993) Taking subjectivity into account. In Alcoff, P. and Potter, E. (eds) *Feminist Epistemologies*. London: Routledge.

Craib, I. (1995) Some comments on the sociology of emotions, *Sociology*, 29, 151–8.

Crossley, N. (1995) Body techniques, agency and intercorporeality: on Goffman's relations in public, *Sociology*, 29, 133–49.

Dickenson, D. and Johnson, M. (1993) *Death, Dying and Bereavement*. London: Sage.

Duncombe, J. and Marsden, D. (1993) Love and intimacy: the gender division of emotion and 'emotion work', *Sociology*, 27, 221–41.

Duncombe, J. and Marsden, D. (1996) 'Extending the social: a response to Ian Craib, *Sociology*, 30, 155–8.

Easthope, A. (1988) *British Post-Structuralism*. London: Routledge.

Finch, J. and Groves, D. (1983) *A Labour of Love: Women, Work and Caring*. London: Routledge.

Fineman, S. (ed) (1993) *Emotion in Organisations*. London: Sage.

Forster, E.M. (1956) *Howard's End*. London: Edward Arnold.

Franks, D. (1991) *Subjectivity and Objectivity in Constructing Emotions as Real*. Virginia Commonwealth University: Richmond VA.

Freud, S. (1935) *Postscript to 'An Autobiographical Study'*. New York: Norton.

Freund, P. (1990). The expressive body: a common ground for the sociology of emotions and health and illness, *Sociology of Health and Illness*, 12, 452–77.

Frey, L. and Adelman, M. (1996) *Dialectical Tests and Fuzzy Boundaries in Studying Communication and Community Building in a Residential Setting for People with AIDS*. Chicago: Department of Communication, Loyola University.

Gabe, J., Calnan, M. and Bury, M. (1991) Introduction. In Gabe, J. *et al* (eds) *The Sociology of the Health Service*. London: Routledge.

Goffman, E. (1968) *Asylums*. Harmondsworth: Penguin.

Hammersley, M. (1992) *What's Wrong with Ethnography?* London: Routledge.

Harding, S. (1991) *Whose Science? Whose Knowledge?* Buckingham: Open University.

Harré, R. (1986) *The Social Construction of Emotions*. Oxford: Basil Blackwell.

Harré, R. and Parrott, G. (1996) *The Emotions: Social, Cultural and Biological Dimensions*. London: Sage.

Hart, E. and Bond, M. (1995) *Action Research for Health and Social Care*. Buckingham: Open University.

Heller, A. (1990) *Can Modernity Survive?* Cambridge: Polity.

Henriques, J., Hollway, W., Urwin, G., Venn, C., and Walkerdine, V. (1984). *Changing the Subject: Psychology, Social Regulation and Subjectivity*. London: Methuen.

Hochschild, A. R. (1983) Comment on Kemper's 'Social constructionist and positivist approaches to the sociology of emotions', *American Journal of Sociology*, 89, 432–4.

Hockey, J. (1993) The acceptable face of human grieving? The clergy's role in managing emotional expression during funerals. In Clark, D. (ed) *The Sociology of Death*. Oxford: Blackwell.

Hunsaker, D. (1983) The social construction of emotion: comment on Kemper, *American Journal of Sociology*, 89, 434–9.

Jackson, S. (1993) 'Even sociologists fall in love, *Sociology*, 27, 201–20.

James, N. (1984) A postscript to nursing. In Bell, C. and Roberts, H. (eds) *Social Researching: Politics, Problems, Practice*. London: Routledge.

James, N. (1989) Emotional labour: skill and work in the social regulation of feelings, *Sociological Review*, 37, 15–42.

James, N. (1993) Divisions of emotional labour: disclosure and cancer. In Fineman, S. (ed) *Emotion in Organisations*. London: Sage.

Jefferys, M. (1996) The development of medical sociology in theory and practice in Western Europe, *European Journal of Public Health*, 6, 94–8.

Kemper, T. (1981) Social constructionist and positivist approaches to the sociology of emotions, *American Journal of Sociology*, 87, 337–62.

Kemper, T. (1990) *Research Agendas in the Sociology of Emotions*. Albany: State University of New York Press.

Kristeva, J. (1982) *Powers of Horror: An Essay on Abjection*. New York: Columbia University Press.

Oakley, A. (1990) *Women and Health*. Edinburgh: Edinburgh University Press.

Ostrowska, A. (1996) The development of medical sociology in Eastern Europe, 1965–1990, *European Journal of Public Health*, 6, 100–4.

Parsons, T. (1951) *The Social System*. London: Routledge, and Kegan Paul.

Polkinghorne, D. (1989) *Methodology for the Human Sciences*. Albany: State University of New York Press.

Scheff, T. and Mahlendorf, U. (1988) Emotion and false consciousness: the analysis of an incident from Werther, *Theory, Culture and Society*, 5, 57–80.

Shweder, R. and LeVine, R. (1984) *Culture Theory: Essays on Mind, Self and Emotion*. Cambridge: Cambridge University Press.

Solomon, R. (1993) *The Passions: Emotions and the Meaning of Life*. Indianapolis: Hackett Publishing Company.

Sontag, S. (1979) *Illness as Metaphor*. London: Allen Lane.

Sontag, S. (1990) *Aids and its Metaphors*. Harmondsworth: Penguin.

Spencer, H. (1897) *The Study of Sociology*. London: Kegan Paul, Trench, Trübner and Co.

Spitzer, W. (1987) State of science 1986: quality of life and functional status as target variables for research, *Journal of Chronic Disease*, 40, 465–71.

Stacey, M. (1988) *The Sociology of Health and Healing*. London: Unwin Hyman.

Stacey, M. (1991) Medical sociology and health policy: an historical overview. In Gabe, J., Bury, M. and Calman, M. (eds) *The Sociology of the Health Service*. London: Routledge.

Thomas, C. (1995) Domestic labour and health: bringing it all back home, *Sociology of Health and Illness*, 17, 323–52.

Turner, B. (1984) *The Body and Society*. Oxford: Blackwell.

Turner, B. (1992) *Regulating Bodies: Essays in Medical Sociology*. London: Routledge.

WHO. (1958) *Constitution of the World Health Organisation*. WHO: Geneva.

WHO. (1995) *The World Health Report 1995: Bridging the Gaps*. Geneva: WHO.

Williams, S. and Bendelow, G. (1996) Emotions and 'sociological imperialism': a rejoinder to Craib, *Sociology*, 30, 145–53.

Wilson, J. (1995) *How to Work with Self Help Groups*. Aldershot: Arena.

Witz, A. (1992) *Patriarchy and Professions*. London: Routledge.

Wouters, C. (1992) On status competition and emotion management: the study of emotions as a new field, *Theory, Culture and Society*, 9, 229–52.

1. Emotions, health and illness: the 'missing link' in medical sociology?

Simon J. Williams and Gillian Bendelow

Introduction: the vicissitudes of emotions in Western thought

The dominance of rationality in Western social and scientific thought has led to the relative neglect or dismissal of emotions as 'irrational', private, inner sensations which have been tied, historically, to women's 'dangerous desires' and 'hysterical bodies'. Even to the present day, emotions are seen to be the very antithesis of the detached scientific mind and its quest for 'objectivity', 'truth' and 'wisdom'; a view in which 'reason rather than emotions has been regarded as the indispensable faculty for acquiring knowledge' (Jaggar 1989: 145).

The vicissitudes of dualism – reason/emotion, mind/body, nature/culture – can be traced back to antiquity. Thus in Plato's scheme of imagery, emotions such as anger or curiosity were seen as irrational urges (galloping horses) that must always be harnessed and controlled by reason (the charioteer) (Jaggar 1989: 145). Similarly, the body, for Plato, 'shackles' and 'enslaves' us, is the source of 'countless distractions' and is liable to 'diseases which overtake and impede us in the pursuit of truth; it fills us . . . with fancies of all kinds, and . . . takes away from us thinking at all' (Plato 1993: 66c). Consequently, the philosophers' task consisted in 'freeing' and 'separating' the soul from the body in the pursuit of knowledge and wisdom.

However, perhaps the figure who stands out most clearly in the history of Western thought as the founder of modern views on the mind and body as separate entities is, of course, the French philosopher Rene Descartes. According to Descartes, mind and body are to be thought of as entirely separate and distinct. Thus for Descartes, my body is simply part of the external world, merely a material form of extension in space, a piece of space; a *res extensa*. In this sense, whilst for Descartes I *have* a body, I never *am* my body. Indeed, in arriving at the *cogito*, Descartes finds it possible to 'think away' everything about himself except the very act of thought itself. Thus, whilst I can conceive of myself as existing without a body, I cannot conceive of myself as existing without conscious awareness. Therefore the very materiality of my body is not part of the quintessential me. Rather I am pure consciousness. Hence Descartes' famous dictum in his *Discourse on Method* (1985/[1637]): '*Cogito, ergo sum*' – I think, therefore I am. The mind, in other words, is entirely distinct from the body according to Descartes.[1]

From this leads the well rehearsed division of the world into subjects who are pure thought, and objects who are pure extension in space. In other words, the famous 'Cartesian dualism' in which there is a bifurcation of mind and matter, subject and object, observer and observed – what Bordo (1986) has appositely termed the 'masculinization of Cartesian thought' (see also Seidler 1994 on the links between reason and masculinity). These views have, in turn, laid the foundations upon which the whole edifice of modern scientific medicine (*i.e.* bio-medicine) as we know it today rests; one which, in keeping with this tradition has, since the late eighteenth century, sought to separate body from mind, reasons from emotions and biology from culture. The body came to be seen as the subject of the natural sciences, including medicine, whilst the mind or *geist* was the topic of the humanities or the cultural sciences (*Geisteswissenschaften*). As a result, the 'sick man disappeared' from medical cosmology from the eighteenth century onwards (Jewson 1976), and allopathic Western medicine has, traditionally speaking, shown little interest in what may be termed the 'lived' as opposed to the 'objective' body (Turner 1992: 32, Leder 1984, 1990, 1992). In short, dualism has been a dominant theme in Western philosophical, Christian and scientific writings and teaching since antiquity and it is these very dualism which modern medicine as we know it today has inherited. Indeed, it would not be too much of an exaggeration to say that medicine, in large part, operates with a peculiarly 'dis-embodied' approach to the patient. In doing so, alongside science more generally, it displays an 'irrational passion for dispassionate rationality' (Rieff 1979).

Clearly, this analysis of the polarised body, whilst revealing, is somewhat oversimplified and does not adequately capture the complexity and heterogeneity of contemporary medical thinking and practice. As Armstrong (1983) has argued, the twentieth century has not merely been marked by a consolidation of Foucault's (1973) reductionist 'clinical gaze', but also by its extension beyond the confines of the clinic and the individual body into its psycho-social spheres and spaces, encompassing forms of biographical medicine which emphasise patient subjectivity and the experience of illness. Similarly, Arney and Neill (1982) have charted the historical transformation in the conceptualisation of pain in childbirth from a one-dimensional space based on physiology, to a two-dimensional space which encompasses subjectivity (see also Nettleton (1992) for a similar argument regarding power, pain and dentistry).

What social constructionist views fail to recognise, however, is that in emphasising this shift, they simply reverse rather than transcend the dualisms. In the hands of social constructionists, the fabricated soul becomes the prison of the body, not the other way round (Falk 1994).

Biological essentialism is therefore exchanged for a form of cultural or discursive essentialism. Indeed, as Armstrong (1987) himself acknowledges, recent developments such as the biopsychosocial model of disease not only display a number of theoretical tensions and limitations, they also involve new, more all-encompassing forms of power, surveillance and control. Moreover, even psychosomatic medicine fails to overcome these dualistic legacies as the term, in common parlance, implies that it is 'all in the mind', thus preserving a mind (psycho) body (somatic) duality (Turner 1992). Similarly, if we move to the level of everyday medical practice, it is also clear that, whether through pressures of time or fundamental beliefs and convictions, a basic dualistic scheme of imagery remains the all too frequent guiding principle (Bendelow 1996, Williams 1996). Here it is the 'somatic' body, rather than the 'body incarnate', which reigns supreme (Frankenberg 1990).

These disembodied views, and the peculiar attitude toward emotions which they display are not, however, simply confined to the realms of medicine and science. Rather, as the forgoing discussion suggests, they have also been deeply embedded in classical and contemporary social theory, as well as the sociology of health and illness. Whilst it is clear that classical sociologists such as Marx, Durkheim, Weber and Simmel, were not blind to the emotional dimensions of their work (Denzin 1984), and that emotions provide a fruitful link between personal troubles and broader public issues of social structure (Mills 1959), it is nonetheless the case that, as with the body more generally, emotions have tended to enjoy a rather 'ethereal existence' in much classical and contemporary sociology. Here, as Freund notes, the Durkheimian legacy that 'social facts' are not reducible to 'biological facts', together with a predominant focus on the rational actor and other unresolved tensions concerning the mind–body–society relationships haunt the sociological landscape; issues which are thrown into cortical relief in the sociology of emotions and the sociology of health and illness (1990: 453). Similarly, Weber equated rationality with freedom, whilst the 'emotional' and 'traditional' were linked to a lack of freedom (Bologh 1990: 122, 132). In short, as Scott and Morgan have rightly argued, within the tradition of social theorising: 'The body, if not irrational, is seen as non-rational. It can become an object of theory only through being disembodied. Theory remains a central and rational enterprise' (1993: 12).

Despite the recent explosion of interest in the body and society (Featherstone et al. 1991, Turner 1984, 1992, Shilling 1993, Grosz 1994) much still remains to be done to 'bring the body back in' in ways which not only satisfactorily resolve the tensions and dilemmas between the biological and the social, nature and culture, reason and emotion, but also avoid the pitfalls of previous crude socio-biological explanations. To date, much of the sociological discussion has been *about* bodies (*i.e.* issues of regulation, representation, restraint etc.) rather than *from* bodies (*i.e.* a more phenomenological emphasis on the body as a structure of on-going lived experience) Csordas (1994a). More generally, as Benton (1991) has recently argued, a number of contemporary social trends and movements are beginning to pose a significant challenge to seemingly 'settled' and 'ossified' conceptual forms in the social science traditions. As a consequence, existing networks of conceptual oppositions such as mind/body, culture/nature,   society/ biology, reason/emotion, object/subject, human/animal, meaning/cause, are beginning to be seen as 'intellectual obstacles' in the way of meeting these challenges.

As this suggests, emotions lie at the juncture of many of these divisions and debates. As writers such as Scheper-Hughes and Lock (1987) argue, emotions form the mediatrix between the individual, social and political body; unified through the concept of the 'mindful body'. Emotions are not only central to debates in mainstream sociological theory, however, they are also crucially important to the sociology of health and illness. Indeed, as Turner (1992) has rightly argued, the very nature of medical sociology, dealing as it does with fundamental aspects of human embodiment such as disease, illness, pain and suffering, offers the possibility for it to become the 'leading edge' of contemporary social theory.

It is this opportunity and challenge which forms the starting point of the present chapter. In particular, having briefly outlined some of the key contemporary debates in the sociology of emotions, we then proceed to illustrate the relevance of this newly emerging field of sociological inquiry to a number of substantive themes and issues within the field of medical sociology such as pain, the social causes of disease, and the growing popularity of holistic therapies in a 'reflexive' age. As we shall argue, not only does the sociological study of emotions shed important new light on these issues, it also offers us a potentially fruitful way out of rigid dichotomous ways of thinking through a unified conception of the 'mindful', emotionally 'expressive' body (Scheper-Hughes 1987, Freund 1990). It is to the first of these issues, namely; recent debates in the sociology of emotions, that we now turn.

The sociology of emotions and the 'problem' of human embodiment

As we have suggested, emotions lie at the juncture of a number of classical and contemporary debates in sociology, including the micro/macro, quantitative/qualitative, managing versus accounting for emotions, and biosocial versus social constructionist perspectives. In addition, considerable attention has been devoted to gender analysis in the study of emotions, as well as the political economy of emotions (Kemper 1990a: 3–23).

Here, as McCarthy notes, central questions include how we relate micro interactional processes of emotion management to broader socio-structural issues of order and conflict; whether or not emotions can be isolated, defined, observed and understood as 'things' in themselves or as 'social constructs'; whether we can circumscribe a distinct, autonomous realm of emotions as 'measurable' phenomena, or whether, instead, emotions are to be seen as cultural phenomena, embedded in beliefs, symbols and language, which in turn are inextricably linked to social and cultural processes. More broadly, a related question concerns whether emotions are culturally specific or universal in nature (1989: 51–2).

For example, regarding the micro/macro debate, Collins (1990) presents a compelling argument that many of the central processes of macro-sociology (*i.e.* social order, statification, conflict) ultimately rest on the much neglected micro-foundation of emotions. For Collins, in classic Durkheimian/Goffmanesque style, social order and solidarity ultimately rest on moral commitments which emerge in the course of 'interaction rituals' and emotional exchanges at the micro level. Conflict, too, rests on an emotional foundation, involving as it does the mobilisation of sentiments of anger toward carriers of opposing social values and interests. Solidarity and conflict perspectives therefore merge in Collins' micro–macro analysis of stratification (Kemper 1990a: 5, see also Kemper 1990b, Denzin 1990, and Gordon 1990 on these micro–macro linkages).

Similarly, concerning the positivism/anti-positivism debate, writers such as Kemper (1990a) have sought to establish patterns of covariance between social structures and interaction, on the one hand, and the emotions that are hypothesised to ensue, on the other. The central thrust of Kemper's position seems to be that emotional outcomes of interaction can be *predicted* on the basis of a model which centres on the social dimensions of power and status. As he states: 'Power and status interactions directly produce emotions' (1990a: 11. See also Kemper 1990b: 207–37). Furthermore, what these approaches share in common is an emphasis on the physiological as well as the social, cognitive and expressive aspects of emotion, in order to pursue what is seen to be a more 'complete' theory of emotions (Kemper 1990a: 11). In contrast, as we shall see, other writers such as Hochschild (1979, 1983, 1990), Denzin (1984, 1990), Clark (1990) and Thoits (1990) stress a mainly qualitative approach. Here, greater attention is devoted to issues such as the self, emotion management, description rather than prediction, and a view of emotion as an on-going structure of lived (bodily) experience: the very antithesis of detached positivistic investigation.

Perhaps the most pertinent debate for our purposes, however, concerns the biological/social divide: an issue which makes the body a central focus of attention. As Kemper (1990a: 20) notes, within the sociology of emotions, the confrontation between the biological and the social is both more focused and more heated than in most sociological subfields. In this respect, whilst few sociologists of emotions would dispute the 'physiological substrate' of emotions, the central question concerns just *how* important it is (Kemper 1990a: 20). At present, it is fair to say that many leading sociologists of emotions, in varying degrees and with different emphases, 'continue to focus on the cognitive and interpretive features of emotional experience and behaviour in contrast to psychological or physiological features of human emotion' (McCarthy 1989: 52).

Within these biology/society debates, approaches to emotions can be conceptualised on a continuum ranging from the 'organismic' at one end to the 'social constructionist' at the other, with 'interactionist' approaches, as the term implies, somewhere in between. Organismic models of emotions include the work of Darwin, Freud and James. In particular, as Hochschild (1983) notes, Darwin's classic book *The Expression of Emotions in Man and Animals* (1955/[1895]), has offered a model of emotions for various other theorists and researchers. Darwin's focus is on emotional expression (*i.e.* physical *gestures* and *displays*) rather than the subjective meanings associated with them. In keeping with Darwin's general theory of evolution, these gestures, he posits, were acquired during a pre-historic period and have survived as residues or 'serviceable associated habits'. Thus, the emotion of love, for example, is seen to be a vestige of what was once the direct act of copulation, whilst the expression of disgust is the vestige of what was once the direct act of 'regurgitating a noxious thing' (Hochschild 1983: 208). Ultimately then, Darwin's theory of emotion is a theory of gesture. As to the question of whether or not these gestures were universal or culturally specific, his own general conclusion was to emphasise that they were innate – as indeed have other more recent writers since Darwin's time such as Ekman (1977, 1982, 1984, Ekman *et al.* 1983). As Hochschild (1983: 208) notes, what is missing from these accounts is any conception of emotion as subjective, and a more subtle and sophisticated notion of how social and cultural factors impinge on emotional experience and expression.

Freud's approach to emotions, in contrast, is somewhat more difficult to characterise, moving as it did through various differing stages. In his early writing he viewed affect as 'dammed-up libido', emphasising tension and anxiety. Here, affect was simply viewed as the manifestation of (repressed) instinct. At the turn of the century, however, Freud came to view affect as a 'concomitant of drive', whilst, by 1923 in *The Ego and the Id*, he stressed instead the mediatory role of the ego between id (drive) and conscious expression: 'Affects were now seen as signals of impending danger (from inside or outside) and as an impetus for action' (Hochschild 1983: 208). Unlike Darwin, however, Freud's focus on psychopathology problematically singled out one particular emotion as the model for all others, namely; anxiety. Moreover, in contrast to Darwin, the meaning of a feeling (*i.e.* the ideational representation of affect) was crucial for Freud, albeit often at an unconscious level. Like Darwin, however, Freud has 'little to say about how cultural rules might (through the superego) apply to the ego's operations (emotion work) on id (feelings)' (Hochschild 1983: 210).

If, for Darwin, emotion is an instinctual gesture with an archaic, evolutionary heritage, and if, at least for the early Freud, emotion (affect) is the manifestation of dammed-up libido, for James in contrast, emotion is the brain's conscious reaction to instinctual visceral change. James, in other words, equates emotion with bodily change and visceral feeling. On this there seemed to be some slight disagreement between James – for whom emotion is conscious feeling and bodily change together – and Lange – for whom emotion is bodily change and feeling secondary. Not enough, however, to prevent the two being referred to together as the James-Lange theory of emotion (1922); a theory which was subsequently discredited by Cannon's (1927) experimental work in which the total separation of the viscera and central nervous system was not found to alter emotional behaviour.

Given these limitations, and the absence of any noteworthy differences in the visceral accompaniments of feelings such as fear and anger (Gerth and Mills 1964), psychologists sought to differentiate between emotions according to *cognitive* factors and therefore laid the basis for social psychology. In other words, this suggested the need to 'go beyond' the organism and the physical environment in order to account for human emotion (Gerth and Mills 1964: 52–3). As Hochschild notes, whilst 'going beyond' does not mean ignoring the importance of physiology in human emotion, 'it does mean working with a more intricate model than organismic theorists propose of how social and cognitive influences join physiological ones' (1983: 211).

In contrast to organismic theories, social constructionist approaches, as the name implies, stress the primarily social as opposed to the biological nature of emotions. In doing so, they too fall foul of the temptation to overstretch their explanatory frameworks (*i.e.* the other extreme of the organic-social spectrum). As in (medical) sociology more generally (Bury 1986), 'social constructionist' approaches to emotion house a variety of differing theoretical perspectives. Nonetheless, what they do all share in common, in varying degrees, is an emphasis on the socially and culturally faceted nature of emotions as 'emergent' phenomena. From this viewpoint, the 'organic moorings' of emotion are at best peripheral, and at worst irrelevant to the sociological enterprise.

Contra organismic theories, emotions, for social constructionists, cannot be studied mechanistically, as in specificity theory. Whilst emotions may be *accompanied* by physiological changes, their existence is not explained in these terms. Indeed, some emotions, it is argued, such as pride and jealousy, seem to have no specific biochemical 'substrate' at all.

Emotions are therefore seen to vary socially and cross culturally in terms of their meaning, experience and expression. As such, with the possible exception of so-called primary emotions such as anger and fear, they are social and cultural constructions. According to this line of reasoning, sociologists should not therefore focus on 'physiological details' until the varieties of emotions, their meaning, functions and relationship to the broader social, moral and ritual order, as well as other aspects of emotional life, have been thoroughly investigated (Harre 1986).

Leading exponents of this social constructionist view include writers such as McCarthy (1989), Harre (1986, 1991) and Jackson (1993) who, from differing vantage points, each seek to elaborate the social or public nature of emotions. McCarthy (1989), for example, seeks to develop what she terms an 'autonomous' (Meadian) sociological perspective on mind, self and emotion as 'emergent' properties: one which will not concede to the psychologist or physiologist exclusive or even primary rights to the domain of emotions. Here the focus is on the fact that, whilst functionally related to the organism, emotions can neither be reduced to, nor explained by, the organism. Rather, emotions are part of the conscious relations, actions and experiences of selves. Seen in these terms 'Emotions are not "inside" bodies, but rather actions we place in our world . . . feelings are *social* . . . constituted and sustained by group processes . . . *irreducible to the bodily organism* and to the particular individual who feels them' (McCarthy 1989: 57, our emphasis). More generally, social constructionist approaches to emotions view human feelings as capable of considerable historical and cultural variation and elaboration.

In a more Wittgensteinian vein, Harre (1986, 1991), argues that the study of emotions involves a focus on a certain kind of social act within a broader moral and cultural order. Seen in these terms, there is no such thing as 'an emotion', rather there are only various ways of acting and feeling emotionally, of displaying one's judgements, attitudes and opinions 'dramatistically' in certain appropriate bodily ways (Harre 1991; 142). Thus, anger, for example, refers not to what someone is, but rather what someone does:

> By reifying anger, we can be tempted into the mistake of thinking that anger is something inside a person exercising its invisible and inaudible influence on what we do. But *to be angry is to have taken on the angry role on a particular occasion as the expression of a moral position.* This role may involve the feeling of appropriate feelings as well as indulging in suitable public conduct. *The bodily feeling is often the somatic expression to oneself of the taking of a moral standpoint* (Harre 1991: 142–3, our emphasis).

As this suggests, emotions are for Harre, and indeed always have been, the bodily enactments of mainly *moral* judgements and attitudes, albeit judgements without premises (*i.e.* judgements which, in large part, are devoid of conscious ratiocination). This, in turn, suggests that the methodological strategy for a social constructionist approach to emotions should focus on: 1. the repertoire of public '*language games*' available in any given culture (*i.e.* what are the emotional vocabularies and under what conditions are they used); 2. the *moral order* within which the moral appraisals which control both the meaning and use of emotional terminologies are themselves meaningful; 3. the *social function* (*i.e.* 'acts') which particular emotions display; 4. the *narrative* forms that the unfolding of the situations revealed in 1., 2. and 3. realise, and finally; 5. the system of *rules* by which these complex forms of social/emotional action are maintained, changed, critically accounted for and taught (Harre 1986: 13). According to Harre, when, and 'only when' all this '*hard work has been done*, are we likely to engage profitably in the tracking of the physiological details of the various bodily perturbations that severally accompany the activities which [the above five points] enable us to understand' (1986: 13).

More recently, Jackson (1993) has extended this social constructionist position to the cultural meaning of love as a neglected emotion in sociological discourse. Building on the arguments that feelings are culturally and historically variable (Lutz 1982, 1986, 1989, Lutz and White 1986, Rosaldo 1984, Stearns and Stearns 1988, Stearns 1994), and that there are complex linguistic and other social pre-conditions for the existence of human emotions (Jaggar 1989), Jackson goes on to argue for an approach to love which: 'similarly regards the emotion itself as just as much cultural as the conventions which surround it, but which still takes seriously the subjective experience of love' (1993: 202).

These issues, in turn, key into broader poststructuralist and postmodernist critiques of the Cartesian rationalist project (and subject); ones which abandon any notion of a core abiding subjectivity (*i.e.* the 'decentred subject') and instead choose to celebrate the body through notions of desire, emotions, the affective life, and 'corporeal intimacies' (Turner 1991). As suggested earlier, the problem with these social constructionist and postmodern approaches, is that ultimately they end up 'decentering' the body itself, which simply becomes a textual product; the result of the endless play of inscription and reinscription on the 'nomadic' body ('without-organs'?) (Fox 1993). As a consequence, the imperialistic tendencies of social constructionists mean that their explanatory frames of reference become 'over-stretched' and the body becomes as 'elusive' versus 'elusory' as ever (Radley 1995). In short, a 'pure' constructionist perspective in the sociology of emotions; 'ignores biological process and presents a disembodied view of human emotions . . . The relationship between body and emotions are not resolved by ignoring the body's relevance or by viewing emotions simply as cognitive products' (Freund 1990: 455).

It is in this sense that interactionist approaches, in our view, represent a significant step forward in the sociological study of emotions, sitting as they do in the analytical space between organismic and social constructionist accounts. Again, as with the previous two approaches, a variety of different theoretical perspectives are housed under this general rubric. Nonetheless, they all share a common approach to emotions which seeks to interlock biological and social factors in a dynamic rather than reductionist, monocausal way. For example, Wentworth and Ryan argue that the most penetrating inquiry into the ontology of emotions can no longer be framed as an *either* nature *or* nurture question. Instead, they propose that 'the reality of emotion is the *interaction* of the biophysical, personal and the social. *Only* in combining can these elements manifest and retain the distinct properties of the compound that is human emotion' (1994: 3).

In seeking to develop this position further they argue that each of these three environments, biophysical, personal and social, is in some way 'social', the latter two in an obvious sense, the former in an interactive manner. As they stress, our biology is not constant, rather it is influenced within one generation and over the long haul of evolution by a variety of noninheritable experiences. Following on from this, innate emotions may be seen as unsophisticated analogues of their later culturally constituted transformations. Moreover, whilst the biophysical, personal and social realms of emotions form a synthesis, the particular influence of each on the resultant synthesis (and therefore on experienced and expressed emotions) is a product of biographical, situational and cultural factors and contingencies (Wentworth and Ryan 1994: 4. See also Lyon's (1989) analysis of respiration as another powerful example of the complex interaction between biology, emotion and culture, and Kemper (1990b) on the links between sociological and biological processes in the formation of human emotion).

Taking these issues further, Wentworth and Yardley (1994) develop the concept of 'deep sociality' (*i.e.* the capacity to make emotionally founded, self to self relationships and, in turn, a profound dependence on them). In this sense, they argue that, through emotion, evolution has yielded a potent medium of attaining both intersubjectivity and a sense that it is imperative to do so. Indeed, in a similar manner to Elias's (1978, 1991a,b) evolutionary analysis of symbol emancipation and the tilting of the balance towards 'learned' rather than 'unlearned' forms of human behaviour and emotional response, Wentworth and Yardley argue that, the greater the sociality of the species, the more emotionality moves to the very centre of information processing and communication. In short, human emotions – linked as they are to evolutionary developments in which the balance between 'pre-wired', 'instinctive' and acquired behaviours has shifted ever more heavily toward the latter – provide the basis for 'deep' forms of sociality. As such, they provide a powerful means of intersubjective communication which possesses the capacity to bind individuals into a social entity and motivate them to perform certain tasks and avoid others (Wentworth and Yardley 1989: 45).

Perhaps the most well known and successful 'interactionist' approach to emotions, however, can be found in the work of Hochschild (1979, 1983, 1990, 1997). For Hochschild, drawing on Freud, emotion is not only a biologically given sense, but also our most important one in signifying 'danger' on the template of prior expectations. Like other senses, emotion is the means through which we know the social world and our relation to it; as such it is crucial to the survival of human beings in group life. Yet as Hochschild also points out, emotion is unique among the senses in being related not only to *action* but also to *cognition* (Hochschild 1983: 219).

In adopting this stance, Hochschild joins three theoretical currents in order to theorise emotions. Drawing on Dewey, Gerth and Mills (1964) and Goffman (1959), within the interactionist tradition, she explores what gets 'done' to emotions and how feelings are permeable to what gets done to them. From Darwin (1955/[1895]), in the organismic tradition, she is able to posit a sense of what is there, impermeable, to be 'done to' (*i.e.* a biologically given sense, which in turn, is related to an orientation to action). Finally, through Freud's work on the 'signal' function of feelings, Hochschild is able to circle back from the organismic to the interactionist tradition, by tracing the way in which social factors influence what we expect and thus what these feelings actually 'signify' (Hochschild 1983: 222). For Hochschild, emotion is 'bodily co-operation with an image, a thought, a memory – a co-operation of which the individual is aware' (1979: 551).

From this starting point, Hochschild (1979, 1983, 1990, 1997) goes on to outline her own 'emotion management' perspective; a perspective which allows her to inspect the relationship between emotional experience, emotion management, feeling rules and ideology. As she explains, feeling rules are the side of ideology which deals with emotions and feelings. Emotion management, in contrast, is the type of work it takes to cope with these feeling rules. In this respect, as she argues, 'meaning–making' jobs, which tend to be more common in the middle class, put more of a premium on the individual's capacity to *do* emotion work. Each class, therefore, 'psychologically' reproduces' the class structure. We shall return to the relevance of Hochschild's work and its subsequent development by Freund (1988, 1990, 1997) later when considering the relationship between emotions and the social causes of disease.

In their differing ways, all these approaches to emotions raise deeper philosophical and ontological questions concerning the problematic status of human embodiment as simultaneously both nature and culture. As Denzin (1984) argues, emotions are embodied experiences; ones which radiate through the body as a structure of on-going lived experience and centrally involved self-feelings which constitute the inner core of emotionality. As a consequence, 'emotion's body', considered as a totality, becomes: 'a moving, feeling complex of sensible feelings, feelings of the lived body, intentional value feelings, and feelings of the self and moral person' (1984: 128). For individuals to understand their own lived emotions, they must experience them socially and reflectively. It is here, according to Denzin, at the intersection between emotions as *embodied* experiences, their socially faceted nature, and their links with feelings of selfhood and personal identity, that a truly sociological perspective and understanding of emotions can most fruitfully be forged.

More generally, in challenging *representational* (*i.e.* constructionist) approaches to the human body, Csordas (1994a,b) argues for an approach to human embodiment as the existential ground of culture and self. In other words, against the notion of the body as a passive object of ideological representation, Csordas proposes instead the *active* subject of embodied being-in-the world. From this viewpoint – one which is not merely about the body but *from* the body – embodiment is neither reducible to representations of the body, to the body as an objectification of power, to the body as a physiological entity, nor to the body as an inalienable centre of individual consciousness. Rather, it becomes instead the existential basis of social and cultural life. Moreover, the interactive, relational character of embodied emotional experience offers a way of moving beyond microanalytic, subjective, internal or individualistic analyses, towards a more 'open-ended horizon' in which embodied agency can be understood as not only individual but also 'institution making' (Csordas, 1994a: 124, Lyon and Barbalet 1994). Here we return full-circle to some of the earlier debates discussed above concerning micro–macro linkages in the sociology of emotions.

Where then does all this leave us? In weaving our way through these complex debates and dilemmas one thing remains clear, namely that, as with the human body more generally, emotion is a complex phenomenon and an 'uncontainable' term in any one domain or discourse. In this respect emotions, in our view, are most fruitfully seen as *embodied* existential modes of being; ones which involve an *active* engagement with the world and an intimate connection with both culture and self (Csordas 1994a,b). Not only do emotions underpin the phenomenological experience of our bodies in health and illness (the 'libidinous structure' of body image in the work of Schilder (1950) and Scheler's (1961/[1912]) phenomenology of feeling), they also provide the basis for social reciprocity and exchange (*cf.* the notion of 'deep sociability' (Wentworth and Yardley 1994)), and the 'link' between personal problems and broader public issues of social structure (Mills 1959). Indeed, to paraphrase Giddens' (1984) structuration theory, social structure may fruitfully be seen as both

the *medium* and *outcome* of the e*motionally embodied practices/techniques*
it recursively organises. In short, the emphasis here is on the active, emotionally expressive body as the basis of self, sociality, meaning, and order
within the broader socio-cultural realms of everyday life and the 'ritualised' forms of interaction and exchange they involve.

Underpinning these arguments, of course, is a broader critique of the
dualist legacies of the past; legacies which, as we have suggested, have
sought to divorce mind from body, nature from culture and reason from
emotion. As Csordas states:

> . . . that the body might be understood as a seat of subjectivity is one
> source of challenge to theories of culture in which mind/subject/culture
> are deployed in parallel with and in contrast to body/object/biology.
> Much of our theorising is heir to the Cartesian legacy in that it privi-
> leges the mind/subject/culture set in the form of representation, whether
> cast in terms of rules and principles . . . signs and symbols . . . text and
> discourse . . . or knowledge and models (1994a: 9).

It is this notion of the emotionally 'expressive' or 'mindful' body as a
lived reality, one which is active in the interactional contexts of power,
conflict and social exchange which, we suggest, strikes at the very heart of
these dualities. Embodiment captures the essential ambiguity (the contradiction between these two terms is intentional) of human beings as both
nature and culture, the transcendence of duality at the pre-objective level
of on-going lived experience, and the existential basis of culture and self.
Here, mind and body, reason and emotion, can only be arbitrarily separated by an act of conscious reflection and objectification.

Having sketched the outlines of these broader debates within the sociology of emotions, together with our own particular position within them, it
is to fuller accounts of their relevance to the sociology of health and illness
that we now turn. In particular, we shall move from the phenomenology
of pain as an emotionally embodied experience, to broader micro–macro
issues concerning the emotionally expressive body in relation to the social
causes of disease and the growth of 'holistic health' in late modernity. In
doing so, we hope to illustrate further how emotions provide the 'missing
link' in (medical) sociology between mind and body, inside and outside,
structure and agency, micro and macro, public and private, and a host of
other dichotomous ways of thinking. Hence, it is to the first of these areas
that we now turn, namely, the phenomenological experience of pain.

Pain and emotions

Pain is never the sole creation of human anatomy or physiology. Rather,
it emerges at the intersection of bodies, minds and culture (Morris 1991).

Moreover, pain is never simply a form of physical suffering, but also encompasses emotional and affective dimensions, feelings which, in turn, are crucially linked to 'gendered' modes of bodily being (Bendelow 1993).

The notion of pain having a substantial emotional component, literally the obverse of pleasure is much older than that of pain being a physiological sensation and can be traced back to Plato's (429–347 BC) deliberations of extremes and opposites in the *World of Forms*. Here he declares pleasure and pain to be the twin passions of the soul, the results of the interactions between earth, air, fire and water. Aristotle (384–322 BC) developed the pain/pleasure principles further, describing them as basic moral drives guiding human action, and believed the pain experience to be a negative passion which had to be conquered by reason. In particular, Aristotle believed that pain was conveyed by the blood to the heart, yet excluded it from his classification of the five senses, instead preferring to describe it as a 'quale' or emotional quality of the soul; a state of feeling and the epitome of 'unpleasantness'. Literature, theology and philosophy abound with considerations of the nature and purpose of pain (amongst many others, see Tillich's (1968) *Systematic Theology* and Kierkegaard's *Works of Love* 1962/[1847]). Within these diverse traditions, the pleasure/pain dichotomy is constantly evoked and reinforced.

In contrast to the dominant biomedical model, pain is a lived, embodied, physical *and* emotional experience. Indeed, as Turner (1992) argues, a phenomenology of the body or 'embodiment' has particular importance for medical sociology as it provides a sensitive and sophisticated perspective on issues such as pain, disability and death. This, in turn, serves to highlight the weakness of the Cartesian legacy for sociology. Indeed, in our view, it is this emphasis upon the phenomenology of the body as a 'lived experience', one where the objective body (*Korper*) is not treated as separate from the inner sensations of the subjective body (*Lieb*), which seems to have particular relevance for the sociology of pain as an 'embodied' emotional and affective experience (Bendelow and Williams 1995a and 1995b).

As Morris states: 'Pain is never entirely a matter of nerves and neurotransmitters but taps into our emotional, psychological, and cultural experience in ways deeply entangled with the meanings we make or invent' (1994: 16). Pain, in other words, can be used to describe not only physical agony but emotional turmoil and spiritual suffering (Leder 1984–5). More broadly, as Scheper-Hughes and Lock argue, emotions affect the way in which the body, illness and pain are experienced and are projected in images of the well and poorly functioning social and body politic. To the extent that emotions entail both 'feelings and cognitive orientations', 'public morality and cultural ideology', they provide an 'important "missing link"' capable of bridging mind and body, individual, society and body politic'. In this respect, explorations of sickness, madness, pain, disability and death are human events which are literally 'seething with emotion' (Scheper-Hughes and Lock 1987: 28–9).

Thus emotion is seen as the mediatrix of the three bodies – phenomenally experienced, social and body politic – which Scheper-Hughes and Lock (1987) identify, and which they unify through the notion of the 'mindful body'. Grief, for instance, is an example of emotional pain which is inseparable from its 'gut churning, nauseating experience', whilst physical pain bears within it a 'component of displeasure, and often of anxiety, sadness and anger that are fully emotional' (Leder 1984–5: 261). On the other hand, pain may also signal something positive. In this respect pain may bring us to an authentic recognition of our own limitations and possibilities. It may also be creative, not only in the sense of childbirth but also in terms of physical, emotional, artistic and spiritual achievements, or it may serve as a catalyst for much needed changes in our lives (Leder 1984–5). Indeed, in the (post)modern world today, pain, it seems, can even function as a 'fashion icon'; one in which 'the ancient arts of body piercing and self-mutilation arrive . . . filtered through pop icons and rock lyrics' (Morris 1994: 24).

In summary, if we are to move beyond dualistic notions of mind and body, reason and emotion, then pain, a fundamental aspect of the human condition, needs to be 'reclaimed' from exclusive biomedical jurisdiction and relocated at the juncture between biology and culture (Morris 1991, 1994). A reconsideration of the place and function of emotions in reconnecting mind and body, culture and meaning is, in our view, central to this enterprise. Beyond this phenomenological level of analysis, however, emotions also serve as an important bridge or 'missing link' between 'personal troubles' and broader 'public issues of social structure': itself the defining hallmark of the 'sociological imagination' (Mills 1959). Hence it is to this broader issue of the micro–macro relationship between the emotionally expressive body, social structure and health that we now turn.

Micro–macro linkages: social, structure, health and the emotionally 'expressive' body

Much has been written about the psycho-social causes of disease and the role which life events, difficulties, and social support play in the onset of physical and mental illness (Brown and Harris 1978, Brown and Harris 1989, Cohen and Syme 1985, Thoits 1995). Nevertheless, little attempt has been made adequately to theorise this relationship, particularly using emotions as the missing link between body, mind and society. A notable exception in this respect is the work of Freund (1982, 1988, 1990, 1997) who sees the 'expressive body' as a common ground for the sociology of emotions and health and illness.

A central part of understanding human emotions for Freund is to see them as existential 'modes of being' (Buytendijk 1974, 1962, 1950), or what Denzin (1984), as we saw earlier, terms human 'emotionality' (see also Wentworth and Ryan 1990). Emotional modes of being involve a fusion of physical and psychic states (Freund 1990: 458). Moreover, as Freund suggests, a sense of being in touch with others, of being (in)validated by them, as well as other emotional modes of being, emerge out of social interaction. Emotional modes of being can be either 'pleasant' or 'unpleasant' and, as Buytendijk (1950) argues, a number of differing modes of feeling exist (Freund 1990).

The crucial issue for our purposes, however, is that these differing modes of emotional being are, in effect, different felt ways of feeling *empowered* or *disempowered* which, in turn, are very much linked to people's conditions of existence throughout their biographies (Freund 1990: 461). It is here, at this nexus, that:

> 'External' social structural factors such as one's position in different systems of hierarchy or various forms of social control can influence the conditions of our existence, how we respond and apprehend these conditions and our sense of embodied self. These conditions can also affect our physical functioning (Freund 1990: 461).

Embodied forms of emotional being and subjectivity, social activity and the socio-structural context, therefore, interpenetrate, and it is this relationship which, Freund argues, comes to be physically as well as emotionally embodied in many different ways. For example, Freund sites irregularity in breathing which may accompany muscular tension and experiences of ontological insecurity and the anger, anxiety or fear that is a part of this insecurity (Freund 1990: 461-2. See also Kelly 1980, and Lyon 1994). Indeed, one may literally be 'scared stiff' (Freund 1990: 462, Buytendijk 1974: 181). Emotions, in other words, are always in some sense embodied. Whilst it is one thing to argue that 'felt' emotions are not always accompanied by psychophysical changes and sensations, it is quite another to argue that moods and emotional states do not have bodily accompaniments and consequences (Freund 1990: 462, Buytendijk 1974: 188). In short, as Freund states:

> Since the body is a means of expressing meaning, including socio-cultural meaning, it is not unrealistic to suppose that people might express somatically the conditions of their existence. Pain, for instance, can express a sense of an existence that weighs heavily on one or a sense of powerlessness . . . Cultural factors can shape the language of the body (1990: 463).

Lynch reaches similar conclusions in his book *The Broken Heart: the Medical Consequences of Loneliness* (1975), in which he presents compelling evidence to demonstrate the links between cardiovascular disease and emotionally distressing life events. In particular, he uses medical technology to demonstrate emotional states (*e.g.* electro-encephalographic (ECG) patterns showing dramatic improvements when a nurse holds a patient's hand). Similarly, as a variety of life-events research shows, emotional states (including psychiatric morbidity) play a 'mediatory' role in the onset of a broad range of physical conditions, from coronary heart disease (CHD) to gastro-intestinal disorders and appendicitis (Brown and Harris 1989).

In order to 'flesh out' these arguments further, Freund draws on Hochschild's (1979, 1983) concepts of 'emotion work' and 'status shields' in the wider context of power, domination and social control. As he notes, one's position in the social hierarchy and the activities involved in insuring social control are two features of social structure that influence feelings. These feelings may, in turn, influence our physiology as well (Freund 1982, 1988, 1990, 1997). In other words, one's position in any system of social hierarchy and the manner in which social relationships are managed both affect and are affected by biochemical states and other aspects of bodyliness (Freund 1990: 465). As Freund suggests, a person's social position and status will determine the resources they have at their disposal in order to define and protect the boundaries of the self and counter the potential for 'invalidation' by powerful and significant others. Relating this more closely to key aspects of contemporary social structure, it therefore follows that those who occupy less powerful positions in the social hierarchy are at greater risk of being invalidated, of feeling instrumentally powerless, insecure, unable to speak one's mind or blameworthy for the distressful feelings experienced. In short, an: '. . . extremely powerless social status increases the likelihood of experiencing "unpleasant" emotionality or emotional modes of being' (Freund 1990: 466).

As Goffman (1959) clearly demonstrates, self presentation and role playing, together with the emotion work that accompanies these activities, can, in and of itself be 'dramaturgically stressful'. If, as Freund (1982, 1990) argues, this stress becomes chronic it may, for instance, affect neurohormonal regulation in the body. Moreover, one's social status affects the degree to which one has 'status shields' available to protect the boundaries and integrity of the self (Hochschild 1979, 1983). Status shields, in other words, protect us from attacks on self and the absence of these is a structural source of feeling powerless; a situation which is more likely to occur amongst lower status persons and be inflicted by those in power (Freund 1982, 1990, Franks 1987, Collins 1990). Having one's feelings ignored or termed irrational is analogous to having one's perceptions invalidated. Less powerful people, therefore, face a structurally in-built handicap in managing social and emotional information, and this handicap may, in turn, contribute to existential fear, anxiety and neurophysiological perturbation (Freund 1990).

More precisely, these social influences on neuro-physiological activity, Freund suggests, may fruitfully be seen as occurring through the agency of an 'ontologically insecure self' (*c.f.* Laing 1965) and the associated negative existential modes of emotional being they generate; issues which, in turn, are linked to dramaturgical stress, the absence of status shields and wider structures of power, domination and control in society. In particular, Freund argues that social relationships may engender a form of 'schizokinesis' (Lynch 1985, Kelly 1980) in which a split occurs between what is shown and consciously experienced, as opposed to what occurs somatically. Here Freund poses two extremely pertinent questions: namely, 'how "deep" can the social construction of feelings go?', and; 'can emotion work eliminate the responses of an unconsciously knowing body?' The implications of his argument and the concept of schizokinesis seem to suggest that the answer to these questions is 'very deep indeed': society affects physiological reactivity deep within the recesses of the human body, although, as the concept of schizokinesis implies, the 'mind' may, consciously at least, be unaware of the 'body's' response. For example, as continued emotional and other kinds of distress alter physiological reactivity, neurohormonally-related functions such as blood pressure may markedly increase in response to a stressor, but not be consciously experienced (Freund 1990: 470). Freund usefully summarises his position in the following terms:

> One's positions, and the roles that accompany them in various systems of social hierarchy, shape the conditions in which one lives. This position influences access to resources. It may also determine the forms of emotional-social control to which one is subject as well as the severity of the impact these controls have on the person . . . Such a process may mean internalising the emotional definitions that others impose on what we are or 'should' be. The physiological aspects of such processes are of interest to those studying emotions. However, these physical aspects may also be seen as examples of ways in which controls are sedimented and fixed in the psycho-soma of the person. Physiological aspects of social activity can also act as a form of feedback that colours the tone of existence. This feedback can *indirectly* serve social control functions. For instance, conditions that create depression . . . construct an emotional mode of being where the motivation to resist is blunted (1990: 470).

As this suggests, the argument here is for a sophisticated and subtle form of 'socialised' or externally 'pliable' biology rather than a reductionist socio-biology; one which accords emotional modes of being a central role, in linking the health and illness of the existential-phenomenologically embodied agent with wider structures of power and domination, civilisation and control in society. Clearly, however, whilst suggestive, many of these insights retain the status of 'working hypotheses' rather than proven facts. As such, they require further rigorous empirical examination, specification and elaboration. Nonetheless, qualifications apart, what Freund does offer us is a potentially very fruitful advance on the now theoretically impoverished debates about the role of life events and psycho-social factors in the aetiology of physical disease and mental illness (Brown and Harris 1989). As we have argued, this notion of the emotionally expressive body, coupled with the important work of Collins on interaction ritual and Hochschild on emotion management, provides a significant step forward in the macro/micro, structure/agency debates which have dogged sociology since its inception.

Holistic health and the 'emotionally reflexive body': liberation or oppression?

Our third chosen area where the sociology of emotions is of relevance to medical sociology concerns the increasing popularity of holistic therapies, seemingly premised upon a non-dualistic ontology, and the growth of social reflexivity in late modernity.

To be sure, as Coward (1989: 43–4) notes, recent years have witnessed a radical change in what is meant by 'health', 'illness' and 'disease'. Now we can set our sights much higher than simply the avoidance of illness. Health instead, is increasingly linked with 'feeling good' and 'looking great', a notion of true 'well-being' which rests on the idea of 'balance' or 'harmony' between body, soul, mind and emotion, as well as satisfactory relationships with other people and society as a whole. Within this context, health becomes an endlessly pursued but rarely achieved goal; one which is inextricably linked to individual attitudes, commitment and personal responsibility (Crawford 1980: 374). This, in turn, links up with broader trends in consumer culture towards the cultivation of the body and self as projects, and the growth of social reflexivity (Featherstone 1991, Giddens 1991, Shilling 1993).

It is within this context that 'holistic' therapies movement comes to the fore. Central to these therapies is the idea that the body can 'heal itself' and that we can only really be well if we achieve a state of true, 'whole person', health: beliefs which have received an enormous boost in recent years from the importation and steady growth of oriental therapies like acupuncture, acupressure and Shiatsu (Coward 1989: 46–9). Here an alliance is forged with the natural healing properties of the body which conventional medicine is seen to have so sorely neglected. These self-healing or teleonomic capacities of the body (*i.e.* the *vis mediacatrix naturae*), are only possible, however, when a state of 'natural balance' or 'harmony' can be restored or found.

As a number of writers have noted (Taylor 1984, Aakster 1986, Lederman 1989, Pietroni 1991, Sharma 1992, 1996, Saks 1995), underpinning this notion of the 'natural healing properties' of the body and the importance of 'harmony' and 'balance', is a focus on 'vital energies'; a focus which links the more accepted therapies such as acupuncture, homeopathy and naturopathy to other more 'marginal' or 'fringe' forms of medicine. Here the proposition is a straightforward one, namely, that 'blockages' of 'imbalances' in the vital energies or life forces which flow through the body result in (a susceptibility to) illness. In acupuncture, for example, an 'imbalance' in the (vigorous) *yin* or the (restraining) *yang* elements is thought to throw the body's life force (*chi*) out of kilter, thus resulting in illness or a deterioration in general well-being. Treatment, therefore, involves the insertion of needles into various energy meridian running through the body in order to rectify such 'imbalances' and restore 'health' and 'well-being'. In short:

> The discourses of alternative therapies seek to recast the imagery of the body and disease by moving away from aggressive military metaphorical conceptualizations of the body . . . to depicting the body as 'natural', as self-regulating and part of a wider ecological balance, with words 'balance', 'harmony', 'regulate', 'spirit' and 'energy' prevailing (Lupton 1994: 128).

As this suggests, emotions are central to holistic forms of therapy and treatment. In many cases, as Coward (1989) observes, this integration is quite subtle, glimpsed only indirectly through discussion of mood, sleep and (vital) energy. In contrast, in other therapies such as Bach flower remedies and aromatherapy, emotions are seen to be central. Indeed, in these forms of treatment, it is far more common to find remedies offered according to a specific set of emotions or 'personality type' than it is to find treatment based on a specific illness. In short, it is attention to emotional state and personality predispositions which, more than anything else; 'inform the idea of "whole person" treatment . . . Previously consigned either to psychotherapy or to astrology, and definitely considered irrelevant to the state of the body, they have now moved into the centre of the picture' (Coward 1989: 71). All the aspects of the person, which 'orthodox' medicine has traditionally regarded as irrelevant, are therefore embodied in these 'alternative' therapeutic traditions.

At one level, this suggests a somewhat rosy picture; an image of ideal health to which we are all supposed to be striving and which, in contrast to orthodox medicine, seeks to integrate not just our bodies and our minds, but also our emotions through a warm embrace with mother 'nature'. What more could one ask for; total health, total well-being, all within our own grasp and under our own personal (read emotional) control? At another level, however, as a number of writers have commented, this Utopian vision of heaven on earth may be more apparent than real. First, it is clear that, whatever the therapy, *personal* responsibility is invariably placed high on the agenda as the means to restore or maintain 'good health' (Crawford 1980). Seen in these terms, health as 'well-being' is translated into a state which has to be 'won back or achieved'. In other words, the 'stresses' and 'strains' of modern life can be 'effectively' controlled according to the 'emotional type' of the individual (Coward 1989: 82). In short, as with health promotion more generally, wittingly or unwittingly, these forms of therapy, and the underlying philosophies upon which they are based, tend to deflect attention away from the wider political economy of health and illness (Crawford 1980, Berliner and Salmon 1980).

Similarly, regarding the notion of 'personality types', there appears to be something of a contradiction. On the one hand a supposedly 'whole person' approach to medicine and healing gives priority to individual control and the ability to 'change'. On the other hand, however, a belief in personality type displays an unhelpful and largely unnecessary degree of 'fatalism'. Indeed, despite protestations to the contrary, the emphasis on the links between personality types, health and illness, often carries with it associations of:

> . . . a static and limited model of a world of fixed emotions and person-
> alities into which human behaviour, characteristics and illness can be
> fitted. In fact, the unresolved tension between calls for change and
> beliefs in fixed personality types has tended to be the way in which
> guilt-provoking and moralistic notions of illness have been able to grow
> (Coward 1989: 73–4).

To this we might also add the comment that, despite the emphasis on the unity of mind and body, an underlying hierarchical form of dualism nonetheless remains, as mind is accorded primacy over body in the 'healing' process.

At a broader level, as Lowenberg and Davis (1994) have recently argued, the 'holistic health movement' contains within it elements which suggest processes of both 'de-medicalization' and 're-medicalization'. Thus whilst the locus of causality is restored to the individual and status differentials between providers and clients are seemingly minimised, suggesting a process of de-medicalisation, the exponential expansion of the 'pathogenic sphere' and remit of the holistic health movement simultaneously suggests a drastic increase in medicalisation in Western society; processes which, in turn, connect with the emergence of the 'psy' complex in late twentieth-century society (Rose 1990, McCarthy 1989). There is also a highly selective and problematic use of the term 'natural' (Coward 1989). In this respect, echoing Armstrong's (1986) earlier critique, Lowenberg and Davis (1994) suggest that the holistic health model subjects an increasing number of areas of everyday life to medical scrutiny and supervision due to its emphasis upon life-style modification and mind–body continuity. Seen in this light, the 'liberatory' potential of 'alternative' therapies and the holistic health movement takes on a more troubling hue, as important elements of 'continuity' rather than contrast with biomedicine and consumer culture are instead thrown into critical relief (Crawford 1980: 370, Sharma 1996). Indeed, even the notion of 'energy' conforms to late capitalist ideologies and imperatives of 'production' (Coward 1989: 57). Moreover, as Saks (1994) suggests, whilst these therapies may pose important challenges to orthodox medicine, they have not, as yet, significantly reduced its dominance. As such, they may perhaps more fruitfully be viewed as 'complementary' rather than 'alternative' (Sharma 1992, 1996). 'Liberation' or 'oppression'?: the tensions of a 'therapeutic' age are therefore thrown into critical relief through a focus on the emotionally reflexive body of late modernity.

Conclusion

A key, albeit somewhat rhetorical, question which flows directly from the foregoing discussion concerns whether or not the Cartesian rationalist actor is 'dead'? This question, in turn, throws into critical relief a number of other contemporary challenges to dominant dualistic modes of thought as we approach the *fin de millenium*. Perhaps the fullest, if somewhat problematic, expression of these issues is the postmodernist/post-structuralist project which has sought to liquidate Cartesian notions of rationality and subjectivity, in favour of an approach which celebrates the emotions, desire, corporeal intimacies and the 'endless deferral of meaning' (Turner 1991).

In contrast to these dominant 'representational' (*i.e.* social constructionist) approaches, our own position within this paper has been to stress the fundamentally *embodied* nature of human emotions as an on-going structure of lived experience, and an *active* mode of being-in-the-world; one which provides the existential basis of culture and self, human sociability and social institutions (Csordas 1994a, Lyon and Barbalet 1994). Here, it is not simply a question of nature *or* culture, biology *or* society, but the 'uncontainability' of human embodiment in either domain or discourse (Grosz 1994). Seen in these terms, it is only through a process of abstraction, objectification and ultimately reification that these domains become analytically separable. Rather, at the pre-objective level of lived experience, these analytical boundaries are wholly blurred: the body is in the mind, society is in the body, and the body is in society. Pain, as a pre-linguistic, pre-objective, emotionally embodied experience, strikes at the very heart of these dualities. More generally, as we have suggested, emotion provides the 'missing link' between personal troubles and broader public issues of social structure: itself the defining hallmark of the 'sociological imagination' (Mills 1959).

Underpinning this anti-dualist argument is a commitment fundamentally to re-think the 'biological' in non-essentialist terms (Benton 1991). To speak of the biological does not necessarily imply an essentialist position, if the notion of the biological is itself reconceptualised in positive rather than negative terms. Our biology is not a constant. Rather it is influenced in complex ways by a host of evolutionary, environmental and social factors. Moreover, it is not simply a constraint or limitation but a source of opportunity as the material basis or vehicle of personhood and being-in-the-world. In other words, human biology supports our most essential characteristics and, if rethought in the ways suggested above, does not (necessarily) contradict structural and cultural views (Wentworth and Ryan 1994: 4). As with the human body more generally, the sociology of emotions provides an important site from which upon which to rethink this biology/society relationship (see Bury 1995 and Williams 1996 for a recent debate on the merits of this case).

To conclude, medical sociology provides a potentially very fertile terrain upon which to fashion a non-dualist ontology of the 'mindful body'; one in which emotions, as mediators of micro–macro relations, play a central role in the human experience and cultural scripts of health, sickness, disability and death. From this viewpoint, existing models of health, illness and disease need to be replaced with more: 'sophisticated models of the dynamic interactions between organic and psychological processes at the level of the individual person, and between persons and their social-relational and bio-physical environments (Benton 1991: 6). Whilst we have chosen to focus on pain, the social causes of disease, and holistic health in order to illustrate these issues, it is equally clear that emotions are central to a number of other areas of medical sociology, including mental health and illness, gender, sexuality and human reproduction, the social organisation of health care, and the ethical dilemmas and issues surrounding the social relations of high technology/new genetic medicine. Indeed, in the context of high-technology medicine, where problems of dualism are becoming acute (Williams 1996), adequate consideration of emotions both demands and necessitates a fundamental rethinking of contemporary medical practice and approaches to the human body; one in which 'immunization from the emotional experiences of one's fellow man [sic] will no longer be seen as either a vital necessity or a particularly virtuous aspect of scientific objectivity' (Lynch 1985: 281). Utopia or reality, only time will tell!

Notes

1 It is clear that Descartes did in fact operate with an albeit limited view of the interaction between mind and body (*i.e.* a form of '*dualistic interactionism*'); one which he sought to locate in the pineal gland – a small portion of the brain. Only here does the mind directly exercise its power over the body like a rider on horseback. (Turner 1992, Leder 1990, Wilson 1975).
2 In this article, beyond the work of Denzin (1984), we have not sought to review or discuss other existential approaches to emotions such as those of Sarte ([1939]/1962). See Crossley (1997) for a fuller discussion of these issues.

References

Aakster, W. (1986) Concepts in alternative medicine, *Social Science and Medicine*, 22, 2: 265–73.

Armstrong, D. (1983) *Political Anatomy of the Body: Medical Knowledge in Britain in the Twentieth Century*. Cambridge: Cambridge University Press.

Armstrong, D. (1986) The problem of the whole-person in holistic medicine, *Holistic Medicine,*. 1: 27–36.

Armstrong, D. (1987) Theoretical tensions in biopsychosocial medicine, *Social Science and Medicine* 25, 11: 213–18.

Arney, W.R. and Neill, J. (1982) The location of pain in childbirth: natural childbirth and the transformation of obstetrics, *Sociology of Health and Illness*, 14, 1: 375–400.

Bendelow, G. (1993) Pain perceptors, gender and emotion, *Sociology of Health and Illness*, 15, 3: 273–94.

Bendelow, G. (1996) A 'failure' of medicine? Lay views of a pain relief clinic. In Wiliams, S.J. and Calnan, M. (eds) *Modern Medicine: the Lay Perspectives and Experiences*. London: UCL Press.

Bendelow, G. and Williams, S.J. (1995a) Transcending the dualisms: towards a sociology of pain, *Sociology of Health and Illness*, 17, 2: 139–65.

Bendelow, G. and Williams, S.J. (1995b) Pain and the mind–body dualism: a sociological approach, *Body and Society*, 1, 2: 82–103.

Benton, T. (1991) Biology and social science: why the return of the repressed should be given a (cautious) welcome, *Sociology*, 25, 1: 1–29.

Berliner, H.S. and Salmon, J.W. (1980) The holistic alternative to scientific medicine: history and analysis, *International Journal of Health Services*, 10, 1: 133–47.

Bologh, R. (1990) *Love or Greatness? Max Weber and Masculine Thinking: A Feminist Inquiry*. London: Unwin Hyman.

Bordo, S. (1989) The masculinisation of Cartesian thought, *Signs*, 11, 3: 433–57.

Brown, G.W. and Harris, T.O. (1978) *Social Origins of Depression*. London: Tavistock.

Brown, G.W. and Harris, T.O. (eds) (1989) *Life Events and Illness*. London: Hyman Unwin.

Bury, M. (1986) Social constructionism and the development of medical sociology, *Sociology of Health and Illness*, 8, 2: 137–69.

Bury, M. (1995) 'The body in question'. BSA Medical Sociology Group plenary, *Medical Sociology News*, 21, 1: 36–48.

Buytendijk, F.J.J. (1950) The phenomenological approach to the problem of feelings and emotions. In Reymert, M.C. (ed) *Feelings and Emotions: the Mooseheart Symposium in Cooperation with the University of Chicago*. New York: McGraw Hill Company Inc.

Buytendijk, F.J.J. (1962) *Pain: Its Modes and Functions*. Trans. by Eda O'Shiel. Chicago: University of Chicago Press.

Buytendijk, F.J.J. (1974) *Prolegomena to an Anthropological Physiology*. Pittsburgh: Duquesne University Press.

Cannon, W. (1927) The James-Lange theory of emotions: a critical examination and alternative theory, *American Journal of Psychiatry*, 138: 1319–30.

Clark, C. (1990) Emotions and micropolitics in everyday life: some patterns and paradoxes of 'place'. In: Kemper, T.J. (ed) *Research Agendas in the Sociology of Emotions*. New York: State University of New York Press.

Cohen, S. and Syme, L.S. (eds) (1985) *Social Support and Health*. London: Academic Press Inc.

Collins, R. (1990) Stratification, emotional energy, and the transient emotions. In Kemper, T.J. (ed) *Research Agendas in the Sociology of Emotions*. New York: State University of New York Press.

Coward, R. (1989) *The Whole Truth*. London: Faber and Faber.

Crawford, R. (1980) Healthism and the medicalization of everyday life, *International Journal of Health Services*, 10: 365–88.

Crossley, N. (1997) Emotions and communicative action. In Bendelow, G. A. and Williams, S.J. (eds) *Emotions in Social Life: Social Theories and Contemporary Issues*. London: Routledge.

Csordas, T.J. (1994a) Introduction: the body as representation and being-in-the-world. In Csordas, T.J. (ed) (1994) *Embodiment and Experience: The Existential Ground of Culture and Self*. Cambridge: Cambridge University Press.

Csordas, T.J. (1994b) Words from the holy: a case study in cultural anthropology. In Csordas, T.J. (ed) (1994) *Embodiment and Experience: the Existential Ground of Culture and Self*. Cambridge: Cambridge University Press.

Darwin, C. (1955/[1895]) *The Expression of Emotions in Man and Animals*. New York: Philosophical Library.

Denzin, N.K. (1984) *On Understanding Emotion*. San Francisco: Josey Bass.

Denzin, N.K. (1990) On understanding emotion: the interpretive-cultural agenda. In Kemper, T.J. (ed) *Research Agendas in the Sociology of Emotions*. New York: State University of New York Press.

Descartes, R. (1985) *The Philosophical Writings of Descartes*. Edited by Cottingham, J., Stoothoff, R. and Murdoch, D. Cambridge: Cambridge University Press.

Ekman, P. (1977) Biological and cultural contributions to the body and facial movement. In Blacking, J. (ed) *Anthropology of the Body*. New York: Academic Press.

Ekman, P. (ed) (1982) *Emotion in the Human Face*. Cambridge NY: Cambridge University Press.

Ekman, P. (1984) *Approaches to Emotion*. Hillsdale, New Jersey: Lawrence Erlbaum.

Ekman, P., Levenson, R.W. and Friesen, W.V. (1983) Autonomic nervous system activity distinguishes among emotions, *Science*, 221: 1208–10.

Elias, N. (1978/[1939]) *The Civilizing Process: Vol 1: the History of Manners.* Oxford: Basil Blackwell.

Elias, N. (1991a) On human beings and their emotions: a process-sociological essay. In Featherstone, M., Hepworth, M. and Turner, B. (eds) *The Body: Social Process and Cultural Theory.* London: Sage.

Falk, P. (1994) *The Consuming Body.* London: Sage.

Elias, N. (1991b) *Symbol Theory.* London: Sage.

Featherstone, M. (1991) The body in consumer culture. In Featherstone, M., Hepworth, M. and Turner, B. (eds) *The Body: Social Process and Cultural Theory.* London: Sage.

Foucault, M. (1973) *The Birth of the Clinic: An Archaeology of Medical Perception.* London: Tavistock.

Fox, N. (1993) *Postmodernism, Sociology and Health.* Milton Keynes: Open University Press.

Frankenberg, R. (1990) Review article: Disease, literature and the body in the era of AIDS – a preliminary exploration, *Sociology of Health and Illness*, 12, 3: 351–60.

Franks, D.D. (1987) Notes on the bodily aspects aspect of emotion: a controversial issue in symbolic interaction. In Denzin, N.K. (ed) *Studies in Symbolic Interaction: Research Annual (1 of 8).* Greenwich, Connecticut: JAI Press.

Freud, S. (1923) *The Ego and the Id.* London: Hogarth Press and the Institute of Psychoanalysis.

Freund, P. (1982) *The Civilized Body: Social Control, Domination and Health.* Philadelphia PA.: Temple University Press.

Freund, P. (1988) Understanding socialized human nature, *Theory and Society.* 17: 839–6.

Freund, P. (1990) The expressive body: a common ground for the sociology of emotions and health and illness, *Sociology of Health and Illness*, 12, 4: 452–77.

Freund, P. (1997) Social performances and their discontents: reflections on the biosocial psychology of role-playing. In Bendelow, G.A. and Williams, S.J. (eds) *Emotions in Social Life: Social Theories and Contemporary Issues.* London: Routledge.

Gerth, H. and Mills, C. Wright (1964) *Character and Social Structure: the Psychology of Social Institutions.* New York: Harcourt, Brace and World.

Giddens, A. (1984) *The Constitution of Society.* Cambridge: Polity Press.

Giddens, A. (1991) *Modernity and Self-Identity.* Cambridge: Polity Press.

Goffman, E. (1959) *The Presentation of Everyday Life.* New York: Doubleday Anchor.

Goffman, E. (1967) *Interaction Ritual: Essays on Face-to-Face Behaviour.* New York: Doubleday, Anchor Books.

Gordon, S. (1990) Social structural effects on emotions. In Kemper, T.J. (ed) *Research Agendas in the Sociology of Emotions.* New York: State University of New York Press.

Grosz, E. (1994) *Volatile Bodies.* Bloomington and Indianapolis: Indiana University Press.

Harre, R. (ed) (1986) *The Social Construction of Emotions.* New York: Basil Blackwell.

Harre, R. (1991) *Physical Being: A Theory of Corporeal Psychology.* Oxford: Blackwell.

Hochschild, A. (1979) Emotion work, feeling rules and social structure, *American Journal of Sociology*, 85: 551–75.

Hochschild, A. (1983) *The Managed Heart: The Commercialisation of Human Feeling.* Berkeley: University of California Press.

Hochschild, A. (1990) Ideology and emotion management: a perspective and path for future research. In Kemper, T.J. (ed) *Research Agendas in the Sociology of Emotions.* New York: State University of New York Press.

Hochschild, A. (1997) The sociology of emotions as a way of seeing. In Bendelow, G.A. and Williams, S.J. (eds) *Emotions in Social Life: Social Theories and Contemporary Issues.* London: Routledge.

Honneth, A. and Joas, H. (1988) *Social Action and Human Nature.* New York: Cambridge University Press.

Jackson, S. (1993) Even sociologists fall in love: an exploration of the sociology of emotions, *Sociology*, 27, 2: 201–20.

Jaggar, A. (1989) Love and knowledge: emotion in feminist epistemology, in Bordo, S. and Jaggar, A. (eds) *Gender/Body/Knowledge: Feminist Reconstructions of Being and Knowing.* New Brunswick/London: Rutgers University Press.

James, W. and Lange, C. (1922) *The Emotions.* Baltimore: Wilkins and Wilkins.

Jewson, N. (1976) The disappearance of the sick man from medical cosmologies: 1770–1870, *Sociology*, 10, 225–44.

Kelly, D. (1980) *Anxiety and Emotions.* Springfield Ill.: Charles C. Thomas Publishers.

Kemper, T. (1990a) Themes and variations in the sociology of emotions. In Kemper, T.J. (ed) *Research Agendas in the Sociology of Emotions.* New York: State University of New York Press.

Kemper, T. (1990b) Social relations and emotions: a structural approach. In Kemper, T.J. (ed) *Research Agendas in the Sociology of Emotions.* New York: State University of New York Press.

Kierkegaard, S. (1962/[1847]) *Works of Love: Some Christian Reflections in the Form of Discourses.* London: Collins.

Laing, R.D. (1995) *The Divided Self.* Harmondsworth: Penguin.

Leder, D. (1984–5) Toward a phenomenology of pain, *The Review of Existential Psychiatry*, 19: 255–66.

Leder, D. (1990) *The Absent Body.* Chicago: Chicago University Press.

Leder, D. (1992) (ed) *The Body in Medical Thought and Practice.* London: Kluwer Academic Publishers.

Ledermann, E.K. (1989) *Your Health in Your Hands: a Case for Natural Medicine.* Bideford: Green Books.

Lowenberg, J.S. and Davis, F. (1994) Beyond medicalisation–demedicalisation: the case of holistic health, *Sociology of Health and Illness*, 16, 5: 579–99.

Lupton, D. (1994) *Medicine as Culture.* London: Sage.

Lutz, C. (1982) The domain of emotion words in Ifaluti, *American Ethnologist.* 9: 31–57.

Lutz, C. (1986) Emotion, thought and estrangement: emotion as a cultural category, *Cultural Anthropology*, 1: 287–309.

Lutz, C. (1989) *Unnatural Emotions.* Chicago: University of Chicago Press.

Lutz, C. and White, G.M. (1986) The anthropology of emotions, *Annual Review of Anthropology*, 15: 405–36.

Lynch, J. (1975) *The Broken Heart: the Medical Consequences of Loneliness.* Basic Books: New York.

Lynch, J. (1983) *The Language of the Heart: The Human Body in Dialogue.* Basic Books: New York.

Lyon, M. (1994) Emotion as mediator of somatic and social processes: the example of respiration. In Wentworth, W.M. and Ryan, J. (eds) *Social Perspectives on Emotion (Vol. 2).* Greenwich, Connecticut: JAI Press Inc.

Lyon, M. and Barbalet, J. (1994) Society's body: emotion and the 'somatization' of social theory. In Csordas, T.J. (ed) (1994) *Embodiment and Experience: The Existential Ground of Culture and Self.* Cambridge: Cambridge University Press.

McCarthy, E. Doyle (1989) Emotions are social things: an essay in the sociology of emotions. In Franks, D.D. and McCarthy, E. Doyle (eds) *The Sociology of Emotions: Original Essays and Research Papers.* Greenwich, Connecticut/ London: JAI Press Inc.

Mills, C. Wright (1959) *The Sociological Imagination.* New York: Oxford University Press.

Morris, D. (1991) *The Culture of Pain.* Berkeley: University of California Press.

Morris, D. (1994) Pain's dominion. *Wilson Quarterly,* Autumn: 8–26.

Nettleton, S. (1992) *Power, Pain and Dentistry.* Milton Keynes: Open University Press.

Pietroni, P. (1991) *The Greening of Medicine.* London: Victor Gollancz Ltd.

Plato (1993) *Phaedo.* Oxford: Oxford University Press.

Plato (1961) *The Collected Dialogues.* Edited by Hamilton, E. and Huntington, C. Princeton NJ: Princeton University Press.

Radley, A. (1995) The elusory body in social constructionist theory. *Body and Society.* 1, 2: 3–24.

Rieff, P. (1979) *Freud: the Mind of a Moralist.* London: Chatto and Windus.

Rosaldo, M. (1984) Towards an anthropology of self and feeling. In Shweder, R.A. and Levine, R.A. (eds) *Culture Theory.* Cambridge: Cambridge University Press.

Rose, N. (1990) *Governing the soul: the shaping of the private self.* London: Routledge.

Saks, M. (1994) The Alternatives to medicine. In Gabe, J., Kelleher, D. and Wiliams, G.H. (eds) *Challenging Medicine.* London: Routledge.

Saks, M. (1995) *Professions and the Public Interest: Medical Power, Altruism and Alternative Medicine.* London: Routledge.

Sarte, J.P. ([1939/1962) *Sketch for a Theory of the Emotions.* London: Methuen.

Seidler, V. (1994) *Unreasonable Men: Masculinity and Social Theory.* London: Routledge.

Scheler, M. ([1912]/1961) *Ressentiment.* New York: The Free Press.

Scheper-Hughes, N. and Lock, M. (1987) The mindful body: a prolegemonon to future work in medical anthropology. *Medical Anthropology Quarterly,* 1, 1: 6–41.

Schilder, P. (1950) *The Image and Appearance of the Human Body.* New York: International Universities Press, Inc.

Scott, S. and Morgan, D. (eds) (1993) *Body Matters.* London: Falmer Press.

Sharma, U. (1992) *Complementary Medicine Today.* London: Routledge.

Sharma, U. (1996) Using complementary therapies: a challenge to orthodox medicine? In Williams, S.J. and Calnan, M. (eds) *Modern Medicine: Lay Perspectives and Experiences*. London: UCL Press.

Shilling, C. (1993) *The Body in Social Theory*. London: Sage.

Stearns, C.Z. and Stearns, P. (1988) *Emotions and Social Change*. New York: Holmes and Meier.

Stearns, P. (1994) *American Cool: Constructing a Twentieth Century American Style*. New York: New York University Press.

Taylor, R. (1984) Alternative medicine and the medical encounter in Britain and the United States. In Salmon, J.W. (ed) *Alternative Medicines: Popular and Policy Perspectives*. London: Tavistock.

Tillich, P. (1968) *Systematic Theology*. Welwyn, Herts: Nisbet.

Thoits, P.A. (1990) Emotional deviance: research agendas. In Kemper, T.J. (ed) *Research Agendas in the Sociology of Emotions*. New York: State University of New York Press.

Thoits, P. (1995) Stress, coping, and social support processes: where are we? What next? *Journal of Health and Social Behaviour*, (Extra Issue): 53–79.

TUrner, B. (1984) *The Body and Society*. Oxford: Blackwell.

Turner, B. (1991) Recent developments in the theory of the body. In Featherstone, M., Hepworth, M. and Turner, B.S. (eds) *The Body: Social Process and Cultural Theory*. London: Sage.

Turner, B. (1992) *Regulating Bodies*. London: Routledge.

Wentworth, W. and Ryan, J. (1990) Balancing body, mind and culture: the place of emotion in social life. In Franks, D. (ed) *Social Perspectives on Emotions*. Greenwich CT: JAI Press.

Wentworth, W. and Ryan, J. (1994) Introduction. In Wentworth, W. and Ryan, J. (eds) *Social Perspective on Emotions*. Greenwich C.T.: JAI Press Inc.

Wentworth, W. and Yardley, D. (1994) Deep sociality: a bioevolutionary perspective on the sociology of emotions. In Wentworth, W. and Ryan, J. (eds) *Social Perspectives on Emotions*. Greenwich C.T.: JAI Press Inc.

Williams, S.J. (1996) The body in question: a rejoinder to Mike Bury. *Medical Sociology News*, 21, 2: 17–22.

Wilson, M.D. (1978) *Descartes*. London: Routledge and Kegan Paul.

2. C. Wright Mills meets Prozac: the relevance of 'social emotion' to the sociology of health and illness

Margot L. Lyon

Introduction: biological versus sociological modes of explanation

The dichotomy between biological and sociological perspectives in the explanation of human behaviour continues to assert itself in contemporary life. This is well demonstrated by recent discourse on depression, partly generated by the market success of new anti-depressant drugs such as Prozac. A prominent instance of this discourse is *Listening to Prozac*, a best-selling book by American psychiatrist Peter D. Kramer published in mid 1993.[1] In Kramer's analysis, depression, and 'affective style' more generally, are reduced to phenomena of the brain, with matters of social and psychological integration subsumed in biology under a 'chemical' understanding of temperament. In a challenge to Kramer's book, later, in a book entitled *Talking Back to Prozac*, published a year later, psychiatrist Peter R. Breggin and Ginger Ross Breggin (1994), refute many of Kramer's claims, arguing that such chemical explanations are oversimplified. Aside from these two books, literally thousands of articles and reviews on Prozac, its uses and consequences, have appeared in major magazines and newspapers since the drug's release first in the American market at the beginning of 1988.

The so-called Prozac debates have frequently been cast in terms of a search for the foundations of the 'modern self', and whether these are to be located in chemical or in socio-psychological phenomena. Putting aside for the moment the question of whether the 'self' should or can be treated as a central organising concept in this way, such debates can be seen to be part of the larger concern with the boundaries between, and the limitations of, biological and social or humanist explanations of human behaviour. This divide, of course, is a reflection of basic level dichotomies such as body/mind, emotion/reason, positivism/constructionism, and so on, which permeate western thought. How these conceptual relationships are perceived and constructed in the social sciences is critical for our understanding of the place of the body (both as individual bodies and as bodies in a collective or group sense) in social life, and conversely for the role of the social in our understanding of the body as a biological entity (see Benton 1991 for a review). These are especially crucial questions in behavioural or social medicine, in epidemiology, and in more recently developed fields such as psychoneuro-immunology, indeed, in the understanding of health and illness in general.

Continuing debates around such issues are indicative of the persistence of the conceptual division between the organic and the social which, despite advances in both social and biological theory, continues to dominate in both social science and in medicine. This conceptual divide between 'the natural' and 'the social' is also reflected in the wider culture, the popular claims for holistic or more metaphysical frameworks notwithstanding. Indeed interest in overarching or holist explanatory frameworks could be seen as a reflection of the concerns arising out of the conventional division in categories. Its continuing persuasiveness has distorted the ways in which biological concepts are understood when they are acknowledged in social analysis and social theory, and therefore the role that biological phenomena may be seen to play in the 'construction' of the individual within society. Similarly, purely sociological categories have limited scope in discourse about bodies. The tendency to flip-flop between two distinct types of explanation depending on the 'dimension' of the phenomenon to be explained, or to simply grant primacy to one form of explanation and ignore the other, does little to encourage the exploration of new models which may bridge or obviate this division and lead to new forms of analysis.

The implications of the separation of the natural and the social in scientific explanation becomes more crucial when one considers how medicine – and thus the very categories through which health and illness is represented and understood – is increasingly being drawn into and implicated in addressing larger structural problems of contemporary society (Zola 1972, O'Neill 1986). The erosion of traditional political and social structural forms in a (post)capitalist world, and the concomitant profound and ever-increasing economic, social, and cultural alienation, generate accelerating pressures (from both individuals and institutions) to find simple and manageable 'solutions' for these problems. In contemporary society, these 'solutions' are frequently thought to be located within individuals, rather than at the level of social structure or institutions. The urge to rectify or overcome the general sense of disenchantment is socially manifest in the many new forms of cultural and bodily regimes focused on individuals, for example, physical training, self-awareness groups, new forms of spiritual development and so forth (*e.g.* McGuire 1988). It is also manifest in the growth of larger social movements, as in the development of new bases of group solidarity and mobilisation such as those grounded in religion, race, or other fundamental identity markers through which individuals seek to become part of a larger entity.

Increasing alienation is thus being manifested in more encompassing and profound forms of the medicalisation of social problems (Freund

1982, 1988). New forms of illness are being called into being, and the boundaries of existing illness definitions extended both within biomedicine and within culture at large. This process does not just occur through the agency of institutional medicine; there is a convergence of the needs of practitioners and of the public from which they are drawn. For example, this promiscuous approach can be detected in the construction of syndromes such as attention deficit disorder, seasonal affective disorder, and post-traumatic stress disorder which have both medical and popular presence (see Young 1995). Characteristic of the process of the medicalisation of social life more generally, explanation for such disorders is sought in, and attributed to, some underlying biological cause. The search for genetic foundations of complex forms of social and behavioural problems is an extension of this. The seeking of explanations for larger societal problems in natural phenomena is also apparent in popular manifestations of scientific developments, such as chaos theory and non-linear dynamics, which have been used to provide explanatory models for things as diverse as variation in personality types to world political strife (Lyon 1993a).

What is needed is a new reference point or perspective from which the assumptions underlying the conceptual division between the natural and the social can be challenged, and which at the same time provides a framework which allows one to go beyond that division. This perspective is to be found in the study of emotion which offers an arena within which, both theoretically and practically, to conceptualise a bridge between natural and social domains (Lyon 1994). Emotion can facilitate this without a retreat either to metaphysics or to reduction. Through emotion, bodily, psychological, and social phenomena can be simultaneously represented and explored. The controversy generated by the widespread prescription of Prozac provides an ideal case. This is because its real neurochemical impact and the wide range of reportedly associated subjective effects – however these are judged – require both their acknowledgement and representation in any account of the experience of persons in their social milieu. The situating of the person in society as taken up by Mills is an equally important step, all the more so when it is acknowledged that this 'situatedness' must be embodied.

The 'Prozac debates'

Prozac is the trade name of a form of fluoxetine hydrochloride manufactured by Distra Products Company, a division of Eli Lilly Company. Fluoxetine hydrochloride is a so-called 5-HT specific antidepressant, that is, it is said to act only on the neurotransmitter serotonin (5-Hydroxytryptophan or 5-HT).[2] Its function is described as selectively blocking the re-uptake of serotonin into presynaptic neurons (where it is metabolised or stored in vesicles), and is thus termed a serotonin specific re-uptake inhibitor (SSRI). This action leaves an excess of active serotonin in the synaptic cleft and at the serotonin receptor sites, causing an increased stimulation of serotonin receptors.

It is argued by the proponents of the SSRIs that 5-HT levels have an important role in the aetiology of depression. As summarised in information provided by Lilly, '[h]uman and animal studies suggest that increased serotonin in these critical areas of the brain modifies certain affective and behavioural disorders' (Eli Lilly and Company 1993: 5). Abnormalities in serotonin activity have been linked to many sorts of symptoms frequently associated with depression, e.g. problems associated with appetite, sexual function, sleep dysfunction, energy levels, memory impairment, as well as low 'self esteem'. The wide range of symptoms or problems included has led to the prescription of Prozac for problems other than those which typically present as clinical depression.

The contribution of the recent fluoxetine antidepressants is said to be their highly selective action such that the drugs in this class are thought to have little effect on other neurotransmitters (such as norepinephrine and dopamine), thus reducing the number and severity of side effects of the drug. Many of the early anti-depressants acted simultaneously on several neurotransmitters, leading to a range of disturbing and sometimes dangerous side-effects.[3] This alone is said to have meant a much wider prescribing profile for the drug, although Breggin and Breggin (1994) note that the newer antidepressants are moving back toward emphasis on their ability to target neurotransmitters other than just serotonin. In addition, the interactions with other common medications are said to be relatively few, although Breggin and Breggin (1994) dispute this. Partly for this reason, the drug has come to be readily prescribed by many physicians, including those working in general practice; indeed this is perhaps its largest market.

Prozac was officially introduced to the U.S. market for the treatment of depression in January 1988. Two years later, by the beginning of 1990, sales of Prozac (at then US$1.60 per capsule) had soared to 350 million dollars, more than the combined amount spent on all types of antidepressants before Prozac came on the market (Cowley et al. 1990: 39). Four years later in early 1994, the market for Prozac was worth US$1.2 billion (Cowley et al. 1994: 42), with more than 11 million people worldwide taking it, over six million of them in the United States. The market for SSRIs has continued to grow not only for Lilly but for other companies making 5-HT specific antidepressants as well, such as Roerig, maker of Zoloft (sertraline hydrochloride), and Smith Kline Beecham, makers of Paxil (paroxetine). The latter were worth another 700 million dollars as of early 1994, and their market is continuing to grow.

The larger context of the Prozac phenomenon

Prozac was presented by the media as a miracle drug. In March, 1990, Newsweek featured Prozac in a lengthy cover article entitled 'The Promise of Prozac' in which it was cast as the 'breakthrough antidepressant' which 'makes patients – and doctors – happy' (Cowley *et al.* 1990: 38–41). In the same issue was an additional article entitled 'Drugs vs. the couch' on the merits of biopsychiatry versus 'talk' psychotherapy (Gelman 1990: 42–4). Its 'promise' led to its use among people in virtually every profession and area of employment. Although initially most often associated with professionals, it is being widely prescribed by general practitioners and psychologists for 'farm hands, maintenance workers and mechanics, people who say they have neither the money nor the inclination to spend months or even years in therapy' (Egan 1994: 16). Compared to sessional therapy, the drug costs little in time and money. Its supporters say that the main threat of the drug is 'to psychologists whose approach to treating depression is years of costly counselling' (Egan 1994: 16). Opponents see it as a mechanical solution, a form of 'spiritual technology' versus the 'true understanding' achieved in more conventional forms of psychotherapy (see Rothman 1994: 36, see also Newsweek 1991).

The enthusiasm for and widespread use of Prozac, perhaps more than many other drugs, fits the description of a legal drug culture. It is seen as a 'normalising' drug. By 1989, Prozac was being widely prescribed for conditions described as panic anxiety, various types of addictions, eating disorders such as bulimia, attention deficit disorders, and obsessive-compulsive disorders (Cowley *et al.* 1990: 39). Many college health clinics prescribe it for a range of routine problems associated with adolescence. Even vets recommend it for anxious dogs: 'Prozac: Rover's Little Helper' says a newspaper headline (Freedland 1994). According to this article, Prozac may help birds and horses, too, but not cats who lack the necessary liver enzyme to break it down.

The few established side effects of Prozac, too, are frequently regarded as positive attributes of the drug. A side effect of weight loss means that more people want it as a 'feel-good diet pill'. The side effect of delayed orgasm has led it to be prescribed for problems with premature ejaculation (Rimer 1993: B8). But its popular image, in America especially, is associated less with specific disorders than with its reputed ability to enhance performance – in one's job, one's social life, one's home life, *etc.* Its reported effect in enhancing confidence, enabling one to focus better, and so apparently to be more successful, makes it in demand by professionals who wish to succeed – or just cope – with the realities of contemporary life (*cf.* Adler 1994, Begley 1994).

Prozac users have a computer bulletin board dedicated to the sharing of experiences of the drug (Rimer 1993: A1). Familiarity with it is so widespread that jokes and cartoons about it abound: Prozac in the White House; Karl Marx on Prozac; Prozac for Bosnians (Rimer 1993: A1); or Hamlet on Prozac (McGrath 1994: 9). 'Prozac is the Dale Carnegie of pharmaceuticals, transforming pessimists into optimists and inducing that state of enthusiasm Americans find so attractive,' says Britain's Chris Petit (Petit 1993; 60). He adds: 'Spot the Prozac-taker became the best game for the holiday . . . There's even a junior pep pill for kids. 'Oh mommy, I feel so bright,' announced one child after a day at school on the stuff' (Petit 1993: 62).

Prozac appeared on the market in the United States at a time when awareness of the illusory nature of the American Dream was almost complete. The declining economy, climbing unemployment, increasing inflation in the late 1980s and early 1990s were seen to be paralleled by a 'psychic slump'. 'Is the country in a depression?' asks Time Magazine in 1990, adding 'when the economy slumps, so does the national psyche' (Elmer-Dewitt 1990: 112–13). Drugstores in the economically most affected areas (New England, the Midwest, the mid-Atlantic states) reported high sales in medications such as Tagamet for ulcers, Halcion for insomnia, and Prozac for depression (Elmer-Dewitt 1990:112). Perhaps economic and existential angst may find some relief in new forms of 'cosmetic psychopharmacology', a term coined by Kramer (1993: xvi). Prozac is seen as a new and 'intimate form of technology', a source of biological 'force' which can give one a leg up in the modern world. In the midst of continuing social alienation, comes not what is sometimes represented as further 'individuation' but, in effect, further alienation of the self – the self as increasingly the object of intervention or reconstruction in a changing world.

This context is not insignificant. It bears on the clear and growing place given to depression in contemporary medicine, as well as the increasingly prominent constructions of a whole host of other problems seen as illnesses of modern life, from anxiety to crime (c.f. Angier 1994). These problems include those said to be frequently associated with depression such as eating disorders, sleep disorders, attention deficit disorders, as well as other less-bounded constructions such as the perceived consequences of low self-esteem and low confidence. This societal context thus bears on the issue, mentioned above, of how social problems are being increasingly and more efficiently medicalised, a process which continues to seek the locus of problems in the individual and thus to mystify the interrelationship between the individual and wider social and economic structures (Zola 1972, O'Neill 1986). In the absence in the general political arena, particularly in America, of direct debate on issues of political economy, the political functions of medicalisation seem clear.

The boundaries of the category of depressive disorders thus continues to expand (Campbell et al. 1994: 271–3), as does the list of other types of 'disorders' for which Prozac is prescribed. According to some commentators, Prozac is commonly prescribed for persons who do not at all fit the criteria for depression, but who are labelled as 'dysthymic', or even 'sub- or borderline dysthymic'. Dysthymia, meaning emotion inappropriate to the circumstances, surely a social judgement, is, in the words of one review, jargon for those who are 'perpetually crabby, under the weather, insecure, malcontent' or simply 'people who realise they're more unhappy than the situation calls for' (Angier 1993: B8). Although this 'diagnostic bracket creep', that is, the expansion of categories of illness 'to match the scope of the medication', has been acknowledged (Kramer 1993: 15), it needs to be added here that the notion of expanding categories can contribute little to the analysis of their content nor toward challenging the categories themselves.

Peter Kramer and the biological basis of being and 'self'
The publicity blurbs for Kramer's best-seller, *Listening to Prozac*, describes it as '[a] psychiatrist discusses mood-changing medications and their effects on a person's self' (New York Times 1994: 22). A profound concern with the construction of self is one key to best-seller status in non-fiction today, at least in the U.S. That a readily available drug might facilitate the realisation of a 'designer self' was perhaps irresistible. By January 1994, *Listening to Prozac* had been on the New York Times Book Review list[4] of hardcover best sellers in the United States for 22 weeks, that is, virtually from the date of its publication in mid-1993. Indeed, Kramer's book made the best seller lists before it was even advertised or reviewed. It has been said that the sales of the book and vastly increased sales of the drug are so closely intertwined that it is impossible to discuss them separately (Rothman 1994: 34). As of mid 1994, *Listening to Prozac* was only outdistanced in number of weeks on the best-seller list by two books which had had earlier releases: *Embraced by the Light* by Betty J. Eadie, with 37 weeks on the list (detailing a 'woman's near death experience'), and *Women Who Run with the Wolves* by Clarissa Pinkola Estes, with 76 weeks (on 'how myths and folk tales can enable women to understand their psyches') (New York Times 1994:22).

Kramer's book has been very important in establishing in the public mind profound claims for the efficacy of Prozac. As described by Kramer through a series of case studies, Prozac does not simply alleviate symptoms; rather, it makes possible a virtual transformation of the self. It is to the question of self that Kramer gives most attention, and to the bases on which the transformation of self might be achieved. These bases, Kramer argues, are biological, indeed chemical, a function of the distribution of particular neurotransmitters. Kramer states that it was the apparent power of the drug profoundly to affect an individual's subjective experience that led him to construct an argument regarding the physiological basis of personality and the implications of this, in turn, for the transformation of psychotherapy.

The title, *Listening to Prozac*, refers to what the author says he learned about the basis of the construction of the self from his patients on Prozac: 'what my patients generally said was that they had learned something about themselves from Prozac. . . . [T]hey believed Prozac revealed what in them was biologically determined and what merely (experience being 'mere' compared to cellular physiology) experiential' (Kramer 1993: xv). In the course of the book, Kramer takes the reader through a series of cases of patients suffering variously from stress, compulsiveness, over-sensitivity, low self-esteem, etc., and describes their transformations under the influence of Prozac. Accustomed to slow changes made by patients through insight they acquired in the course of psychotherapy, Kramer was astounded by the instant change in personality through medication. '[W]ith Prozac I had seen patient after patient become . . . "better than well" ' (*ibid*). 'Prozac seemed to give social confidence to the habitually timid, to make the sensitive brash, to lend the introvert the social skills of a salesman', says Kramer (1993: xv). The effect of the drug, Kramer says, was global. It transformed rather than healed (1993: 113). The new selves created were the 'real' selves. It is in such terms that Kramer justifies Prozac's use in patients who for the most part could not conventionally be defined as ill.

More important here, however, is another meaning given to the notion of 'listening' to drugs. The term for Kramer also refers to the notion that one may infer the causes of illness by observing a person's response to a particular substance. What Kramer heard, as spoken through his patients, had less to do with biographies or culture than with what he saw as the signals of biology: 'Spending time with patients who responded to Prozac had transformed my views about what makes people the way they are. I had come to see inborn, biologically determined temperament where before I had seen slowly acquired, history-laden character' (1993: xv).

For Kramer, Prozac works at the level of the individual through chemically assisting in the production and therefore 'revelation' of the 'real self'. But what is the basis of such a judgement that this 'self' constitutes a 'true self'? Any argument about a 'true self' has to have some underpinning in a larger perspective on the constitution of self in the context of human society if it is to have more than just subjective existence. (This, of course, forces us to put aside the issue of what in fact constitutes 'self', as well as the fact that the constitution of any 'self' is a function of persons in relation, not something inherent in individuals, a matter to which I will return.) To this end, Kramer develops an argument about the location of illness not just in chemical malfunction but in the biology of the species and the determinants of what he terms 'affective temperament' rather than 'social temperament' (Kramer 1993: 166–7). Drawing on the work of Michael T. McGuire, a UCLA psychiatrist working on non-human primate and human behaviour, Kramer argues that the very biology of our species is determinative of what are seen as 'affective traits' such as shyness or inhibition. These traits, however, have varying social consequences in different types of societies, that is, they would be seen as successful or unsuccessful modes of behaviour depending on the society in which a person was located (Kramer 1993: 169). The social and cultural contexts of being, in Kramer's scheme, thus figure primarily in terms of how a particular 'strategy or mode of behaviour . . . is not rewarded in contemporary society' (Kramer 1993: 169). '[O]ur culture favors one interpersonal style over another' (Kramer 1993: xv). Those who are biochemically 'out of synch' with a particular style are disadvantaged in that culture, and so are diagnosed as 'dysthymic' or 'subaffective dysthymic'. Thus, social relations are reduced to whether an individual's temperament – which for Kramer (and McGuire) is a matter of individual physiology but rooted in the history of the species – fits with the demands of a given society. Society is therefore treated as external to or separate from the individual.

Kramer accepts that the events of life, *e.g.* trauma, make for 'scars' in the mind, in memory, as is clear from his consideration of the case of Daniel, a survivor of Nazi death camps, who first presents with depression in his early sixties (1993: 137–42). Such trauma results in 'changed anatomy and chemistry within the brain' and when Daniel suffers from depression, this is evidence for a physiological event in terms of Kramer's 'concept of progressive damage to transmitter systems' (1993: 141). In Kramer's view it is this chemical change which can be treated, and it is this which enables Daniel to read differently in a creative way, or perhaps 'overwrite' his history (*cf.* Rothman's discussion of this point 1994: 36).

Kramer acknowledges that the 'availability of medication, and the medication-supported predominance of biological models, influences the way we are likely to frame a human predicament' (Kramer 1993: 141). But his view of illness, as outlined above, also prevents the addressing of other, and finer, distinctions in the representation of behaviour; for example, how behaviour grounded in what is often termed 'character', a concept which can encompass individual histories as well as capacities or agency, might be distinguished from temperament. Nor does he address how social and cultural processes play an important part in the shaping and determining of behaviour and temperament according to the varying position (*e.g.* according to class, race, gender) of persons within those structures. Society appears on the scene for Kramer, as noted above, in the form of demands of the dominant culture which favours particular individual psychic 'styles', styles which are pre-determined. The underlying explanation for behaviour is thus biochemical and genetic although the impact of social and cultural context on an individual may vary. The primacy given to biological explanation in the structure of such an argument raises the question of different 'levels' or domains of description, and therefore the role of biology in the explanation of social and cultural phenomena. Must one domain be treated as causally prior to the other?

The concept of 'functional autonomy' and the medicalisation of social life
The argument about the origins and locus of illness in 'neurochemical fit' between an individual and society can be seen to constitute a sophisticated form of medicalisation of problems which have as much basis in contemporary social life as in any of its 'chemical' implications. The consequences of modern life for individuals are being increasingly defined and treated through illness constructions grounded in the neurochemical features of individuals. As this occurs (whether within institutional medicine or outside it in the larger cultural context), the social relations in which that individual is implicated can only be further mystified through a more abstract chemical model of being. But biological explanation, in turn, has also been further mystified in that the rapid expansion of developments in biopsychiatry has resulted, paradoxically, in a simplification and a narrowing of the theoretical scope of models of illness in medicine.

This reduction has been facilitated especially through the increasingly common application of the notion of 'functional autonomy' to illness categories and behaviour. Functional autonomy in medicine refers to how illness categories come to be treated as though they are autonomous in the contexts in which they exist and through which they may have been produced. It is one thing to apply this to diseases which have clearly defined, discrete symptomology and clear causal histories. It is another to do so in reference to general or vague psychological categories such as 'dysthymia'. In psychiatry and psychology today, an increasing range of forms of behaviour or experience have been given the status of independent illness entities – frequently through their inclusion within the expanding boundaries of existing illness categories such as depression – and therefore regarded as treatable with newly available medications. Kramer's reasoning regarding the autonomy of the categories with which he deals relies mainly on the work of Donald Klein, a researcher who has used drug responses in seriously ill patients to work backward toward making diagnoses of particular disorders (Kramer 1993, Chapter 4). Kramer (1993: 75) quotes Klein on functional autonomy, who holds that 'a cause engenders an adaptive response (function) that persists after the termination of the cause (autonomy).' Thus, for example, in Klein's research on hysteroid dysphorics, he states: '[r]egardless of its origins [*i.e.* of the original disorder], the [subsequent] vulnerability to loss had a life of its own in adulthood' (Klein quoted in Kramer 1993: 75). But it would seem a very different question as to whether constructs such as mild depression (and their associated types of affect such as low self esteem) can, once experienced, be taken as 'functionally autonomous' in the contexts in which they arise and exist.

The question of the functional autonomy of what are defined as 'emotional' disorders mirrors the larger emphasis in Western society on control of the body which is part of the rational bias in Western thought. But what is seen as having to be controlled is emotion, and more importantly, the locus of control is seen to be the self. With the SSRIs, if we read Kramer, one's old self, one's old patterns of reaction, can be treated as a sort of emotional false consciousness and the 'real self' can assert itself. Emotion – the 'wrong' kind of it as variously defined as that is – is labelled as potentially pathological. With Prozac, control (and therefore rationality) can then be reasserted (cf. Kirmayer 1988).

Regardless of whether or not the concept of functional autonomy can be validly applied in the case of routine mood reactions, it has proved attractive and enhanced the attractiveness of biological treatment (Kramer 1993: 75). Given the availability of many new drugs, its application has added impetus to the search for discrete neurochemically-based representations for an increasing range of human experience and behaviour. When drugs are available and deemed capable of altering behaviour, then 'disorders' of behaviour are seen everywhere as is well demonstrated in the literature on medicalisation, and as Kramer himself acknowledges (Kramer 1993: 85). As a result of the availability of Prozac and similar drugs, and the claims made about their broad efficacy, a seemingly infinite number of 'problems' are being defined and explained in terms of 'defects' in serotonin levels. Yet, concepts such as low self-esteem, over-sensitivity, mild depression, and various other 'mood disorders' are so loosely constructed and associated with such a wide variety of signs and symptoms, that subsuming them within a chemical framework based on a single neurotransmitter can contribute little either to the understanding of the neural correlates of human emotional experience, or to the understanding of the increasing social and psychological concern with such moods in modern society. As an analytical (or methodological) category, 'functional autonomy' thus serves the interests of biological reduction. Developments in biopsychiatry, then, seem to continue to lead medicine away from the social, and contribute to the continuing process of the medicalisation of profound social-structural problems in modern society.

To ask whether, on the basis of the effects of SSRI drugs such as Prozac, the cause of depression or other disorders can be sought in and attributed to serotonin uptake problems, and that therefore, such illnesses can be treated as autonomous, is to frame incorrectly the question of cause. That is, it cannot contribute to causal understanding in a larger sense. Such a model is insufficient to encompass, for example, the question of the ontology of suffering (Kleinman and Kleinman 1991), or the question of a changing sense of the self in illness. As will be seen later, one of the apparent consequences of the use of Prozac is a reduction in the sense of the social connectedness of self. A parallel illustration is provided by the relationship of pain to aspirin: although aspirin relieves pain, the cause of pain could hardly be said to be too little aspirin in the system, and the notion of 'listening to aspirin' is patently absurd (Oatley 1994: 6). Information about the correlates of illness, biological *and* social, needs to be determined through knowledge of the person concerned in the context of his/her milieu, as well as through the use of relevant biological measures. The concept of functional autonomy denies the continuing interplay between the individual and the social which pertains at all times and which has both biological and psychosocial dimensions. If we are not to deny the validity of the social and the physiological dimensions of this relationship, we must establish a framework within which the importance of biology, of the real, physical effects of a drug, as well as the role of social context, are encompassed.

A response to Kramer's 'chemical' account
In a challenge to Kramer's book entitled *Talking Back to Prozac* (1994), psychiatrist Peter R. Breggin and Ginger Ross Breggin respond to Kramer's account of the chemical basis of depression. Breggin and Breggin do not deny that depression has physiological dimensions, but they argue that one must not confuse that fact with arguments about the primary biological origins of depression (Breggin and Breggin 1994: 185–6). Rather, drawing in part on sociological perspectives, they stress the importance of social and psychological phenomena – the milieu in which a person is reared and lives. The Breggins draw a parallel with states of arousal and agree that emotional arousal, for example the fear of being mugged or the joy of seeing a loved one, create physical responses. Yet these responses are not therefore evidence of a simple physical cause of these states or reactions, rather that they are complex in their ontology.

The Breggins also continue to hold that drugs are not necessarily superior to psychotherapy in the treatment of depression and many other types of disorders (Breggin and Breggin 1994: 205). They argue that the sheer power of Prozac to transform is in part due to the unprecedented publicity given to claims of its benefits and efficacy, and that this reputation for efficacy exceeds any real bases for it. Thus, a good deal of its reputed effect is because of the 'placebo effect'. For the Breggins, the 'hype' on Prozac works together with its neurophysiological effects and the low level of unpleasant side effects to create a powerful combination such that the positive mood changes in the context of a person's overall experience are cast into 'higher relief'.[5]

But how are we to encompass the neurophysiological effects of such a drug in a framework which also can fully acknowledge the importance of a sociologically grounded perspective? The ability of Prozac to effect changes in serotonin levels and therefore in behaviour and subjective experience cannot be ignored. Yet how do changes in neurotransmitters translate in terms of observed or reported subjective qualities? This question cannot be answered in any conclusive way. Some authors argue that Prozac's positive effects are due to its ability to induce a mild euphoria which undergirds confidence, promotes energy, and so aids in decision making and the taking of action (see Kramer 1993: 167 for an example). Breggin and Breggin suggest that SSRIs may provide a sense of a jump in physical energy which may help in cases of mild depressive mood disorders (Breggin and Breggin 1994: 207). This quality, apparently, may be rooted in the fact that serotonin also figures in the action of neurons in muscle tissue. Such action would seem to fit well with the more visceral subjective effects described by some of Kramer's subjects. But such explanations beg the question.

Using data from various sources, Breggin and Breggin attempt to build a larger argument about the drug's action. They argue that the effects of SSRIs on serotonin and dopamine[6] correlate with a reduction in 'sensitivity', that is, the capacity to love and to experience self awareness (Breggin and Breggin 1994: 210): 'Put simply, the SSRIs are anti-empathic agents. That means they are anti-life – anti-human in the fullest sense' (Breggin and Breggin 1994: 210). This may be the key to how such drugs work, they argue. The blunting of feeling or empathy involves the self as object as well as others. It aids in the disconnection from the depressed self and thus enhances euphoria, and it lessens the empathic or sympathetic regard of others. Psychiatric drugs remove 'our fine-tuning toward ourselves and others . . . In reducing emotional fine tuning, empathy is the first to go' (Breggin and Breggin 1994: 211). A person can thus achieve distance from, care less about, the milieu which makes them lonely, self-loathing, cold, fearful (Breggin and Breggin 1994: 211). Drugs, they say, 'are euthanasia of the soul' (Breggin and Breggin 1994: 212).

Social emotion and resituating the person

The task here is to resituate the organism in such a way as to give voice simultaneously to sociological and biological accounts of depression (or other dimensions of human experience). This is not to deny that the biological and the sociological are distinct domains of knowledge drawing on different forms of information, and that each constitutes a different mode of explanation. To do so would be to commit a category error. Yet to deny the existence of a relationship between them would be absurd. The means of 'locating' this relationship, of finding an arena in which it can be coherently approached, is thus the central problem.

The effort to bridge such apparently disparate domains often takes the form of giving primacy to one mode of explanation, *i.e.* material over social or vice versa, which only serves to reinforce the distinction between biological and sociological explanation. This also tends toward making one domain prior to the other which in turn implies a causal relationship between the two. Biochemical modes of explanation, for example, if treated as causally prior to any other mode of explanation might therefore be seen to provide the explanatory basis for more complex forms of behaviour. In social science, on the other hand, explanation which relies solely on social and cultural construction of any particular phenomenon tends to ignore or at least marginalise the biological realm, and in some cases, to treat the social or cultural realm as prior and even causative. The extreme position in the social construction of emotions, for example, would argue that all emotions are social products and that natural phenomena have little relevance in their understanding (Thoits 1989: 320). In the case of depression, the reputed profound physical and psychological effects of SSRIs such as Prozac typically tend to overwhelm or marginalise sociological modes of explanation: The social becomes mere superstructure to physical nature's structures, and forms of behaviour are treated as outward expressions of underlying chemical complexity. This, in effect, denies a place for sociological forms of explanation, and therefore the importance of social agency in bodily being, and in effect, reduces the scope of sociological perspectives to questions of interpretation and critique.

The apparent efficacy of biopsychiatry has strengthened the dominance of biochemical explanation and helped to reinforce the already sharp divide. But, for our purposes here, it can also be said that new developments in biopsychiatry and the problems raised in the interpretation of its complex effects, bring into even higher relief the realisation that neither biological nor social reduction provide an adequate framework for embracing the unity of bodily and social domains. Both the body's intrusive presence in what is defined as depression and the relationship between this and the complexities of human social experience provide an ever more urgent challenge. Thus, to move beyond the dichotomies which underlie the opposition between, say, the psychobiological and the psychosocial, any adequate account must be able to situate or resituate individuals within the context of social life in the larger (not just psychological) sense. And, it must do so in a framework that can demonstrate how that relationship between person and society may be embodied in the full sense of the term.

A central concern of C. Wright Mills' work was to situate a person's experience within a larger social framework. In the first chapter of *The Sociological Imagination* (1959), Mills discussed the ways in which a sociological perspective enables an understanding of the relationship between history and biography, that is, the link between individual experience and the larger social context in which each person exists. Mills refers to 'the personal troubles of milieu' and the 'public issues of social structure' as 'perhaps the most fruitful distinction with which the sociological imagination works' (Mills 1959: 8): 'Troubles occur within the character of the individual and within the range of his immediate relations with others; they have to do with his self and with those limited areas of social life of which he is directly and personally aware' (Mills 1959: 8). Public issues on the other hand 'have to do with matters that transcend these local environments of the individual and the range of his inner life . . . They have to do with . . . the ways in which various milieux overlap and interpenetrate to form the larger structure of social and historical life' (Mills 1959: 8).

Mills's argument that in the modern world there is a need to understand personal problems from the perspective of their connections with the social and historical context in which they emerge, is as true of 'medical' problems as it is of social phenomena. This realisation, however, requires us to address the question of how the social realm is to be embodied. To represent the situatedness of understanding of human existence requires a concept which can give form to the relationship between the social structural milieu in which humans live, their subjective experience, and the flesh through which that existence is lived (Lyon 1993b). It is this dilemma for which the study of emotion provides a means to overcome the profound division between the two modes of explanation without denying the fundamental differences between the two. Emotion is such a concept because emotion is both a bodily and a social phenomenon; it is through bodies that people feel and act. Further, although in Western society we are accustomed to thinking of emotion as interior to the individual, as a matter for psychology, it is in human social life that emotions in fact arise, for the capacity to experience emotion is part of, and necessary to, the human social capacity. Emotion can thus provide an alternative analytical framework that both challenges assumptions regarding the division between biology and being, *and* provides a new perspective on the interrelationship of these different orders of phenomena.

Emotion is social
The capacity for the experience of emotion is integral to the very existence and maintenance of social life and is thus universal. The human (and higher primate) affective capacity is both demonstrated in, and crucial to, the formation of strong relational/affective bonds with others (Bowlby 1969, 1980), bonds which undergird social life and thus, ultimately, are an important aspect of the fabric of society. Emotion is equally as important as, and inextricably linked to, the capacity for so-called logical or rational functions, and it is also implicate in instrumental action. Emotion is at the foundation of human sociality, and indeed the affective systems developed in evolution were precisely for the mediation of social relationships (Reynolds 1981: 82). The implications of the social nature of emotion are frequently overlooked in approaches which give emphasis to its role in

individual psychological experience, and which thus tend to locate emotion solely in the individual organism. An adequate representation of emotion must go beyond primarily individual and psychological modes of description.

Feeling arises in the context of social relationships, whether or not that feeling comes to be within one's awareness, and whether or not one can consciously articulate it. It is through emotion that social and historical processes and individual experience are linked, although Mills does not explicitly theorise this. This social nature of emotion has implications for how we understand its importance both in human experience and human agency in social processes.[7] Mills's perspective is thus extended through the theorising of emotion.

As an aspect of the organism's very being, emotion has a role in the organisation of actions – actions through which relations are structured and generated. Just as important is the role that social relations themselves play in generating emotion, including relations in the sense of our place within larger social structural forms. Emotion therefore can be seen to have a social ontology, whatever we may wish to say about its biological or psychological dimensions. Emotions move us but they do so by virtue of the social situations in which we find ourselves, or imagine ourselves to be. The work of Kemper, for example, explores the relationship between emotions and outcomes of social interaction, including attention to the physiological dimensions of this relationship. This perspective allows as well for the role of culture and socialisation. Kemper has demonstrated that 'an extremely large class of human emotions results from real, anticipated, imagined, or recollected outcomes of social relationships' (Kemper 1978: 32). Kemper focuses on what he sees as the two central dimensions of social relationships, i.e. relations of power and status. Power involves the 'control of one actor by another and degrees of positive social relations'; status involves the 'voluntary giving of benefits, rewards, privileges' (Kemper 1978: 32). Emotions such as fear, anger, depression, and satisfaction, to use Kemper's terms, result from the outcome of the power-status relations. The work of Collins (1984) goes beyond a focus on the individual and considers the importance of feelings in coalitions, e.g. feelings of membership. Emotional group identification for Collins is accomplished through sets of what he terms 'interaction ritual chains'. Another, although less empirically precise, way of conceiving the links between emotion and social structure is the idea of 'emotional modes of being' proposed by Buytendijk (Buytendijk 1974, Freund 1990: 452). The term refers to the way in which relationships or aspects of social structure are experienced by individuals both cognitively and bodily. What is important here is that the concept of emotion enables a theoretical articulation of the social structural context, subjectivity, and bodily being. Perhaps most important is the understanding that the social context of emotion, its social ontology, is crucial to the constitution of emotional being in the individual.

Emotion is bodily

The next issue to be considered – and one which has greater implications for the question of the understanding of health and illness – is how we conceptualise the place of biology in reference to the social basis of emotion. A model of biological functioning as mechanistic and independent from social life is clearly not sufficient. Again, emotion provides a link between the body and the social world, for emotion is, by its very nature, both bodily and social. Further, the role of emotion in the mediation of social relationships must be conceptualised through the body. The bodily aspects of emotion in the context of social life have been considered by a number of writers (some recent sources include Kemper 1987, Lyon 1994, Barbalet 1994, Lyon and Barbalet 1994). The body is thus the agent of social experience, just as it is necessary implicated in action and communication.

The study of emotion therefore permits regard of the body not just as subject to social processes but as an embodied agent in their creation. To ignore the importance of the body in its biological incarnation is to refuse to consider the interrelationship between it and psychological and sociocultural processes. And, to ignore the social dimensions of bodily being is to objectify and mechanise the body. The concept of emotion thus requires us to, and provides a means to, address the juncture between biological, individual and social domains.[8]

The study of emotion necessarily moves us beyond purely physicalist descriptions of human experience for these alone cannot address the processes through which physiological phenomena are both generated and made manifest. As emotion serves to organise social processes, this process of organisation includes also its physiological dimensions. While we may use different domains of description (biological, psychological, social), these do not necessarily equate with levels in the 'processing' of experience.[9] Bodily being and experience are always social, always a function of persons in relation. Emotion is thus an aspect of being in the world. Although it includes bodily components, emotion takes us beyond both individual and bodily domains and shows how the social is implicated in individual life (*cf*. Lyon and Barbalet 1994).

Emotion, social relations, the body and the 'self'

Mills's articulation of the relationship between 'private troubles' and 'public issues' is thus extended and given fuller form through an understanding of the central role of emotion in the explanation of human behaviour. This approach moves us beyond a view of emotion as primarily an attribute of individuals, whether this is through Kramer's development of the notion of a biologically-based 'affective temperament', or through psychologically-oriented approaches in the social sciences. A social emotions perspective involves a view of emotion as foundational to the very fabric of social life, and as simultaneously constitutive of the life of individuals and constituted by the agency of individuals in that social milieu.

Yet the conceptual categories of western medicine and western social science and society more generally are grounded in assumptions which treat the individual as an autonomous entity, independent of and even prior to society (Gordon 1988). This results in an objectification of the categories of both self and body. As in the example provided by Kramer's analysis of depression, the self is seen as the locus of disorder and treatment, as well as, ultimately, the locus of explanation. The 'causes' of contemporary problems, whatever their ontology, can then be defined as a function of chemical imbalance within individuals. How life in society is implicated in the modulation of neurochemical functioning is moot, as we saw in Kramer's treatment of the case of Daniel. Society is seen as substantially irrelevant to questions of the conceptualisation of illness categories as well as to questions of cause and treatment.

One could see in the greater emphasis being placed today on new drug therapies and the expansion of the categories of socio-psychological 'disorders' associated with contemporary life, a continuing process of the objectification of the individual and ultimately the individual's further alienation. In a sort of 'object relations' analysis of biological explanation and treatment, a chemical (e.g. serotonin) becomes an 'object' which mediates in both physical and symbolic terms the relationship between self and world This is seen to be accomplished in a 'real' biological sense, in that the SSRIs do effect changes in the level of neurotransmitters, however these level changes may be interpreted by patient or physician, as well as in the symbolic sense, that is, in that the drug is seen to make possible a 'new' or 'optimal' self which is seen as prior to the construction and control of the world external to it.

One can thus observe in the Prozac phenomenon an example of the perceived process of the transformation of subject ('self') into object ('ideal self'). That is, the drug is seen to facilitate the symbolic (and 'actual') transformation of the self and therefore the production or reproduction of a form of ideal relations. Thus, a drug such as Prozac is seen as a chemical basis for a binding relationship between a person and their ideal self in the world, a sort of technological prosthesis for the individual's psychological, and therefore ultimately social, life.

But the fact is that neither an individual organism nor the 'self' that a person constructs is autonomous. The role of the structure of society in the bodily and subjective life of individuals and groups cannot be denied. It is only from this sociological perspective that any conceptualisation of a 'self' makes sense, as well as any possibility of its existential realisation.

The self comes into being and is continually formed and reformed by virtue of its location in a social milieu. And, in that the self-in-context entails also a bodily dimension, so this point is especially important in the consideration of health and illness. Just as one's identity is not independent of society and culture, one's health is not simply a project of the 'self' (Gordon 1988: 36).

This is well demonstrated in sociological perspectives on depression. Though well established, such perspectives seem to be losing ground in a climate in which new developments in biopsychiatry dominate, partly fuelled by the drug industry and the wider marketing profile of newer low-side-effect drugs. But this larger literature must not be dismissed. What is today referred to as depression is a complex yet persistent construct with a long history (Jackson 1986). Its evolutionary origins and its transformations through the course of development of human society are also a complex question. In evolutionary terms, depression is considered to be grounded in a special-purpose form of appraisal system, responding to clues in the environment that cause an individual to withdraw from social contact. In the context of contemporary life, one observer has stated that the system might perhaps be seen to work too well (Brown and Harris 1978, Brown 1994). There is no room here to attempt to give an account of various evolutionary and sociological approaches to depression. Nor is there room to discuss the changes in the forms of description given to the mood shifts, psychomotor changes and other disturbances which have been associated with depression at varying times and in varying socio-cultural and historical contexts.

It is sufficient to state here that studies of depression support the importance of the social-environmental context in creating the conditions for depression, and for its resolve, as well as for how it is represented in medicine and in society and culture more generally (Brown and Harris 1978, Jackson 1986, Kleinman and Good 1985). Such a statement does not preclude the importance of the biological domain. Brown, for example, holds that the brain and the social system can be considered as almost one, are in effect united, and that the biology of depression is the mirror of psychosocial factors (Brown 1994). He argues that the study of depression must look at the conjunction of biology, attachment, support, and what he terms 'bad luck', that is, negative consequences arising from social, cultural and economic components of individuals' lives.

Emotion provides an arena in which to explore these matters. Such an expanded view of emotion has more to do with our intercommunication in the widest sense, with our very being in the context of relationships with others (whether through direct interaction or institutions), than with the dominant cultural notion of emotion as constituent of some 'inner core'. And its bodily dimensions provide the framework for the examination of social-relational bases of illness and illness constructions.

Notes

1 The book had its origins in columns written by Kramer for a trade paper for psychiatrists beginning in 1990. Kramer, a Rhode Island psychiatrist on the teaching staff at Brown University, was intrigued by the transformations his patients achieved through the use of Prozac. As popular press coverage of the Prozac phenomenon increased, Kramer was frequently cited and increasingly called upon for comments. The early case accounts in the trade paper with additional interpretive material became the basis of the book, *Listening to Prozac*.
2 Serotonin is a transmitter stored in vesicles in the presynaptic neurons. On nerve impulse, it is released by a presynaptic neuron, and passes into the space (synaptic cleft) between two neurons (termed the presynaptic and postsynaptic neurons) where it stimulates serotonin receptors located on the phospholipid neuronal membrane of the postsynaptic neuron. This stimulation or activation generates an impulse, which facilitates a physiologic response. Serotonin is actively transported back out of the synaptic cleft by what is termed a serotonin 'uptake pump' across the presynaptic neuron membrane. It is then either metabolised by the enzyme monoamine oxidase (MAO), contained in mitochondria in the neuron, or it is stored in vesicles inside the neuron. Fluoxetine's action is said to be to block the uptake pump, thus leaving a surplus of active serotonin in the synaptic junction and at the serotonin receptor sites, causing an increased stimulation of serotonin receptors (Eli Lilly and Company 1993: 5).
3 Blockade of the uptake of the neurotransmitter, norepinephrine, for example, is associated with tremor, tachycardia, and ejaculatory dysfunction. Blockade of the uptake of dopamine, another transmitter, is associated with psychomotor activation, antiparkinsonian effect, and aggravation of psychosis. Further, various of the monoamine oxidase (MAO) inhibitors associated with the metabolising of serotonin were found to be highly toxic. WIth Prozac, according to Lilly's claims, neither prescribing doctors nor patients have to be concerned with some of the more unpleasant and debilitating side effects characteristic of some of the older anti-depressants.
4 Not just a city or regional list, the New York Times Book Review best seller list is based on sales figures at '3,050 bookstores plus wholesalers serving 28,000 other retailers (gift shops, department stores, newsstands, supermarkets), statistically weighted to represent sales in all such outlets nationwide' (New York Times 1994: 22).
5 Breggin and Breggin (1994: 205) cite a book by Seymour Fisher and Roger Greenberg (1989), which argues for a complex understanding of placebo effect. For example, it is known that the use, in conjunction with the inert placebo proper, of harmless substances such as atropine which induce very definite physical sensations, can greatly enhance the 'placebo effect'.
6 Breggin and Breggin argue that, contrary to statements on specificity, there is evidence that not just serotonin is involved in the action of the SSRIs such as Prozac, but that the levels of other neurotransmitters (particularly dopamine) may be affected by the drugs due to the nature of neural structure and action and the interrelationship between various transmitter systems in some areas of the brain (1994: 210).

The action of neurotransmitters, of course, is a far more complex question than can be or is typically represented in the literature on Prozac and other antidepressants which link depression and other disorders to serotonin levels. For a review of literature on neurochemistry and emotion systems see Panksepp (1986, 1993) and LeDoux (1993). Panksepp, for example, notes that there are a great number of different receptor systems for serotonin implying real complexity in terms of the behavioural and emotive processes affected (1993).

7 The link between social relations and the production of emotion is addressed in the work of a number of sociologists including Durkheim 1915, Goffman, *e.g.* 1959, 1967, Collins 1981, 1990, Scheff 1988, 1990, Kemper 1978, and Barbalet 1992, 1993, 1995. Hochschild (*e.g.* 1979) explicitly uses Mills and the social interactionists to make a constructionist argument about the link between specific sociohistorical contexts and individual feeling arising in those contexts. For Hochschild, such a link is accomplished via cultural rules, 'feeling rules', which pertain in particular role slots and which guide what people think or do about their feelings.

8 The bodily dimensions of emotion cannot be denied, although at no time can they be entirely consciously experienced or articulated. For example, we may be unaware of minor changes in blood pressure, respiratory patterns and endocrine levels during 'states' of arousal. Yet, we all have physical feelings associated with emotion of which we *are* aware in certain situations. We could speak here as well of the interconnectedness of cognitive categories and bodily experience. Johnson (1987), for example, shows how basic-level semantic categories are grounded in perceptual and bodily experience, experience which occurs in the context of social and cultural life. Thus, we could extend Johnson's perspective to consider how these experiences which generate particular categories emerge from social relations.

9 Leventhal, a psychologist, asks how the physical level might be represented in the 'mind', for example, and how the 'interconnection' between 'levels' might best be understood (Leventhal 1994). One might ask whether the physical is best conceptualised as a level of description, or a medium for 'processing'.

References

Adler, J. (1994) A dose of virtual Prozac, *Newsweek*. 7 February 1994, 43.

Angier, N. (1993) Drug works, but questions remain, *New York Times*. 13 December 1993, B8.

Angier, N. (1994) Elementary, Dr Watson. The neurotransmitters did it (looking to biology for the causes of crime), *New York Times* (Section 4: The Week in Review). 23 January 1994, 1, 3.

Barbalet, J.M. (1992) A macro-sociology of emotion: class resentment, *Sociological Theory*, 10, 2, 150–63.

Barbalet, J.M. (1993) Confidence: time and emotion in the sociology of action, *Journal for the Theory of Social Behavior*, 23, 2, 229–48.

Barbalet, J.M. (1994) Ritual emotion and bodywork: a note on the uses of Durkheim, *Social Perspectives on Emotion*, 2: 111–23. Greenwich, CT.: JA Press.

Barbalet, J.M. (1995) Climates of fear and socio-political change, *Journal for the Theory of Social Behavior*, 25, 1, 15–34.

Begley, S. (1994) One pill makes you larger, and one pill makes you smaller . . . beyond Prozac, *Newsweek*, 7 February 1994: 36–40.

Benton, T. (1991) Biology and social science: why the return of the repressed should be given a (cautious) welcome, *Sociology*, 25, 1, 1–29.

Bowlby, J. (1969) *Attachment and Loss*. Volume 1 (*Attachment*). London: Penguin Books. (2nd Edition 1984).

Bowlby, J. (1980) *Attachment and Loss*. Volume 3 (*Loss: Sadness and Depression*). London: Penguin Books.

Breggin, P.R. and Breggin, G.R. (1994) *Talking Back to Prozac: What Doctors Aren't Telling You About Today's Most Controversial Drug*. New York: St. Martin's Press.

Brown, G.W. (1994) Depression and emotion. Distinguished Address VIIIth Conference of the International Society for Research on Emotions. University of Cambridge, England. 15 July 1994.

Brown, G.W. and Harris, T.O. (1978) *The Social Origins of Depression: A Study of Psychiatric Disorder in Women*. London: Tavistock.

Buytendijk, F. (1974) *Prolegomena to an Anthropological Physiology*. Pittsburgh: Duquesne University Press.

Campbell, I.C., Marsden, K. and Powell, J.F. (1994) Editorial: Shifting depression, *Psychological Medicine*, 24, 271–3.

Collins, R. (1981) On the micro-foundations of macro-sociology, *American Journal of Sociology* 86, 984–1014.

Collins, R. (1984) The role of emotion in social structure. In Scherer, K.R. and Ekman, P. (eds) *Approaches to Emotion*. Hillsdale, NJ: Lawrence Erlbaum and Associates.

Collins, R. (1990) Stratification, emotional energy, and the transient emotions. In Kemper, T.D. (ed) *Research Agendas in the Sociology of Emotions*. Albany: State University of New York Press.

Cowley, G. (with others) (1990) The promise of Prozac, *Newsweek*, 26 March, 38–41.

Cowley, G. (1994) The culture of Prozac: how a treatment for depression became as familiar as Kleenex and as socially acceptable as spring water, *Newsweek*, 7 February, 41–2.

Durkheim, E. (1965–1915) *The Elementary Forms of the Religious Life*. New York: The Free Press.

Egan, T. (1994) A Washington city full of Prozac, *The New York Times International*, 30 January, 16.

Eli Lilly and Company (1993) *Prozac Comprehensive Monograph*. Dista Products Company, a Division of Eli Lilly and Company.

Elmer-Dewitt, P. (1990) Is the country in a depression?: when the economy slumps, so does the national psyche, *Time*, 3 December, 112–13.

Freedland, J. (1994) Prozac: rover's little helper. *Canberra Times*, 18 August (originally published in *The Guardian*).

Freund, P.E.S. (1982) *The Civilized Body*. Philadelphia: Temple University Press.

Freund, P.E.S. (1988) Bringing society into the body: understanding socialized human nature, *Theory and Society*. 17, 839–64.

Freund, P.E.S. (1990) The expressive body: a common ground for the sociology of emotions and health and illness, *Sociology of Health and Illness*, 12, 4, 452–77.

Gelman, D. (1990) Drugs vs. the couch: the discovery of new medications for emotional disorders stirs a debate between traditional talk therapists and the advocates of 'biopsychiatry', *Newsweek*. 26 March, 42–3.

Goffman, E. (1959) *The Presentation of Self in Everyday Life*. New York: Doubleday.

Goffman, E. (1967) *Interaction Ritual*. Garden City, NY: Doubleday/Anchor.

Gordon, D.R. (1988) Tenacious assumptions in Western medicine. In Lock, M. and Gordon, D.R. (eds) *Biomedicine Examined*. Dordrecht: Kluwer Academic Publishers.

Hochschild, A. (1979) Emotion work, feeling rules and social structure, *American Journal of Sociology*, 85, 3, 551–75.

Jackson, S.W. (1986) *Melancholia and Depression: From Hippocratic Times to Modern Times*. New Haven, CT: Yale University Press.

Johnson, M. (1987) *The Body in the Mind*. Chicago: University of Chicago Press.

Kemper, T.D. (1978) *A Social Interactional Theory of Emotions*. New York: Wiley.

Kemper, T.D. (1987) How many emotions are there? Wedding the social and the autonomic components, *American Journal of Sociology*, 93, 263–89.

Kirmayer, L.J. (1988) Mind and body as metaphors: hidden values in biomedicine. In Lock, M. and Gordon, D.R. (eds) *Biomedicine Examined*. Dordrecht: Kluwer Academic Publishers.

Kleinman, A. and Kleinman, J. (1991) Suffering and its professional transformation toward an ethnography of experience, *Culture, Medicine, and Psychiatry*, 15: 275–302.

Kleinman, A. and Good, B. (eds) (1985) *Culture and Depression: Studies in the Anthropology and Cross-Cultural Psychiatry of Affect and Disorder*. Berkeley: University of California Press.

Kramer, P. (1993) *Listening to Prozac*. New York: Viking.

LeDoux, J.E. (1993) Emotional networks in the brain. In Lewis, M. and Haviland, J.M. (eds) *Handbook of Emotions*. New York: The Guilford Press.

Levanthal, H. (1994) Multiple levels of cognition in the emotion process, *Proceedings of the VIIIth Conference of the International Society for Research on Emotions*. University of Cambridge, 14–17 July 1994.

Lyon, M.L. (1993a) Complexity and emergence: the seduction and reduction of non-linear models in the social sciences. In Green, D.G. and Bossomaier, T.J. (eds) *Complex Systems: From Biology to Computation*. Amsterdam: IOS Press.

Lyon, M.L. (1993b) Psychoneuroimmunology: the problem of the situatedness of illness and the conceptualization of healing, *Culture, Medicine and Psychiatry*, 17, 1, 77–97.

Lyon, M.L. (1994) Emotion as mediator of somatic and social processes: the example of respiration, *Social Perspectives on Emotion*, 2, 83–108. Greenwich, CT.: JAI Press.

Lyon, M.L. (1995) Missing emotion: the limitations of cultural constructionism in the study of emotion, *Cultural Anthropology*, 10, 2, 244–63.

Lyon, M.L. and Barbalet, J.M. (1994) Society's body: emotion and the 'somatization' of social theory. In Csordas, T.J. (ed) *Embodiment and Experience: The Existential Ground of Culture and Self*. Cambridge: Cambridge University Press.

McGrath, D.G. (1994) The happy Dane, *The New Republic*. 24 January, 9.

McGuire, M.B. (1988) *Ritual Healing in Suburban America*. New Brunswick: Rutgers University Press.

Mills, C.W. (1959) *The Sociological Imagination*. N.W.: Grove Press.

New York Times (1994) *New York Times Book Review*, 23 January, 22.

Newsweek Magazine (1991) A Prozac backlash: does America's favorite antidepressant make sane people crazy? Despite a string of dramatic accusations, the jury is still out. *Newsweek*, 1 April, 64–7.

Oatley, K. (1994) Prozac. *International Society for Research on Emotion Newsletter*, 8, 3, 6.

O'Neill, J. (1986) The medicalization of social control, *The Canadian Review of Sociology and Anthropology*, 23, 350–64.

Panksepp, J. (1986) The neurochemistry of behavior, *Annual Review of Psychology*, 37, 77–107.

Panksepp, J. (1993) Neurochemical control of moods and emotions: amino acids to neuropeptides. In Lewis, M. and Haviland, J.M. (eds) *Handbook of Emotions*. New York: The Guilford Press.

Petit, C. (1993) The Prozac zone, *The Independent on Sunday*, 12 September, 60–2.

Reynolds, P.C. (1981) *On the Evolution of Human Behavior: The Argument from Animals to Man*. Berkeley: University of California.

Rimer, S. (1993) With millions taking Prozac, a legal drug culture arises, *New York Times*, 13 December, A1, B8.

Rothman, D.J. (1994) Shiny happy people: the problem with 'cosmetic psychopharmacology', *The New Republic*, 10, 7, 14 February, 34–8.

Scheff, T.J. (1988) Shame and conformity: the deference-emotion system, *American Sociological Review*, 53, 395–406.

Scheff, T.J. (1990) *Microsociology: Discourse, Emotion, and Social Structure*. Chicago: University of Chicago Press.

Thoits, P.A. (1989) The sociology of emotions. *Annual Review of Sociology*, 15, 317–42.

Young, A. (1995) *The Harmony of Illusions: Inventing Post-Traumatic Stress Disorder*. Princeton: Princeton University Press.

Zola, I.K. (1972) Medicine as an institution of social control, *Sociological Review*, 20, 487–503.

3. Teenage pregnancy, romantic love and social science: an uneasy relationship

Andrew Finlay

Introduction

David Armstrong describes how in the post war period sociologists, 'in close alliance with medicine, opened up areas of the health experiences of ordinary people through surveys of health attitudes, of illness behaviour, of drug taking and of symptom prevalence'. He argues that 'more recently' the 'medical gaze' has increasingly focused on 'individual idiosyncrasies, personal meanings and subjectivity' (1983: 114). This extended medical gaze might appear to afford sociologists and anthropologists working in the context of health service research scope to consider the role of emotion in health behaviour. Reflecting on recent research on teenage pregnancy and adolescent sexuality, I am less sanguine.

This chapter re-examines health services research on teenage pregnancy in the light of recent work in the sociology of emotion. I was prompted to write it because, having recently coordinated a study of teenage pregnancy, I had become increasingly uneasy with a pivotal dichotomy around which much of this research turns; namely that between planned and unplanned pregnancy.[1] The study had a number of elements, but the main one consisted of semi-structured interviews with 62 pregnant teenagers. My unease with the dichotomy between planned and unplanned pregnancy arose from the suspicion that these were not truly 'emic' categories for most respondents. Although they understood the terms, respondents would probably not have used them had the interviewer not introduced them. It is possible that the dichotomy may obscure important aspects of the experience of being young, single and pregnant, particularly the emotional aspect.

Hochschild (1983: 201) and others, have identified a general tendency for social scientists to ignore emotion or subsume it under other categories and to focus narrowly on cognitive rationality and measurable 'facts'. This chapter begins by showing how these general tendencies manifest themselves in health services research on teenage pregnancy. The centrality of a dichotomy between planned and unplanned pregnancy is one manifestation of this tendency, but I also examine the ways in which researchers appropriate sociological analyses of the effects of romantic love on young women's contraceptive behaviour. Having reviewed health services research I re-examine the relationship between love, sex and contraceptive behaviour using illustrative material from the study which I was involved in. Notions of romantic love are notable by their absence from respondents' explanations of how they came to be pregnant, and the remainder of the chapter is an attempt to assess the significance of this absence.

There are two possible explanations for the absence of any mention of love from respondents' accounts. One is that it is an artifact of the way in which the research was carried out. I am thinking particularly of the possibility that the rationalistic language of family planning which we, following previous health services researchers, used in the interview schedule may have pre-empted the expression of feeling on the part of respondents. The second possibility is that the absence of love is symptomatic of a broader 'transformation of intimacy' described by Giddens (1992). The purpose of this article is not primarily to arrive at definitive conclusions regarding the changing nature of intimacy – the study was not designed for this purpose – but to illustrate both the promise of a sociology of the emotions and some of the obstacles to its development in the context of an extended medical gaze.

Health services research on teenage pregnancy

There is a large and growing literature on the antecedents and consequences of teenage pregnancy in the United States of America and the United Kingdom. The literature on the consequences of teenage pregnancy encompasses health and socio-economic considerations. Comment on the latter has been fuelled on both sides of the Atlantic by Charles Murray's controversial ideas about single parenthood and the emergence of an underclass (1990). The literature on the antecedents of teenage pregnancy – that is, adolescent sexual and contraceptive behaviour – has been augmented by research which is designed to inform estimates of the spread of HIV. This brief review does not attempt encompass all of this work; rather, the focus is on research carried out with the aim of influencing health service practice and policy with respect to teenage pregnancy; that is, what I have called health services research. However, I will draw on the broader literature to add weight to particular points.

The size of the literature in The United States and in the United Kingdom seems to be linked to the fact that both countries share 'an overwhelmingly negative social construction of teenage motherhood' (Phoenix 1993: 74). Arney and Bergen (1984) argue that this negative social construction has changed over the years. Drawing on an analysis of the *Reader's Digest* and the *American Journal of Public Health* from 1940 to 1980 they describe a change in discourse about teenage pregnancy:

In broad strokes our claim is that pregnant adolescents used to be a moral problem. Now they are a technical problem. They have not lost their problematic status, but a moral problem invokes a different kind of solution than does a technical problem (1984: 11).

I am not sure how far Arney and Bergen's analysis can be generalised. Indeed, it seems to me that they underestimate the enduring permeability between moral and technical discourses (Finlay and Shaw 1993). Nevertheless their analysis of the tensions between moral and technical discourses on teenage pregnancy can be used to illuminate the backdrop to the research upon which this article is based and, perhaps, to health services research on teenage pregnancy in the United Kingdom more generally.

Angela McRobbie (1989) described attitudes to teenage motherhood in the United Kingdom during the 1980s as constituting a 'subdued moral panic'. In Northern Ireland the issue came to the boil in the early 1990s when the Director of Public Health (EHSSB 1990) at the Eastern Health and Social Services Board announced a decision to invite the Brook Advisory Service to set up a clinic in Belfast. The decision to invite Brook provoked fierce opposition from a loose coalition which cut across Northern Ireland's usual religious and political divisions. In addition to pro-life groups, the opposition to Brook included clergy from the Roman Catholic Church and from several of the Protestant denominations. Representatives from some of the main Nationalist and Unionist parties also joined the campaign against Brook. The campaign focused on the fact that Brook provides an advice and contraceptive service to young people which is non-judgmental and confidential: this was seen to violate parents' rights to bring up their children according to their own moral and religious beliefs (see Finlay and Shaw 1993: 26).

Most of the protagonists in the controversy – the health professionals who decided to invite Brook and those who campaigned against the decision – shared a common concern about the increasing numbers of births being registered by unmarried teenagers in Northern Ireland. Indeed, it was this same concern which prompted the Western Health and Social Services Board (WHSSB) to commission the research upon which this article is based. Although the controversy surrounding Brook was focused on the Belfast area, this research was restricted to the WHSSB area which is in the West of Northern Ireland, adjacent to the border with the Irish Republic. It is a largely rural area, but includes one small city, Derry or Londonderry,[2] and several substantial towns.

Despite – or perhaps because of – the controversy surrounding teenage pregnancy, public health professionals in Britain and Northern Ireland have, with varying degrees of success, been careful to avoid moralistic or emotive language and to phrase their concern in technical or scientific terms (Finlay and Shaw 1993). They tend to stress that their concern is not the fact that most pregnant teenagers are unmarried, but is based on the assumption that most pregnancies to unmarried teenagers are unplanned, and also unwanted, and on evidence which links such pregnancies with a range of adverse social and health outcomes for both mother and child (see EHSSB 1990: 30, WHSSB 1990, Peckham 1992, Macintyre and Cunningham-Burley 1993). In line with this concern there has been a considerable amount of research aimed at measuring the level of unplanned/unwanted pregnancy, providing information on which women are more likely to have unplanned pregnancies, and identifying the factors involved (Peckham 1992: 4–7). Ultimately, the aim of such health services research is to inform strategies or reducing unplanned pregnancies.

It is noteworthy that Charles Murray, the American social policy expert who has influenced public debate both in the United States and in Britain, shares the health professionals' preoccupation with pregnancy planning. The difference is that for health professionals the problem with teenage pregnancy is that most of them are unplanned; for Murray it is that they are planned so as to gain access to council housing and welfare (Murray 1990). It is also worth mentioning that unlike the health professionals Murray does not eschew a moral tone.

Given that the problematic character of teenage pregnancy is defined by health professionals in terms of a dichotomy between planned and unplanned pregnancy, it is not surprising that health services researchers tend to emphasise the cognitive, and to a lesser extent, the situational and social factors that prevent teenagers, usually the female, from making rational decisions about having sex and the use of contraception. These factors include a lack of accurate information, poor access to contraception, lack of the communication and interpersonal skills needed to negotiate effective use of contraceptives, and conflicts over sexual activity (Adler and Tschann 1993: 144).

There is some recognition among health services researchers that this emphasis on the cognitive to the exclusion of the affective may be problematic. For example, Peckham (1992: 7) quotes Cheetham:

> This is a complicated and muddled world where unplanned pregnancies may be wanted, where wanted children may emerge from unwanted pregnancies, where the off-spring of wanted pregnancies may be rejected, where infatuation with infants grows cold and where children may be wanted solely to meet their parents pathological needs (1977: 3).[3]

Macintyre and Cunningham-Burley (1993: 61) have also commented on the way in which 'commentators often conflate aspects of teenage pregnancy that are analytically and empirically distinct'. Given these uncertainties, some researchers prefer the phrase unintentional pregnancy to unplanned pregnancy. Ann Cartwright, prefers 'unintentional' because, 'Intending to do something is possibly rather less definite than planning to do so: planning may seem to imply taking action, intending more a state of mind' (1988: 249). Adler and Tschann are more explicit. They argue that although apparently unintended some teenage pregnancies may be the result of conscious or pre-conscious motivation, and discuss theoretical models of motivation for pregnancy which include a role for 'feelings' (1993: 146). But, in the context of health services research, these definitional problems and qualifications tend to be dismissed in the name of pragmatism. Having quoted Cheetham, Peckham writes: 'Whilst it is difficult to define what is meant by an unplanned or unwanted pregnancy it is generally accepted to be beneficial to try and reduce the number of such pregnancies'. (1992: 7).

It is possible to discern an implicit recognition of a role for emotion in discussion of aspects of youth culture which militates against planned sexual activity. To use Peckham as an example again: 'For many young people planned or premeditated sex combined with an expectation of contraceptive use is equated with low sexual morals' (1992: 23; see also Phoenix 1991, Hudson and Ineichen 1991). This argument is an allusion to McRobbie's seminal work on the role of romantic love in the culture of working class girls. The relation between love, sex and contraception which she posits is as follows. According to the code of romantic love, it is not acceptable for a young woman to desire or plan to have sex: having sex is only acceptable if you are in love and 'get carried away'. For a young woman to be on the pill or carrying condoms would be to 'risk savage criticism since such calculated, premeditated action totally contravenes the dominant code of romance' (1978: 98–9). One sociologist writing in the context of a review of research on HIV-related risk behaviour comments that this code 'makes it preferable for some women to fall pregnant through unpremeditated sex than to go on the pill and be labelled as promiscuous' (Wight 1992: 15). Stevi Jackson (1982) and Sue Lees (1986, 1992) take this kind of analysis further. Lees argues that 'nice girls cannot have sexual desire outside of love', and cites Deirdre Wilson to the effect that the existence of a love attachment prior to sex is a 'fundamental rule governing' young women's sexual behaviour as it offers 'some protection from a reputation of sluttishness' (1986: 50–1).

Thus, notwithstanding the overweening emphasis on cognition and measurable facts in health services research on teenage pregnancy, there is some recognition that emotions might be relevant. Occasional allusions are made to sociological analyses of the effect of romantic love on young women's sexual and contraceptive behaviour. However, emotions remain largely uncharted territory in research on teenage pregnancy.

Although I have not included a systematic review of research on adolescent sexual behaviour in the context of HIV/AIDS in this article, it is worth noting that the general tendency to ignore emotional categories such as love seems to be reproduced here. This is true even of sociologically sophisticated work such as that conducted under the auspices of the Women, Risk and Aids Project (WRAP). The WRAP researchers argue that 'if we are to understand young people's sexual relationships we must attend to the power relations within which sexual identities, beliefs and practices are embedded' (Holland *et al.* 1990: 336). The importance of this insight makes the apparent absence of a systematic exploration of emotional categories all the more unfortunate. Margrit Eichler's work may be relevant here. She rejects the notion that 'romantic love can compensate for the lack of wifely power' (1981: 214), but points out that 'sentiments and internalised moral precepts may reverse the effect of an asymmetrical interspousal dependency at the socio-structural level' (1981: 213).

In the next section, I will re-examine our respondents' explanations of how they came to be pregnant in the light of McRobbie's and Lees' analysis of the code of romantic love and subsequent work in the sociology of emotion. One of the central insights to emerge from this work is that emotions are not purely involuntary, biologically-given, affective states; rather they are socially constructed to some degree or, at least, permeable to social and cultural influence (see Harre 1986 and Hochschild 1983). There are differences as to the role of biology and the relationship between the social and the biological, but, even a critic of social constructionism like Craib who believes that 'there is a range of emotions common to all humans, perhaps rooted in our biological make up', accepts 'that the available register of emotions, forms of emotional experiencing and expression, as well as the wider meanings of emotions, vary culturally and historically' (1995: 152).

With these insights in mind it is worth noting that McRobbie's argument about the role of romantic love in young women's contraceptive decision-making was developed in the late 1970s, and draws on evidence from an earlier article written by Melville in the early 1970s. Although Lees' work is more recent, her comments on the role of love in adolescent girls sexuality draws heavily on an article written by Deirdre Wilson in 1978: it is possible that the culture, language and perhaps even the experience of love have changed since the early 1970s.

Notions of love and explanations of conception

The data presented below are derived from 62 semi-structured interviews with pregnant teenagers. Respondents were selected from the total population of pregnant women under the age of 20 who presented at antenatal clinics in the study area during the period between 1 September 1992 and 1 September 1993. Socio-demographic data on these women were collected by means of a short questionnaire administered by mid-wives at the ante-natal clinics. Each women was also asked if they would be willing to be interviewed in greater depth. Using the information gathered on the questionnaire, respondents were selected on a quota basis so as to be broadly representative of the larger population in terms of age, class, religion and marital status. Those who were selected for in-depth interview were contacted again by telephone or by letter to arrange a time and a place for the interview. The interviews were carried out in the latter stages of pregnancy (second or third trimester). All but five interviews were carried out in the respondents' own homes. The interviewer in each case was a young (early twenties) female member of the research team. Interviews typically lasted between one and two hours.

Following previous research on teenage pregnancy, a key aim of our study was to explore the extent to which pregnancies to unmarried teenagers were in fact unplanned and unwanted. Although we were aware of some the reservations about terminology mentioned above, and despite our concern to allow teenagers to talk about their situation in their own terms, we tended to take the notions of planned and unplanned pregnancy somewhat for granted. Typically, the interviews began with broad open-ended questions relating to lifestyle, education, family, employment and their current situation. If respondents did not elaborate on their pregnancy during this phase of the interview, and most did not, the interviewer invited them to classify their pregnancies as planned or unplanned before asking them more detailed questions about their relationship with the putative father, their sexual and contraceptive behaviour around the time of conception and what happened after they found out that they were pregnant.

Most of the 62 young women we interviewed were content to use the words planned and unplanned to describe their pregnancies. We classified approximately ten of our respondents' pregnancies as planned and approximately 40 as unplanned. However, with hindsight, I doubt that they would have used these terms to describe their pregnancies had not the interviewer introduced them. Some of the remaining twelve respondents resisted such categorisation; for example, they preferred to describe their pregnancies as 'sort of planned' or said that they had wanted a baby at some point in their lives and that they were 'not bothered' when. Only one women used the word 'unplanned' spontaneously, and it is perhaps significant that she was from a middle class background and was describing how she had had to postpone her plans to go to art college because of her unplanned pregnancy.

It is in this sense that I have suggested that the categories 'planned pregnancy' and 'unplanned pregnancy' are not truly emic categories. The realisation that our respondents would not have used these categories had we not introduced them led me to re-examine the interview transcripts. We had gathered a considerable amount of data about our respondents' sexual histories, their relationships, and the circumstances in which they had conceived. Reading through this material, I was stuck by the fact that although all but one of our respondents claimed to have conceived in the context of some kind of ongoing relationship and although all but 14 were still involved with the putative father at the time when they were interviewed, only two mentioned love for their partner when explaining how they came to be pregnant.

> We were only going out over a year, but it's long enough you know, that when about four months, you know, I want him, and we are in love and talked about it, both of us. It was me who brought it up at the start about having it, the baby, and I says 'we'll do [but] wait a while, a bit longer'. We didn't wait that much longer, but [laughs] . . . (062S).

> It was planned at the start. He loved me and it just happened . . . (060S).

It is noteworthy that both of these respondents were among the minority of respondents who described their pregnancies as planned.

Bearing in mind the evidence presented by Angela McRobbie and by Sue Lees regarding the pervasiveness of a code of romantic love among young women and the prior importance of love to sex, it would appear to be quite remarkable that only two respondents mentioned love for the putative father when explaining how they came to be pregnant.

Notwithstanding the relative absence of love, it is possible to detect echoes of the cultural motif described by McRobbie (1978) and Lees (1986) in the interview transcripts. One such echo is a reluctance to organise contraception in advance of sexual activity for fear of harming ones reputation. This is evident in some respondents' explanations of why they were not using the pill, but was particularly noticeable in respect of the condom. Most respondents were either indifferent to, or approved of, the idea of women carrying condoms; however, very few said that they themselves would do so. In part, this reluctance simply reflects the fact that it is men who wear condoms: as one respondent said: 'it would seem OK for a guy [to carry them], but it would seem funny for a girl: it wouldn't be right for a girl' (116E). However, fear for one's reputation was the preeminent reason for their reluctance to carry condoms. Lees discusses the risk to reputation in terms of the distinction between 'slag' and 'drag'. The former 'depict[s] a girl who is promiscuous and sleeps around' (1986: 43). Our respondents did not use the term slag, but, as the following quotes show, the risks involved are essentially the same as that identified by Lees. They were asked 'who do you think of a girl carrying condoms?'

> I think girls are afraid to carry them in case fellas [think they] are pushy, you know, or they are easy like. (045A).

If she is not going steady, I don't think she should carry them with her. I mean, a one-night stand, I would never do anything on a one-night stand: fellas would regard such a girl as wanting it. (056E).

I don't a wild lot to tell you the truth. Just like tramps. That annoys me that . . . just out looking to get something. (057L).

A couple of my friends carry condoms . . . its up to them . . . but I wouldn't . . . even think about it . . . I think its up to fellas to carry them things.
Question: what would fellas think . . .?
Answer: a real good thing there something like that. They all think different but they probably think dirty things, you know, most of them would. (062S).

Despite this general reluctance to be seen to have prepared for sex, 15 out of the 40 respondents who described their pregnancies as unplanned claimed that they had been consistent in their use of some form of birth control and attributed their pregnancy to its failure. The remaining 25 respondents said that they had not been using any method of birth control consistently or ever. They usually had well-rehearsed explanations as to why they had not been using any method of birth control. The contraceptive pill often featured. One of the most common explanations was that they had been discouraged from getting the contraceptive pill for fear of people, particularly their mothers, finding out. Another common explanation involved the contraceptive pill and its real or supposed side effects: either the respondent had stopped taking the pill because of side-effects or had been discouraged from getting the contraceptive pill because they had been told about its side-effects. Other explanations included the refusal of a GP to prescribe the pill without parental consent, and the refusal or inability of their sexual partner to use condoms.

Explanations of why respondents persisted in having sex without contraception were more hesitant; nevertheless, it is possible to identity two main types. One type of explanation involved a denial of fertility: 'I didn't think that I would have got pregnant, I suppose everybody does at some stage, but no, not me' (153A). This kind of fertility denial (Hyde 1995: 25) is worthy of further exploration; particularly the idea that some respondents seem to believe that they would not become pregnant until they wished to or were socially ready.

From the perspective of this paper, however, the second type of explanation is more interesting. In this type of explanation, sex is presented as something which 'just happens' in the heat of the moment. For example, one respondent explained why she continued having sex after she had stopped taking the pill in the following way:

Just not thinking . . . me and my boyfriend were just minding somebody's house, and it [sex] just happened. We got carried away. (039L)

Other examples include: 'it [sex] was just quick and you don't think about them things [contraception]' (001A), or 'it all went so quick you know: I didn't really think at the time' (129O).

The resonance with the data from the late 1970s presented both by McRobbie and Lees is obvious. However, it is notable that none of our respondents mention love as the emotion which carried them away. In the next section I attempt to assess the significance of this absence.

The absence of love: methodological shortcomings or the changing nature of intimacy?

At the outset of this article, I noted two possible explanations for the puzzling absence of love from our respondents' explanations of how they came to be pregnant. One is that it is an artifact of the way in which the research was carried out. The second possibility is that the absence of love is symptomatic of some kind of 'transformation of intimacy' such as that described by Anthony Giddens (1992).

There is a sense in which it only becomes possible to pose the latter explanation in the light of the idea that emotions are permeable to social and cultural influence. Thus, Giddens distinguishes romantic love and passionate love. He regards the latter as 'a generic connection between love and sexual attachment' which is 'universal'. The former is more 'culturally specific': it 'began to make its presence felt from the late eighteenth century onwards' and is currently undergoing further transformations (1992: 37–8). According to Giddens, 'the romantic love complex . . . has now become weakened by some of the very influences it helped create' (1992: 59). He discusses these influences in terms of the emergence of the 'pure relationship' and 'plastic sexuality' (1992: 2). A 'pure relationship' is defined as 'a relationship of sexual and emotional equality' (1992: 2). The phrase 'plastic sexuality' refers to the freeing of sex from reproduction which 'has its origins in the tendency, initiated somewhere in the late eighteenth century, strictly to limit family size; but . . . [which] becomes further developed later as the result of the spread of modern contraception and new reproductive technologies' (1992: 2). Giddens regards young women as the pioneers of the 'pure relationship'.

Giddens is not the only writer to remark upon the changing nature of intimacy. The British National Survey of Sexual Attitudes and Lifestyles, provides further evidence for a decline in 'romanticism': 'the proportion of women who mention being in love as the main precipitating factor [associated with first sexual intercourse] continues a slow decline through all the age groups, from more than half the sample of 45–49 years olds (51.6 per cent) to little more than a third (37.5 per cent) of women aged 16–24' (Wellings et al.1994: 77). McRobbie, in the thirteen years since her earlier analysis of youth subculture, has noticed 'real and remarkable shifts in the world of girls magazines', the 'most notable is the decline of romance' (1991: 135). In the stories, girl-characters are 'less passive . . . they are less the victims of romance than they once were in the world of *Jackie* in the 1970s . . . these shifts could also be attributed to a wider climate of greater sexual equality which rejects and resists 'sloppy romance' as out-dated and old fashioned' (1991: 148).

With McRobbie's more recent work in mind, it is worth drawing the reader's attention to one of the respondents mentioned above (001A). For the sake of clarity, let us refer to the respondent and her partner by the pseudonyms Ann and Fintan. Ann said that she had been 'going out' with Fintan 'off and on' for about two years. She said that their relationship had finished because he did not 'want anything to do with the baby'. This was unusual – the single women in our sample were usually single by choice: they had terminated the relationship. Fintan had been Ann's first sexual partner, and she was asked 'Why did you decide to have sex with him?'. She answered: 'Well, I thought I liked him, he used to say he loved me [laughs], but he mustn't'. In the light of what McRobbie says about 'sloppy romance' being 'out-dated and old fashioned' in the world of girls magazines (1991: 148) it becomes apparent that Ann's laughter has a self-mocking tone.

Some writers have queried the thesis that intimacy is in the process of being transformed. Jackson, although an advocate of the view that 'love has changed historically' (1993: 203), argues that the 'the decline in romantic fiction in teenage magazines noted by McRobbie (1992) is unlikely to herald the decline of the culture of romance' (1993:215). Other writers have queried specific aspects of Giddens's argument (Duncombe and Marsden 1996, Craib 1995). Given these doubts, it is all the more important that I address the methodological issues alluded to at the outset of the article.

The interviews were retrospective, and it is therefore possible that the way in which respondents discussed how they came to be pregnant was influenced by a subsequent events. For example, the fact that respondents were pregnant would appear to set them apart from the young women discussed by McRobbie and Lees. An unexpected pregnancy can place a huge strain on a relationship. Our respondents were no exception; nevertheless, as I mentioned in the previous section, all but 14 described themselves as part of an ongoing relationship with the putative father and some even described how the trauma of finding out about, and dealing with, the pregnancy had brought them closer together. In this context, the absence of love from our respondents' accounts is still surprising.

Given that this chapter has its origins in the realisation that the terms 'planned pregnancy' and 'unplanned pregnancy' were not truly emic, I must also consider the possibility that the use of these terms in our interview schedule distorted our findings by eliciting responses which emphasised the cognitive and rational aspects of behaviour over the emotional. The validity of uncorroborated data derived from interviews has long been a matter of concern. In a recent review article in the *New York Review of Books* (20 April 1995), Richard Lewontin criticises research on sexual behaviour in America conducted by the National Opinion Research Center (Lauman *et al.*, 1994 and Michael *et al.*, 1994), for failing to deal adequately with the problem of self-report and the possibility that respondents might seek to manipulate the impression that interviewers have of them. Laumann *et al.* responded in the following issue by arguing that any tendency for their respondents to 'create a favourable self image' in interviews would have been off-set by 'the privacy, confidentiality and anonymity of our respondents' (25 May 1995: 43). The implication is that people only attempt to create a 'favourable self-image' when 'public disclosure' is involved. Against this, Lewontin argues that:

> People do not tell themselves the truth about their own lives. The need to create a satisfying narrative out of an inconsistent and often irrational and disappointing jumble of feelings and events leads each of us to write and re-write our autobiographies . . . these stories . . . become the basis for further conscious manipulation and manufacture when we have exchange with other human beings (25 May 1995: 44).

From a different perspective – that of a group therapist and a sociologist – Ian Craib has drawn attention to 'the extraordinary difficulty in distinguishing between one's own emotions and those of others and how readily people tell you what you want to hear' (1995: 157). For this and other reasons, Craib expresses methodological doubts about the sociology of emotions. Short of training as psychotherapists or spending a year getting to know their respondents, 'how do sociologists talk to people about their feelings in a way that can perhaps take them to reality behind the ideology'? By implication, he identifies the latter – 'the discourses of emotion . . . the stereotyping, the ideology of emotional life' (1993: 155) – rather than the former as being amenable to sociology. Like Lewontin, he calls on sociologists to be more circumspect about the phenomena they are studying.

In the context in which our study was carried out, one might expect that respondents would have been particularly keen to create a favourable impression. A considerable degree of stigma still adheres to teenage pregnancy. Moreover, as pointed out above, teenage pregnancy was the focus of fierce local controversy around the time that the research was being carried out. The material presented in the previous section provides evidence that some respondents were concerned to create a favourable impression. It is probably not insignificant that more than a third of the respondents who described their pregnancies as unplanned (15 out of 40 or 37.5 per cent) blamed their pregnancy on a failure in a method of birth control rather than upon any real or imagined shortcoming of their own. And those respondents who had not been using any method of birth control usually gave well rehearsed explanations as to why they had not.

Our study did not, in Craib's terms, get beneath the discourse or ideology to the 'reality' (whatever that is) of respondents' emotional experience.[4] In the circumstances of the study, there is little doubt that many respondents were concerned to create a favourable impression; that is, to protect their reputation. The fact that concerns about reputation influenced what respondents said during the interviews does not undermine my argument that the material presented here is symptomatic of some broader transformation; rather, it strengthens it. For the point is that in contrast to the situation described by McRobbie (1978) and Lees (1986) remarkably few respondents sought to protect their reputation by explaining how they came to be pregnant in terms of a discourse of romantic love. Even those who talked about having been carried away did not claim to have been carried away by love.

If the analysis presented above supports the idea that some kind of transformation of intimacy is in train, it also suggests that Giddens overstates the extent of the transformation that has occurred and understates the complexity of the phenomenon. The absence of love from respondents' explanations of how they came to be pregnant is suggestive of a diminution in the potency of a discourse of romantic love; however, their views on contraception, particularly regarding the idea of young women carrying condoms, suggest that it still exercises some hold. It is probably more acceptable for one respondent to take precautions than it was for their older sisters, but it is still not acceptable for a young woman to be seen to anticipate sex, let alone desire it. All this would seem to be highly relevant to those responsible for devising sex education programmes; however, that is a subject which is beyond the scope of this chapter.

Conclusion

Even if the reader is not convinced that the data can bear the full weight that I have placed on them, I hope that the foregoing 'story' of health services research on teenage pregnancy and adolescent sexual behaviour successfully demonstrates both the promise of a sociology of the emotions and some of the obstacles to its development. It is a familiar enough story: the tendency for social scientists to neglect emotions or subsume them in other categories has been much commented upon. Arguably, however, this neglect is particularly damaging in the case of research on reproductive behaviour. Although an understanding of the emotions is relevant to the full range of social relationships and social behaviour, it is perhaps especially relevant to understanding reproductive behaviour. Hochschild (1983: 21–2) argues that with the commercialisation of feeling and the development of 'an instrumental stance towards feeling' in 'our time', then 'we come to treat spontaneous feeling . . . as if it was scarce and precious, we raise it up as a virtue' (1983: 68). In this context, people – even some of our youthful respondents – come to regard their sex lives as a haven of spontaneous, authentic feeling in an increasingly rationalistic and instrumental world.

Although I have focused on the role of love in teenager's explanations of how they came to be pregnant, this is not the only relevant emotional category. Love has a particular relevance in the context of the literature, but other emotions are probably equally important: fear, concupiscence, envy, loneliness and so forth. I need hardly add that this is true not only for teenagers but for adults too.

The idea that emotions are susceptible to social and cultural influence opens up the possibility of a sociology of the emotions. However, the tendency for social scientists to ignore emotions cannot be explained in terms of a failure to grasp their relevance to social life and behaviour; more likely it is rooted in the difficulties involved in researching them. In the course of the debate in the *New York Review of Books* which I referred to earlier, Richard Sennet (25 May 1995: 43) criticises 'positivistic sociological research' for failing to probe 'subjects which resist quantification'; he notes that 'the usual disclaimer is that while such matters as the relation of sex and love may be important, they cannot be scientifically researched'.

In the context of health services research on reproductive behaviour, the development of a medical gaze which takes in 'individual idiosyncrasies, personal meanings and subjectivity' (Armstrong 1983: 114) and which is more open to qualitative approaches, may appear to offer greater scope to probe subjects such as the emotions which 'resist quantification'. In the mainstream research-methods literature, there would appear to be a complacent assumption that qualitative methods are appropriate to the study of emotions. For example, the index to the *Handbook of Qualitative Research* (Denzin and Lincoln 1994) has one reference to emotions. It is to a chapter by Hamilton. He writes,

> All qualitative traditions give as much attention to the inner as well as the outer states of human activity. Jacob (1987, table 1) for instance notes the 'subjective perceptions', 'emotions', 'reflective interpretations', and 'mental standards' that can be included within the 'characteristics' of qualitative research (1994: 66).

However, the experience recounted in this article suggests that even with a qualitative approach serious problems remain. Like all qualitative researchers, my colleagues and I began with the idea of 'letting the respondent speak for her self'. We were interested in the subjective aspects of pregnancy. And yet, somehow, in the event we found ourselves imposing the categories 'planned pregnancy' and 'unplanned pregnancy' on respondents. This attests to the power of the technical or scientific discourse on teenage pregnancy described by Arney and Begen (1984) and to the insidious nature of rationalistic categories. The medical gaze may now seek to encompass the personal and the subjective, qualitative methods may be more acceptable in the context of health services research, but as Arney and Bergen point out 'Using the language of scientific discourse to map emotionality and desire [which] seems to involve us in a language of Reason that need never speak about itself' (1984: 18).

In this context, those of us who are keen to develop a sociology of the emotions, need to take seriously Craib's warning about a particular form of social constructionism which 'gives priority to cognition . . the danger . . . is that emotions will be reduced to ideas: they will have no autonomy from the rational world with which they co-exist.' (1995: 153). It is possible that the problem may no longer be that emotions are neglected so much as apprehended in a reductionist way.[5]

However, I do not share Craib's pessimism about the possibility of a sociology of the emotions. Inadvertently, we found ourselves imposing, in Arney and Begen's terms, a 'language of Reason' on our respondents. This article grew out of a self-critical reflection on how this imposition might have affected our findings. It seems that the 'language of Reason' can speak about itself: it is called reflexivity.

Notes

1 The research was commissioned by the Western Health and Social Services Board in Northern Ireland (WHSSB). It was carried out by a team of researchers associated with the Centre for Health and Social Research at the University of Ulster: Dorothy Whittington, Nicola Shaw and Monica McWilliams (see Finlay et al. 1995). The research was a team effort and I therefore refer to it in the first person plural; however, the views expressed in the article are the responsibility of the author. Early versions of the paper upon which the article is based where read at seminars organised by the Department of Sociology, Trinity College Dublin and by the Sociology and Politics Society, University College Galway. I would like to acknowledge the helpful comments made by participants at those seminars, by the editors of the monograph and by the anonymous referees.

2 The name of the city is contested by some of its inhabitants. Those from the Protestant or British Unionist tradition tend to prefer Londonderry. Those from the Roman Catholic or Irish Nationalist tradition prefer Derry.

3 It is, perhaps, significant that Cheetham comes from a social services background.

4 It might be worth developing Hochschild's (1983) ideas about 'feeling rules' and the management of emotion as the basis for a credible sociological understanding of the gap between what Craib describes as the discourse or ideology of emotion and the reality of emotional experience.

5 This is not to deny that the long-standing tendency in Western thought to exaggerate the distance between cognition and emotion (James 1989: 17) is also dangerous.

References

Adler, N.E. and Tschann, J.M. (1993) Conscious and preconscious motivation for pregnancy among female adolescents. In Lawson, A. and Rhode, D.L. (eds) *The Politics of Pregnancy: Adolescent Sexuality and Public Policy*. New Haven – London: Yale University Press.

Armstrong, D. (1983) *Political Anatomy of the Body Medical Knowledge in Britain in the Twentieth Century*. Cambridge: Cambridge University Press.

Arney, W.R. and Bergen, B.J. (1984) Power and visibility: the invention of teenage pregnancy, *Social Science and Medicine*, 18, 1, 11–19.

Cartwright, A. (1988) Unintended pregnancies that lead to babies, *Social Science and Medicine*, 27, 3, 249–59.

Cheetham, J. (1977) *Unwanted Pregnancy and Counselling*. London: Routledge and Kegan Paul.

Craib, I. (1995) Some comments on the sociology of the emotions, *Sociology*, 29, 1, 151–8.

Denzin, N.K. and Lincoln, Y.S. (eds) (1994) *Handbook of Qualitative Research*. Sage.

Duncombe, J. and Marsden, D. (1996) Extending the social: a response to Ian Craib, *Sociology*, 30, 1, 155–8.

EHSSB Director of Public Health (1990) *Public Health Matters Annual Report 1989*. Belfast: Eastern Health and Social Service Board.

Eichler, M. (1981) Power, dependency, love and the sexual division of labour a critique of the decision-making approach to family power and an alternative approach with an appendix: on washing my dirty linen in public, *Women's Studies Quarterly*, 4, 2, 201–19.

Finlay, A. and Shaw, N. (1993) Brook in Belfast and the 'problem' of teenage pregnancy, *Critical Public Health*, 4, 2, 24–30.

Finlay, A., Shaw, N, Whittington, D. and McWilliams, M. (1995) *Adolescent Reproductive Behaviour In the Western Health and Social Services Board Area – Executive Summary*. Coleraine-Londonderry: University of Ulster/Western Health and Social Services Board, 1–8.

Giddens, A. (1992) *The Transformation of Intimacy Sexuality, Love and Eroticism in Modern Societies*. Cambridge: Polity Press.

Hamilton, D. (1994) Transitions, preferences, and postures in applied qualitative research. In Denzin, N.K. and Lincoln, Y.S. (eds) *Handbook of Qualitative Research*. London: Sage Publications.

Harre, R. (ed) (1986) *The Social Construction of Emotions*. Oxford: Basil Blackwell.

Hochschild, A.R. (1983) *The Managed Heart Commercialization of Human Feeling*. London: University of California Press.

Holland, J., Ramazanoglu, C., Scott, S., Sharpe, S. and Thompson, R. (1990) Sex, gender and power: young women's sexuality in the shadow of AIDS, *Sociology of Health and Illness*, 12, 3, 336–50.

Hudson, F. and Ineichen, B. (1991) *Taking it Lying Down Sexuality and Teenage Motherhood*. London: Macmillan.

Hyde, A. (1995) Younger and older women's contraceptive practices in the lead up to their pregnancies, *Northern Exposure*, Spring Symposium of the Scottish Society of Family Planning Nurses. Inverness.

Jackson, S. (1982) *Childhood and Sexuality*. Oxford: Blackwell.

Jackson, S. (1993) Even sociologists fall in love: an exploration in the sociology of emotions, *Sociology*, 27, 2, 201–20.

Jacob, E. (1987) Qualitative research traditions a review, *Review of Educational Research*, 57, 1–50.

James, N. (1989) Emotional labour: skill and work in the social regulation of feelings, *Sociological Review*, 37, 1, 15–42.

Laumann, E.O., Gagnon, J.H., Michael, R.T. and Michaels, S. (1994) *The Social Organization of Sexuality: Sexual Practices in the United States*. London: University of Chicago Press.

Laumann, E.O., Gagnon, J.H., Michael, R.T. and Michaels, S. (25 May 1995) 'Sex, lies, and social science' an exchange, *The New York Review of Books*, XLII, 9, 43–4.

Lees, S. (1986) *Losing Out Sexuality and Adolescent Girls*. London: Hutchinson.

Lees, S. (1992) *Sugar and Spice Sexuality and Adolescent Girls*. London: Penguin.

Lewontin, R.C. (20 April 1995) Sex, Lies and Social Science, *The New York Review of Books*, XLII, 7, 24–9.

Lewontin, R.C. (25 May 1995) 'Sex, Lies, and Social Science': An Exchange, *The New York Review of Books*, XLII, 9, 43–4.

Macintyre, S. and Cunningham-Burley, S. (1993) Teenage pregnancy as a social problem: a perspective from the United Kingdom. In Lawson, A. and Rhodes, D.L. (eds) *The Politics of Pregnancy: Adolescent Sexuality and Public Policy*. London: Yale University Press.

McRobbie, A. (1978) Working class girls and the culture of femininity. In Women's Studies Group, Centre for Contemporary Cultural Studies, University of Birmingham, *Women Take Issue. Aspects of Women's Subordination*. London: Hutchinson.

McRobbie, A. (1989) Motherhood a teenage job, *The Guardian* 5 September.

McRobbie, A. (1991) *Feminism and Youth Culture From 'Jackie' to 'Just Seventeen'*. London: Macmillan.

Melville, J. (1974) *New Society*, 28 March.

Michael, R.T., Gagnon, J.H., Laumann, E.O. and Kolata, G. (1994) *Sex in America: A Definitive Survey*. London: Little, Brown.

Murray, C. (1990) *The Emerging British Under-Class*. London: IEA Health and Welfare Unit.

Peckham, S. (1992) *Unplanned Pregnancy and Teenage Pregnancy A Review*. Wessex Research Consortium, Institute for Health Policy Studies, University of Southampton.

Phoenix, A. (1991) *Young Mothers?* Cambridge: Polity Press.

Phoenix, A. (1993) The social construction of teenage motherhood: a black and white issue. In Lawson, A. and Rhodes, D.L. (eds) *The Politics of Pregnancy: Adolescent Sexuality and Public Policy*. London: Yale University Press.

Sennett, R. (25 May 1995) 'Sex, lies, and social science': an exchange, *The New York Review of Books*, XLII, 9, 43–4.

Wellings, K., Field, J., Johnson, A.M. and Wadsworth, J. (1994) *Sexual Behaviour in Britain: the National Survey of Sexual Attitudes and Lifestyles*. Harmondsworth, Penguin.

WHSSB Director of Public Health (1990) *Health Accounts 1989: A Time for Change*, Annual Report. Londonderry,: Western Health and Social Services.

Wight, D. (1992) Impediments to safer heterosexual sex: a review of research with young people, *AIDS CARE*, 4, 1, 11–23.

Wilson, D. (1978) Sexual codes and conduct. In Smart, C. and Smart, B. (eds) *Women, Sexuality and Social Control*. London: Routledge and Kegan Paul.

4. Fieldworker feelings as data: 'emotion work' and 'feeling rules' in first person accounts of sociological fieldwork

Elizabeth H. Young and Raymond M. Lee

Introduction

The personal dimension in fieldwork has become an increasingly documented focus in methodological writing (Emerson 1981), and first person accounts of fieldwork have become popular. Such accounts have a variety of forms ranging from the heroic (Van Maanen 1988) to the confessional (Johnson 1975), from the personal and autobiographical (Wilkins 1993) to the more detached and descriptive (Whyte 1981). Accounts often refer, directly or indirectly, to emotions experienced by the fieldworker during fieldwork. In particular, feelings of stress, anxiety, and physical discomfort associated with fieldwork are well-documented in the methodological literature (Hammersley 1984, Sanders 1980, Cannon 1989).

Descriptions of fieldwork have been criticised for being anecdotal and lacking a comparative theoretical base (Dingwall 1980). To try and understand more fully the role of emotions in fieldwork, we suggest that the methodological basis upon which first person accounts are generated needs to be examined. More particularly, this chapter examines how far Hochschild's concepts of 'emotion work' and 'feeling rules' can be used to inform first person accounts of fieldwork. Hochschild describes 'emotion work' as 'the act of trying to change in degree or quality an emotion or feeling' (Hochschild 1979: 561). Emotion work can be accomplished by evocation, the attempt to create a desired feeling, or by suppression, the attempt to diminish an undesired feeling. Hochschild outlines three techniques for carrying out such work. These are cognitive, bodily and expressive. She goes on to suggest that emotion work is directed by 'feeling rules', the social guidelines that influence how we try to feel. These feeling rules are related to particular perspectives or ideologies or, as Hochschild puts it, feeling rules are 'the bottom side of ideology'. We suggest that sets of feeling rules are associated with particular methodological perspectives and we argue that the emotion work involved in fieldwork may be more problematic if the field experience challenges implicit methodological tenets held by the fieldworker. In these situations there are no clear feeling rules by which to operate. The fieldworker is left asking 'How should I feel?' or 'Do my feelings fit?'

In what follows, an account of the first author's fieldwork is presented and then used to illustrate the complex relationship between emotions felt and emotions acknowledged. We argue that the production of first person fieldwork accounts is part of the process of doing research and as such the accounts should be treated as raw data which require further reflective analysis. Their value comes when they are analysed as data in an attempt to gain a sociological understanding of the work carried out by a practising fieldworker, in the same way that any group of people's accounts would be studied by sociologists. The accounts have to be theorised and contextualised. Following from this we go on to work with Hochschild's suggestion that emotion work can be carried out by others on the self. We suggest that reflective work on first person accounts can be carried out by the fieldworker her/himself or as a collaborative exercise.[1] We conclude with a consideration of the potential of providing fieldworkers with a variety of more structured ways, including debriefing sessions, to reflect on their feelings within a sociological context.

We begin by reviewing how the role of emotion has been treated within a number of methodological traditions. We begin with a comment by Hochschild who observes, 'The focus of Mead and Blumer on conscious, active and responsive gestures might have been most fruitful had, not their focus on deeds and thoughts almost entirely obscured the importance of feelings' (1979: 555). This lack of interest in emotions carried over into the methodological writings associated with the 'neo-Chicagoan' tradition, the dominant postwar approach to field research in sociology associated with writers like Everett Hughes, Howard Becker, Herbert Gans and others. Fieldwork accounts in this tradition rarely make explicit the role of emotions in fieldwork. There is the occasional suggestion that fieldworkers may self-select themselves on what might be emotional grounds. Gans (1982: 60) observes for example that 'My hunch is that fieldwork attracts a person who, in Everett Hughes' words, "is alienated from his own background", who is not entirely comfortable in his new roles, or who is otherwise detached from his own society; the individual who is more comfortable as an observer than as a participant'. Generally, however, fieldwork accounts tend to describe 'fieldwork troubles' and methods for their resolution. (See Whyte 1981 for a classic example of this genre.) This is a tradition which encourages the normalisation of feelings. That is, the researcher becomes accepting of the local research setting, and in doing so associated emotional problems are overcome. To facilitate this normalisation as well as to prevent 'overrapport' the neo-Chicagoans tended to advocate a marginal role for the researcher (Miller 1952), and the fieldwork accounts they provide tend towards a retrospective and detached description of problems overcome. The emotion work undertaken by the field worker is minimised, perhaps hidden in a semi-embarrassed way in a somewhat sanitised account:

One of my mentors has commented that what typically goes into 'how the study was done' are 'the second worst things that happened'. I am inclined to believe that his generalization is correct. What person with an eye to his future, and who wishes others to think positively of him, is going to relate anything about himself that is morally or professionally discrediting in any important way? This is especially the case since field work tends to be performed by youngish persons who have longer futures to think about and less security about the shape of those futures. We delude ourselves if we expect very many field workers actually to 'tell all' in print (Lofland 1971: 132–3).

By contrast, a later generation of fieldworkers associated with what became known as 'existential sociology' (Adler and Adler 1987) saw emotion as being central to the research process. Johnson (1975) carried out participant observation on child welfare procedures in a social work agency. In an excerpt from his fieldwork diary Johnson describes an epiphany which moved him towards a growing awareness of and greater commitment to bridging the gap between rational self-presentation of fieldwork and the private feelings of the fieldworker. A dramatic and emotional custody case had just finished in which the court had found against Johnson's client. He goes on:

> And how did the cool, objective, calculatingly rational social scientist react to all this? Having quickly analyzed all of the formally rational courses of action open to me, and feeling confident that I had controlled for all spurious relations, I also began to cry. As we say in the trade, I presented the appearance of one who had lost all self control. And then, when alone on the grounds of the juvenile facility several minutes later I presented the appearance of a formally rational (expletive deleted) social scientist beating his (deleted) fist against a tree. Shortly after that, I doubled over and puked my guts out. What am I doing here anyway? To hell with the appearance of sociology and the horse it rode in on! (1975: 158–9).

The emotional experiences of the fieldworker have a central role to play in feminist methodology. In an account of her fieldwork experience with pregnant women, Wilkins describes her deep anxiety about carrying out the fieldwork:

> I displayed all the physiological symptoms of acute anxiety: including sweating, mind blitzing and a dry mouth. I resorted to taking a 'panic pack' on my observational outings: this included talcum powder, antiperspirant, changes of clothes, chocolate bars and mints (1993: 95).

However, this emotion work was theoretically contextualised for her when she discovered the feminist literature on methodology. Wilkins felt she had 'come home' on reading this literature; it made explicit for her a set of feeling rules and provided a theoretical justification for feeling as she did. This literature embraces the emotional sensibility of the fieldworker and the respondent. A distinguishing factor is common identity – woman to woman, sisterhood, common experience and capitalising on 'person-hood' (Finch 1984, Oakley 1981, Stanley and Wise 1983). Derived from this is a focus on the personal relationship between the interviewer and the interviewee, rather than on the research setting. The assumption in this is that women, researchers and respondents, have a common experience which is fundamental to the research; difference is counteracted by common experience. The analysis of fieldwork in this tradition is often accomplished through autobiography (Stanley 1992).

There is some tendency for each of the methodological traditions described above to emphasise particular aspects of the fieldwork process. The neo-Chicagoans tended to focus on researcher *involvement* in the research process and with those being studied. Existential sociologists tend to emphasise the *comfort* of the researcher as indexed by feelings of stress, anxiety, the presence of physical ailments and so on. For feminist sociologists, *identification* with those studied is a central concern. We would argue that in so doing, each tradition emphasises different feeling rules and mandates different kinds of emotion work. Of course, categorising fieldwork experiences into neat methodological packages is problematic (Hunt 1989). As Devereux (1967: 134) points out 'The influence of . . . scientist's ideology on his (*sic*) work is particularly difficult to explore, partly because he has little interest in, or awareness of, his own ideology'. In any case, fieldworkers do not always have an allegiance to a particular methodological perspective. Or the experience of fieldwork, and coping with unexpected situations, can challenge previously held methodological allegiances. Nevertheless, we suggest that certain kinds of emotion work may need to be done where the feeling rules associated with various methodological approaches come into conflict, and that the tensions between involvement, comfort and identification need to be managed. As Hochschild states 'Sets of feeling rules contend for a place in people's minds as a governing standard with which to compare the actual lived experience' (1979: 567).

One difficulty in examining the role of emotions in fieldwork relates to the status of first person accounts themselves. In the published accounts there seems to be a tendency for fieldworkers both to overanalyse and to underanalyse their own feelings. Thus, analytic procrastination may be attributed, for example, to deep conflicts over the researcher's sexuality (see *e.g.* Kreiger 1985), rather than being seen as a common aspect of many work situations, the delaying of the inevitable start to a substantial task. Alternatively, anxiety-reducing rituals associated with fieldwork tasks (Wilkins 1993) may be glossed as 'needs', rather than as the 'neurotic symptoms' likely to be seen by a psychoanalytically-oriented commentator like Hunt (1989). What we have in mind here is that first person accounts often contain statements of causal attribution (I felt X *because of* Y). the difficulty is that alternative accounts or explanations for these processes are rarely offered in the first person account. Alternative explanations have to come from the reader. Usually there is little basis for preferring one interpretation over another. Traditionally in qualitative research of this kind appeal is made to 'ethnographic authority' the argument that the fieldworker was there and has better purchase on what happened than a third party. The point we want to make is that there may be all sorts of reasons why fieldworkers may not be reliable informants on their own actions.[2] No claim is made that the account given in this chapter escapes problems of over- or underanalysis, but in order to try to understand more fully the role of emotions in fieldwork we suggest the methodology by which first person accounts are generated needs to be examined.

Because of the sensitive nature of the research discussed here, the emotional impact of the study on the fieldworker (and on the respondents) was a central concern. Emotional reactions to the research were charted in a fieldwork diary and in debriefing interviews which the first author held with her supervisor.[3] In what follows we reflect on an account distilled from this material. In so doing we treat the fieldwork account as data. However, returning to the account and using it as a source of data to explore the ideas of emotion work and feeling rules in fieldwork involves a complex set of relationships. Reading again the diary and transcripts, this time with a theoretical agenda on the part of the first author, could lead to accusations of selection and reconstruction. However it can be argued that returning to a research account and using that as a source of data makes more explicit the actual processes often undertaken in research writing (Kreiger 1985). Kohli, when considering the process of research account writing, points out that what is salient in the present is used to select and construct in the text relevant elements of the past (Kohli 1981). Working with another author, not involved in the fieldwork or the research management, adds another dimension. It, hopefully, enables a form of secondary analysis to be applied to the fieldwork account.

The research described below in the first person account was concerned with the role of friendship for women who were dying. In this study issues to do with the meaning of death and the boundaries of friendship were explored. This involved interviewing dying women and their nominated friends. Included in these interviews were questions about borrowing and lending money and help with intimate caring tasks. The work was an attempt to get closer to a sociological understanding of the dying experience from the dying person's perspective and the perspective of a friend, rather than relying on retrospective accounts from family members. It was felt that insights, valuable to the research community and palliative care practitioners, could be obtained by utilising this prospective approach. However, the research team was aware of the sensitive nature of such a direct approach and in order to mitigate any possible adverse effects worked very closely with the hospice staff at each fieldwork site. In the following section the first author's account of this fieldwork is presented. As a direct, account it is written in the first person singular.

The fieldwork account

Writing in the first person for my fieldwork diary feels strange to me. The professional is very obviously becoming the personal. This first person account feels like crossing over boundaries. As well as keeping a diary, I am also having debriefing interviews with my manager and supervisor.[4] These interviews are tape recorded and transcribed. The debriefing interviews bring out of me things I haven't previously written or consciously thought about. I have had three of these interviews over the fieldwork period. The second interview which took place two-thirds of the way through the fieldwork starts with me saying: 'I don't know what I want to say but I know I need to talk. . . .'. I have become less self-conscious as the months have gone by. The diary has become a vent for letting off steam and working out what I feel about the fieldwork, and the debriefing sessions are a welcome space to talk about me and my research. So, having begun to get over the self-conscious act of writing the diary and talking about myself, I then begin to exploit that very self-consciousness. In fact, doing this takes me nearer to, and further away, from my feelings about the whole thing. I don't want to overplay the sensitive nature of the research topic, dramatise my experiences, or hide behind the potential sensationalism of the topic. One thing I do know I feel is that first person accounts of fieldwork can leave the reader with the drama of the research experience but without the methodological substance. The more sensitive the research topic the more potential to do this.

  The dilemma I mentioned above, about professional forays into my feelings via the fieldwork diary and debriefing interviews, are somewhat resolved for me by thinking, that instead of just 'baring my soul', I am attempting to ground the experiences in a sociological context. For me it is too personal to vent my feelings to a professional audience without some end product. I am also more than aware of presentation of self to peers. I'm not knowingly going to make myself seem foolish. I really want to be able to extrapolate from some of my feelings and experiences of fieldwork to a wider sociological arena – otherwise I feel I am not capitalising on the privileged position of interviewing women who are dying.

I am carrying out a series of depth interviews with dying women, their friends if they nominate a friend, and in a possible third of a series of three interviews, a dual interview with the friend and the dying woman. So I am not 'in the field' in the true ethnographic sense. I often have to travel to conduct interviews. Whether on the train or in the car, the journey itself feels significant. I am away from my normal contacts and routines. I am thinking about the interview. The car particularly becomes like a microcosm, a small world of my own. I carry food and drink, not least because for the majority of my fieldwork time I have been pregnant or breastfeeding. I have the tapes of previous interviews playing and, after the interview, I stop and write in the diary as a way of finishing the interview. So, for me, I am in the field, and this is particularly the case if I am away overnight.

Although the ethnographic literature on fieldwork has a very practical grounded style which makes it is very readable and very absorbing, it is not of direct relevance to me for two main reasons. Firstly, I am not carrying out participant observation. Most of the literature on fieldwork seems to be about participant observation rather then a series of depth or long interviews. Secondly, I cannot live with, and live like, women who are dying in their own homes. In the immediate sense I am not dying. Any attempt at relating on this level would be crass and insensitive. In fact this feeling has been supported many times by the women themselves who do not like people who say 'I know how you feel'. Platitudes like this were referred to with frustration and sometimes anger.

I was finalising details of the research design at the same time as submitting applications to local ethical committees for four fieldwork locations. Local ethical committee approval was required as I was randomly sampling patients' names from hospice home care patient lists. Ethical considerations were uppermost in the research team's mind. As a result, the research design was influenced by our understanding of what would be deemed ethical. After a long question and answer session with one of the ethical committees, the details of the research design and consent form appeared to me to be secondary to the committee. Their decision, after lengthy deliberations, seemed to be based on whether they could trust me as the researcher. My initial reaction was pleasure as they had accepted the proposal. But the emphasis on me and my sensitivities to the interviewees felt quite onerous. I felt I couldn't hide behind procedures as set out in the research design. My judgement was being put on the line. In particular they had wanted reassurances that I would not use the question 'What does your death mean to you?' if I didn't feel it was appropriate. But there were no prescribed indicators for 'inappropriateness' on which I could rely.

This emphasis on the sensitivity of the research begins with introducing the research to the potential interviewee and gaining consent. It became clear very quickly that while women were consenting at the beginning of the interview, they had no real conception of what was in store. I felt this was not because of any knowing deception on my part but because the women were unaware of what they felt until actually asked. So I developed the technique of obtaining consent from the woman throughout the interview. Every time we moved on to a new topic or the line of questioning became more intense I checked with the woman if she wanted to go on. In the interviews women used my checking whether they wanted to continue as a breathing space in which they composed themselves before continuing. Women who were talking freely seemed to appreciate that, by ·checking with them, I was acknowledging the effort it required from them to talk. The women who were more reticent caused me to question my interviewing skills. Should I be probing more? Would another interviewer manage to elicit fuller responses? Was I backing off because I was a sensitive interviewer who was taking my lead from the woman, or was I feeling uncomfortable myself and therefore backing off? I began to realise that I had to be more conscious about what made *me* feel comfortable in the interview setting. Was my feeling comfortable and at ease, a good enough indicator of whether to probe or not? Was my feeling comfortable going to result in an ethical interview? It was only very near the end of the fieldwork when I was having a debriefing interview that it dawned upon me that the relationship between my comfort factor and the interview was complex and significant.

This is illustrated by the interview with Cheryl, one of the respondents who was dying.[5] Cheryl said, right at the beginning of the interview, that she would not be happy borrowing money from friends and that she had never had any experience of doing so. She went on to say that as far as money was concerned she was very independent. Further into the interview she explained how a friend had paid for her to have an operation which cost £2,000. This piece of information came in the middle of a long description by Cheryl of the onset of her illness. I was immediately aware of the apparent discrepancy in the two pieces of information Cheryl had proffered about money transactions. However, I chose not to follow this up at any time throughout the rest of the interview. I was not secure in that interview situation because I sensed that Cheryl was not completely relaxed. I didn't want to embarrass her, or myself, by drawing attention to the potential conflicting pieces of information. There may well have been a very plausible explanation. But I decided the risk of probing was too great, potentially too exposing.

The second interview was with a dying woman, Katherine. Before the interview started Katherine had said that she was interested in research and had herself carried out some interviews. I felt comfortable that she had an understanding of the research process and this would enable her to consent or not from an informed standpoint. I interviewed her in two sessions because she had a lot to say and each interview took approximately two hours. Three-quarters of the way through the first interview Katherine had said that her friend Helen had protected her when she had an episode of illness. Helen had done this by not talking about any of her own problems. As Katherine became stronger Helen had talked more about her own life. Very near the end of the first interview Katherine had talked about how she had been irritated by her husband's attempts to protect her, for example, by not even letting her load the washing machine or be involved in decisions about whether their son should take extra French at school. I picked up on this and asked Katherine how she reconciled her different reactions to her husband and to Helen. At the beginning of the second interview I had the opportunity to ask her how she had felt following the first interview. She said that she had felt disturbed by her different reactions to her friend and to her husband and this had troubled her. Later she reported to her MacMillan nurse that she had been quite troubled by this exposure. I had felt comfortable during the interview and so I had followed up on something I felt was interesting. By coincidence, because I was visiting Katherine twice, I had the opportunity of finding out how she had felt about my interviewing. My comfort factor was not a good indicator of interviewee comfort. Was it insensitive to probe with Katherine? Was it bad interviewing not to probe with Cheryl?

The importance and sensitivity of the research topic seemed to make everyone focus on doing a 'good job'. My problem was knowing what that was. I began to think about the 'good' interview. What is a good interview? I knew about the technical references to interviewing skills. I had been on depth interviewing courses. I had experience of interviewing in several setting. But the 'good' interview remained illusory and this became a major source of anxiety for me. In fact it wasn't only me that was aware of this, the women judged themselves as 'good' interviewees, or not, in terms of their perceived ability to express themselves. They were often keen to do justice to the subject matter, which because of its existential nature, was often difficult for them. This was all compounded as both the women and I knew I couldn't go back to them at a later date since many of them would have died.

I am also getting clues about my interviewing technique from the women talking in the interviews about their relationships. This realisation made my reading of the literature on relationships between interviewer and interviewee very focused. I could not relate to the interviewee on the level of our common health status and other characteristics like gender, race and age, felt secondary to the topic. I feel I am the professional researcher come to do a job when I go and interview and I sense that is what the women expect. This 'apartness' from those who are dying has been, and continues to be, a pervading theme in any methodological or theoretical aspect of my work. The chasm between a dying woman and a healthy woman interviewer makes other commonalities seem, if not banal, secondary. To compensate for this 'separateness', I tend to talk after the more formal interview in a social way by including information about myself which I had purposefully withheld during the actual interview.

The fact that I was obviously pregnant when doing some of the field-work provided a point of contact for a lot of the women and myself. Within the research team we had discussed whether this would be an advantage or a disadvantage. Would it be seen as such an obvious sign of new life to a dying woman? In actual fact it seemed to be facilitating. In two cases I revisited the women for a dual interview after the baby was born, having interviewed them first separately when I was 8 months pregnant – and huge. The women had not realised I was pregnant. Understandably, they had been so absorbed in their own agendas they did not notice. However, it proved to be much harder when returning to the field after maternity leave. On more than one occasion, when I talked about my baby as part of the presentation of myself, I was greeted by some quite hostile responses. The women felt I should not be working with a young baby. To them it seemed like a wasted opportunity, some-thing acutely pertinent to dying women. From an interviewing point of view I had not lost any data, as the exchange happened at the end of the meeting. But I felt awful, I had taken so much, and what I had offered had been rejected. I learnt to be very selective when imparting informa-tion about myself. So, even at that stage of the interview when I was being more social, I was very circumspect. Everything I talked about was taken from the women. For example one woman had a camper van and had talked about this in the interview. My husband has a camper van. It was a safe topic of conversation. It was not however something I would have chosen as representing me. It placed me in a very peripheral part of my life.

My first interview was problematic. As a social interaction it happened without obvious mishaps. I went through all my question areas and felt comfortable enough to raise or to respond to Cynthia's references to her illness and her death. There were no breakdowns, an agreement that she would approach her friend about an interview, cups of tea and chat about Christmas as it was 2 weeks before Christmas. Three days later I was told that Cynthia had had, a previously booked, counselling session after my interview with her. In this session it became apparent that the research had uncovered a lot of painful areas for her. Her daughters were also angry because their mother was upset. The nurses were extremely support-ive of me and did not seem at all concerned by this turn of events. They felt Cynthia's reaction was typical of a counselling response; after expo-sure, the person withdraws. I am *not* a counsellor or therapist. It wasn't clear to me what in the interview was responsible for sparking off this response. That was worrying in itself. I was being insensitive and didn't know how. I then, by chance, bumped into Cynthia at the hospice and we talked in a private room. She was quite reticent because she knew her daughters had been on the phone to the hospice and that 'her case' was being discussed.

It transpired that at the end of the research interview I had asked for demographic details, a lot of which I thought I already knew. I thought she had two daughters. So I said as a way of confirmation 'and you have two daughters is that right?' She hesitated momentarily and then said that in fact she had another child. That child had not been mentioned at all during the main body of the interview and I was aware of that, but I did not ask any more questions. We were in the process of winding up the interview and, although this could have been interesting, it was not obviously apparent that it would have any bearing on her friendships, illness and forthcoming death. It transpired that she was not in communication with the third child and this was a cause of great concern and pain to her. It was this simple structured question about her children which left her upset after I had gone. Asking 'simple facts' like age, who you live with, number of living children and last occupation were designed to wind up the interview in a lighter fashion. The obvious is not always the sensitive. The balance of working in this sensitive area and keeping regard to confidentiality is much more complex than on first consideration. I was told in some detail about Cynthia's situation in a debriefing session with the nurses in order to put the interview into perspective for me. They had obviously talked to the counsellor. However, I realised that I couldn't ask about Cynthia too many times during the following weeks. The nurses gave the impression that this incident was par for the course and I needed to be able to deal with it in order to do this type of research. So I quickly stopped referring to the case even though I desperately wanted to know that it was all right, whatever all right was. I had to maintain my professional credibility. This has been repeated in other settings. Nurses have implied that over-concern on my part about emotional responses in patients is inappropriate. Their view is that some response in the patient is natural given their circumstances.

I have been shaken by other people's response to the research topic. People sometimes draw their breathe in when they hear the research topic. I do not have such a clear response. Right from the start I have felt committed to the idea that dying women as a group should be involved in research just as any other group in the population. I have felt privileged to be in the position of interviewing women who are near the end of their life. It allows me to be privy to women's thoughts at a time when these thoughts are not generally exposed. It has been very inspiring. In some cases I have left interviews feeling so very moved by the woman's story, overwhelmed by a general sense of emotion – numb, not positive or negative, impossible to define except by its pervasiveness. The women's stories are often complex and involve an intermeshed series of life events which have involved their friends. Their forthcoming death is only a part of the story. In a sense I suppose this work is deemed sensitive because so many people do not have access to dying people. But with the privilege of access comes awesome responsibility. I began to feel that I was insensitive, hard, unsympathetic and callous. I was not having physical symptoms as a result of the research. I was not breaking down in tears regularly during or after the interviews. In some cases I didn't even like the women. Interviewers sometimes use first person accounts of fieldwork to 'confess' to not liking some respondents. It is particularly difficult to confess to not liking a dying person. If the majority of people you are interviewing over a period of time are dying, this fact in some senses loses its significance.

Underpinning all these concerns is a sense that whatever I feel *it is data*. This is reassuring, up to a point. Perhaps the research will not be properly finished for me until I am dying. But, in the meantime, I am still left with the sense of risk that this type of research involves. If any of the women regret being involved in the research they have so little time to resolve their concerns. The interviews felt very much like the women rehearsing their biography for perhaps the last time. If it came out wrong, or was misinterpreted by me, they would have very little time to resolve their feelings. Therein lies the peculiar risk of this research.

Joint reflections on the fieldwork account

In this section both authors reflect on the fieldwork account presented above, using it as an established text to be analysed.

The fieldwork account is permeated with a sense of struggle and search. We suggest that the search is for appropriate rules for feelings. Young states that she wants to 'ground her research experience in a sociological context'. By having access to the feeling rules associated with a particular sociological approach her feelings could be more easily managed. The struggle described in the account is with the management of the potentially conflicting sets of feeling rules. The awareness and management of this searching and struggling constitutes the emotion work being carried out. As Hochschild observes, emotion work is an active stance, it requires effort. The effort or work is exacerbated by making it public and attempting to deal with the vulnerability and exposure that writing in the first person in a professional context creates: 'The professional is very obviously becoming the personal. This first person account feels like crossing over boundaries'. There is an immediate sensitivity to the level of involvement required.

The potentially emotive nature of this particular research subject is referred to in the account. 'In some cases I have left interviews feeling so very moved by the woman's story, overwhelmed by a general sense of emotion – numb, not positive or negative, impossible to define except by its pervasiveness'. But interestingly the sensitivities of talking to dying women and their friends is not the predominant theme in the account and this Young acknowledges when she describes other peoples' reactions to the research topic as being different from her own. 'People sometimes draw their breath in when they hear the research topic. I do not have such a clear response'. There is a sense that physical symptoms, of anxiety for instance, indicate desired feelings which she should evoke. She refers to feeling 'hard, unsympathetic and callous' because she was not experiencing physical symptoms. In a similar way she acknowledges that not liking some dying respondents may be a feeling that she should attempt to suppress. These concerns imply expectations about what should be felt.

A lot of the emotion work described in the account is related to an awareness that her feelings did not necessarily fit with documented expectations of fieldworker feelings. We interpret her reading of the ethnographic literature as a search for appropriate feeling rules. But her reading, instead of making her feel comfortable, or as if she 'had come home', as Wilkins did on discovering a feminist literature, provides only partial insights. She is left to manage sets of potentially conflicting feeling rules. So we see that she particularly rejects as inappropriate the feminist notion of identification when considering her relationship with the dying women. She says 'In the immediate sense I am not dying. Any attempt at relating on this level would be crass and insensitive. . . . I could not relate to the interviewee on the level of our common health status and other characteristics like gender, race and age, felt secondary to the topic'.

In the same way she struggles with placement strategies finding them to be problematic when used in the field, 'On more than one occasion, when I talked about my baby as part of the presentation of myself, I was greeted by some quite hostile responses'. In some cases, she only understands the nature of the feeling rules governing her own emotions when different feeling rules are invoked by others. This is illustrated by the interview with Katherine when Young's feelings of comfort led her to probe further. Katherine expressed unease concerning the emotions generated for her by this probing (access to feelings of interviewees after the interview are relatively rare in research). Significantly this insight about the comfort of the interviewee and probing became apparent to her during a debriefing interview with her supervisor. 'It was only very near the end of the fieldwork when I was having a debriefing interview that it dawned upon me that the relationship between my comfort factor and the interview was complex and significant'. As Hochschild observes, emotion work can be done by others on the self. In this context the debriefing interviews made her aware of conflicting emotions; her own emotional comfort, the desire to 'do a good interview' in a sensitive situation, and her feelings for the respondents.

One can also see something of the same in the response the nurses made to the interview with Cynthia. The situation of a dying woman reacting with pain to a rehearsal of her biography was familiar to them. They had a response to this situation, based on their own profession's feeling rules, and could do the emotion work required. Young had no such clear rules to guide her. Perhaps significantly, she speaks of needing to maintain professional credibility at that point in the research. Her concern over seeming foolish to peers also implies that there is a proper, sociologically acceptable, way to feel. These examples suggest that professions, including sociology, may be to some extent defined by the feeling rules that underpin them.

A series of questions are posed throughout the account. These are connected with the technical skills required to do 'a good interview', a topic that seems at the root of many of the anxieties expressed. The methods chosen for the interviews did not provide in themselves a safeguard for her feelings. Judgements about probing and exposure of feelings and vulnerabilities are decisions peculiar to each interview. As stated in the account 'I couldn't hide behind procedures as set out in the research design . . . there were no prescribed indicators for inappropriateness on which I could rely'. She goes on to say that 'the "good" interview remained illusory and this became a major source of anxiety for me'. She is left with a set of unresolved tensions and no allegiance to a particular methodological approach. Hochschild refers to the dynamics of contending sets of rules and the potential for there to be a vacuum as one set become deconventionalised and other sets are not reconventionalised. In this situation the fieldworker is left asking 'How should I feel?' or 'Do my feelings fit?'. This tension may be more productive than an allegiance to a particular set of interviewing rules or techniques as good interviewing practice does not necessarily result in the production of the good interview.

Conclusion

In this chapter we have related Hochschild's concepts of emotion work and feeling rules to the endeavour of sociological fieldwork as documented in first person fieldwork accounts. In particular we have made use of Young's fieldwork experiences when interviewing women who were dying. The sensitivity of this particular research topic may have highlighted the emotion work undertaken during and after fieldwork. However, we feel the association between emotion work and feeling rules applies to fieldwork accounts in general. To an extent, the 'classic' accounts of fieldwork are ironized by feminist methodologists and by writers like Johnson and the Adlers. Ironically, the cool detached research-as-work orientation typical of the neo-Chicagoan tradition in fact hid a range of emotional responses to the fieldwork situation. We have suggested that this ironization needs to go further. Part of the reflexive process involves understanding the emotional implications of our own methodological preferences, and how they might interact and conflict.

The emotions expressed in fieldwork accounts tend to be negatively cast, or they express difficulties which are finally managed. This is partly because such accounts tend inevitably to describe a process or a journey (James 1984). A rosy picture of comfort and harmony may read as self-satisfied. Although fieldwork accounts are often written by novice fieldworkers who are describing a rite of passage into their profession (Lee 1993), it is not enough to say how difficult fieldwork can be for an individual. The roots of the difficulty have to be explored. The analysis above has made explicit the conscious awareness or sociological introspection which is a necessary part of writing a first person account. It provides a 'way in' to the mass of feelings expressed in these accounts and a means of putting some theoretical perspective on them. For us, the emotion work that is done in research is best seen as an attempt to *manage* the feeling rules implicit in *different* methodological perspectives.

We have argued that first person fieldwork accounts capture the dissonance between what fieldworkers feel they ought to feel and what they admit to feeling. The difficulties or the stress portrayed in these accounts reflect the emotion work undertaken in attempting to manage the tensions between involvement, comfort and identification. We suspect that tensions of this kind are inherent in fieldwork. Our experience suggests that what is important is to provide a variety of forums for grappling with these tensions for example though structured debriefing interviews and the use of first person accounts as data for secondary analysis. Such forums do not ensure that the conflict between comfort, involvement and identification is resolved in a particular way. Indeed, just the opposite. Because the emotion work on this project was partly done collectively, differing approaches to resolving the tensions were always on offer. In fact, there may be something to be said for not fully resolving emotional issues in research. To do so may risk resolving the competing pulls of comfort, involvement and identification in a complacent way which solves some problems but potentially exacerbates others.

Notes

1 This paper arose out of a series of discussions between the authors in which an attempt was made to identify theoretical bases for the understanding of the role

of emotions in fieldwork. The starting point for the discussions was the first author's fieldwork account. This was written by the first author at the end of the fieldwork using her fieldwork diary and the transcripts from the debriefing interviews with her supervisor. The intention from the start of the research project was to keep a diary, carry out debriefing interviews and to write a first person account. The ideas for this chapter were developed after the first person account of the fieldwork had been written. Chapter drafts which theorised and contextualised the first person account were passed backwards and forwards between the authors in order to develop the arguments presented. The actual fieldwork account was not altered at this stage. It was treated as an established text to be analysed.

2 To be clear, in talking about over or under-analysis we are not referring to the volume of analysis carried out by a particular fieldworker on a particular topic. Nor do we have any view on the 'correct' interpretation of the examples we have given. The point we make is a methodological one about the adequacy of first person accounts.

3 When the words supervisor or manager appear in the first person account these do not refer to the second author. He is a collaborator and joint author of this chapter but was not directly involved in the original research.

4 Three debriefing interviews took place during the fieldwork period. A topic guide was used by the interviewer and the focus of the interviews was on the emotional aspects of the fieldwork. Particular fieldwork interviews were discussed in some detail.

5 All the names used in this account are pseudonyms.

References

Adler, P. and Adler, P. (1987) *Membership Roles in Field Research*. Newbury Park, CA: Sage.

Cannon, S. (1989) Social research in stressful settings: difficulties for the sociologist studying the treatment of breast cancer, *Sociology of Health and Illness*, 11, 1, 62–77.

Devereux, G. (1967) *From Anxiety to Method in Behavioral Science*. Paris: Moulton and Co.

Dingwall, R. (1980) Ethics and ethnography, *Sociological Review*, 28, 4, 871–91.

Emerson, R. (1981) Observational fieldwork, *Annual Review of Sociology*, 7, 351–78.

Finch, J. (1984) 'It's great to have someone to talk to': the ethics and politics of interviewing women. In Bell, C. and Roberts, H. (eds) *Social Researching: Politics, Problems and Practice*. London: Routledge and Kegan Paul.

Gans, H. (1982) The participant observer as human being: observations on the personal aspects of fieldwork. In Burgess, R. (ed) *Field Research: A Sourcebook and Field Manual*. London: Hyman.

Hammersley, M. (1984) The researcher exposed: a natural history. In Burgess, R.G. (ed) *The Research Process in Educational Studies: Ten Case Studies*. Lewes: Falmer.

Hochschild, A. (1979) Emotion work, feeling rules and social structure, *American Journal of Sociology*, 85, 3, 551–75.

Hunt, J. (1989) *Psychoanalytic Aspects of Fieldwork*. London: Sage.

James, N. (1984) A postscript to nursing. In Bell, C. and Roberts, H. (eds) *Social Researching: Politics, Problems and Practice.* London: Routledge and Kegan Paul.

Johnson, J. (1975) *Doing Field Research*. New York: The Free Press.

Kohli, M. (1981) Biography: account, text, method. In Bertaux, D. (ed) *Biography and Society: The Life History Approach in the Social Sciences*. Beverly Hills: Sage.

Krieger, S. (1985) Beyond subjectivity: the use of self in social science, *Qualitative Sociology*, 8, 4, 309–24.

Lee, R. (1993) *Doing Research on Sensitive Topics.* London: Sage.

Lofland, J. (1971) *Analysing Social Settings: A Guide to Qualitative Observation and Analysis*. Belmont, CA: Wadsworth.

Miller, S. (1952) The participant observer and over-rapport, *American Sociological Review*, 17, 97–9.

Oakley, A. (1981) Interviewing women: a contradiction in terms. In Roberts, H. (ed) *Doing Feminist Research*, London: Routledge and Kegan Paul.

Sanders, C. (1980) Rope burns: impediments to the achievement of basic comfort early in the field research experience. In Shaffir, W., Stebbins, R. and Turowitz, A. (eds) *Fieldwork Experience: Qualitative Approaches to Social Research*. New York: St Martins Press.

Stanley, L. and Wise, S. (1983) *Breaking Out: Feminist Consciousness and Feminist Research*. London: Routledge and Kegan Paul.

Stanley, L. (1992) *The Auto/Biographical I: Theory and Practice of Feminist Auto/Biography*. Manchester: Manchester University Press.

Van Maanen, J. (1988) *Tales of the Field*. Chicago: University of Chicago Press.

Whyte, W.F. (1981) *Street Corner Society*. Chicago: University of Chicago Press. 3rd edition, revised and expanded.

Wilkins, R. (1993) Taking it personally: a note on emotions and autobiography, *Sociology*, 27, 1, 93–100.

5. Emotion work, order, and emotional power in care assistant work

Geraldine Lee Treweek

Introduction

Understanding the world as an emotional space has become a central concern for sociology, especially in the study of service sector, health and 'caring' occupations. A paramount issue has been the debate around women and emotional labour (Hochschild 1983, James 1989). This chapter contributes to the existing literature by examining the particular case of a residential care home for older people and the emotion work of the care assistants. This is emotion work not only in the context of providing care and support but also in creating order. Care in homes for older people takes place within a difficult emotional context. Many residents enter after their personal circumstances have changed, such as after bereavement or illness, and some will have chosen residential care as a last resort. They may experience mixed emotions in the move from their domestic homes, and care assistant work helps provide order in this transition.

Society in general tends to view care as involving positive emotion work, such as nurturance, comfort and protection, which are beneficial for recipients. But emotion work as explored in this chapter is a dynamic mechanism for creating social order in the residential setting and is presented as involving both nurture and control. To the care assistant this work involves the 'best interests' of residents and from an outsider's perspective it may seem innocuous. However, I argue that emotion skills are harnessed by workers to allow them to get through their work and create order in the home. Although care assistants are of low status and their emotion work is generally unrecognised by employers, the need for order in homes is a shared value. This chapter provides a description and interpretation of the interior of residential care work as a complex set of emotional activities and understandings.

To avoid confusion the term *emotion work* is used to examine the job of the care assistant. Tolich (1993: 377–8) argues that Hochschild (1983) developed the terms emotional labour and emotion work to distinguish between emotions performed in the work place and emotions performed in the private domestic sphere. He views this public/private division as illusory, as it suggests that emotion used in public roles is imposed upon the worker, whereas in private settings emotion work is genuine and autonomous. Similarly, I use the term emotion work to avoid the connotations of enforced emotional behaviour that I perceive to be attached to the concept of emotional labour. Although there were certain expectations contained in the care assistant job description, the emotion work they displayed was not defined by management. The work group had developed an independent emotional order and way of responding to residents.

The chapter begins with an outline of the research methodology used and a discussion of sociological literature centred on women, emotional work, power and social control. Next, I discuss the character of emotions within the residential home, and the care assistants' perceptions of emotions at work. Illustrating this are the assistants' view that all emotions need to be controlled and that this is a central component of their work. The chapter then examines the assistants' use of typifications of emotional states, used to order residents, and gives three illustrative typification groups: 'the lovelies', 'the disliked' and 'the confused'. The chapter concludes with a discussion of these findings, and also indicates how research on emotion work can benefit from ethnographic approaches.

Methods

Ethnographic research was carried out in Hazelford Lodge residential home,[1] a privately owned establishment for older people sited in the West Country (Lee Treweek 1994). The research focused upon the experience of women working as care assistants and was undertaken through non-participant observation of shifts, in-depth interviews with staff and analysis of documents such as day and communication books. A close research relationship was maintained with staff and residents for two years. It is usually difficult to gain access to private homes, but Hazelford was owned by friends of my family and the initial contact with the owner was undertaken by my mother. Next, I negotiated with the Matron who granted full access to all areas of the home. I also asked the individual care assistants and residents if they were opposed to my presence, both before the research proper had begun and later as the need arose. Although my first point of access, the owners, could potentially have presented difficulties in my relationship with the care assistants, none were experienced. Indeed, my active interest in their work was often welcomed.

Much of the data were collected over 179 hours of non-participant observation carried out over four weeks in 1992. This allowed me to view a continuous period of work; follow the day-to-day work of the carers and see the development and outcome of events over this time. Observation was organised to cover mornings, afternoons, evenings and nights. After each hour of observation I took time out to write up events and conversations. This gave me a verbatim account which was written up in full on the same day. At the same time a research diary was kept as a reflexive account of the research and in which I recorded themes as they emerged from the research process. The analysis involved reading the data and creating files of themes to allow a more detailed sorting of material on a second re-reading. At the end of this basic analysis I had ten key themes which were recurrent within the data and which were examined in more depth. This chapter is only one of a number of possible accounts of work at Hazelford Lodge. However, at the end of the research I presented some of my findings to the care assistants and was pleasantly surprised at their recognition of events and the structure of home life.

In common with other homes in the local area, Hazelford Lodge's clientele were physically able, and the majority were mentally capable. Similarly, Hazelford employed only care assistants of which there were twenty, ten of whom were full-time. All were female, white and recruited from the local area. There was a Matron who oversaw their work but she did not have a nursing or social work qualification and had risen from the general rank of care assistant after ten years experience. She undertook the same chores as the other assistants. Only one care assistant had a relevant formal qualification which was a National Vocational Qualification in care: Grade One. Hazelford Lodge was presented by the proprietors as one of the better residential homes in the local area and charged rates accordingly.

During the two years of contact with Hazelford Lodge a strong rapport was formed between myself and the staff. Over time I became the recipient of the assistants' emotion work and when physically and emotionally tired with the everyday drudgery of data collection, I was carried by their enthusiasm. At other times I provided support, such as spending time with a bereaved care assistant discussing her feelings. Although the good relationships I had with the assistants made data collection a mutually satisfying experience, I often felt stifled by their attempts to look after me. For example, on leaving the home I would often find leftovers wrapped in tin foil surreptitiously deposited in my bag. On one occasion I was infuriated when a care assistant not much older than myself took a piece of toast away from me and said that I 'wasn't buttering it properly' and that I 'needed looking after'. The collection of data was simultaneously emotionally stimulating and yet demanding, perhaps reflecting the general experience of carrying out qualitative social research.

Emotional labour, emotional work and women

In feminist analyses of power, attention has been drawn to the powerlessness of women; in relation either to men or to the system of patriarchal values embodied in contemporary western societies and institutions (Barrett 1980, Rowbotham 1972). Current understandings of women and emotion at work are mainly derived from feminist perspectives on emotional labour. Central to these arguments is the notion that women's emotion skills have become commodities which are bought and sold within the public sphere. However, despite their usefulness these skills are often not recognised in wage levels. More recently, women's abilities to define and organise power within specific settings has been identified as an important issue (Curtis 1991, Evers 1981, Lorentzon 1989).

In Hochschild (1983) and James's (1989) work emotional labour is presented as a commodity mainly associated with the skills of women. It is work used to create a certain relationship with the recipient and to manage that individual in a particular way. In the case of Hochschild's air hostesses the format of this management is advocated by the airline management and imparted through training. It is in the airlines' interests to keep customers happy through creating workers who facilitate and order emotion. In Hochschild's view this work is non-autonomous and estranges the individual from their own feelings during their work. James (1989) argues that the skills of working with emotion, maintaining the emotional composure of other people and presenting a particular emotional front, are essential activities in the work place. The logical conclusion of such ideas is that damage, distress or deceit is forced upon the emotional labourer by the nature of what they are expected to do and by the contradictions of self and role. This account appears to suggest that emotional labour is for *all* of those expected to do it an enforced behaviour in the workplace.

However, there are clear difficulties in asserting such a generalised view and this is reflected in recent work on the concept of emotional labour (Tolich 1993, Wharton 1993). Wharton highlights two major changes in the perception and presentation of emotional labour within sociology. First, she notes a greater recognition of the complexities of the relationships involved in emotional labour, and the importance of moving away from accounts which present emotional labour as leading to, 'uniformly negative consequences for workers' (Wharton 1993: 205). Secondly, she rejects the notion that undertaking emotional labour necessarily involves an assault upon the giver's private self, or produces a discrepancy between the labourer's self, role, and emotion.

In this chapter, I use the example of care assistant work to illustrate the importance of the autonomous use of emotion work in residential care of older people. By autonomous I mean emotion displayed by workers which operates independently from formal training or management rules. For the care assistants, emotion work was a useful resource in organising and making sense of work in the home. Their emotion work often involved negative emotional behaviours towards the residents, such as control and coercion. These activities are not traditionally associated with women's emotion work, but neither can they be conceptualised as abuse; these are part of the hidden side of care. However, emotion work in the domestic sphere is not only about facilitation and nurturance but involves emotionally ordering individuals through a variety of means. James notes perceptively that women's emotion work in the domestic sphere includes much more than provision of support and involves a range of emotional tools,

This work can be carried on in a number of ways, by listening, gentle persuasion, by firm direction, by discomforting the person and by force (1989: 24).

This quote highlights the proposition that emotion work can involve negative behaviours towards the recipient, as well as more positive ones. Within a broad construction of emotion work, verbal coercion and emotional manipulation can be as much a part of emotion work as loving, facilitating and caring. Therefore, emotions and control cannot necessarily be constructed in all contexts as opposing points on a continuum, and they may be best perceived as sides of the same coin. From this perspective emotion work can be seen as a means of creating order and a method of control.

Power, care and social control

Residential settings have been the object of sociological interest for many years (Bloor 1986, Goffman 1961, Kings et al. 1971). However, it is quite hard to locate contemporary residential care for the elderly within the traditional sociological debates. For example, residential homes, although sharing some features, are not the same as the total institutions that feature in Goffman's (1961) Asylums. It is difficult to argue that residential care raises the same social control issues as institutional living for those suffering from forms of mental illness, for people with learning disabilities or children in community homes. The aims of residential homes for older people are not to reform, treat or punish older people and the circumstances for the passage into residenthood are somewhat different. However, what can be said is that some older people do not wish to go into residential care, do not choose the home they go to and may be admitted by relatives or others, rather than through their own choice (Challis and Bartlett 1986). Furthermore, as Willcocks (1987: 146–7) notes, the very existence of homes, functions as a way of limiting the demands of older people upon the state and welfare. She argues that many older people do not ask for support or services for fear that they might be 'put away'.

On a micro-scale within these homes the nature and function of social control has been identified (Paterson 1977, Willcocks *et al.* 19878). Thus, research has highlighted the social organisation and the routines which serve to order the older individuals within residential settings. However, the notion of emotion work as a means of ordering older people in residential care has tended to be overlooked. In research about other health settings, emotion work, as an aspect of social control, and the way that emotion work may serve to empower health and care labourers, is becoming more visible. For example, Curtis's (1991) ethnographic study of midwives focused upon the creation of an emotional order. Evers' (1981) work on long-stay hospitalised elder care showed that those patients who complied with the ward order were rewarded with emotional support. In health and care settings power may be said to be based (at least partially) on the provision, or denial, of need. Lorentzon (1989) defines this as 'nurturant power' and notes it as a particularly feminised form. The power of women who undertake health work is enacted through the ability to provide for or deny other peoples physical and emotional needs. However, it has to be noted that this is not a one-way process because recipients of care in these settings can also utilise emotion to control staff and other care recipients. Health and care settings provide us with a very complex set of emotional relationships and understandings to disentangle. Therefore although we do not have a well formed tradition of combining power and care, we now have research that provide a basis for considering emotion as at least part of social control mechanisms within health and social care contexts.

In addition, Foucault's (1988) notion of 'pastoral care' can be developed to examine the basis of power relationships within car e settings. The more familiar Foucauldian concepts of 'surveillance' and the 'gaze' can be successfully combined with the notion of pastoral care to examine the particular case of residential settings. Foucault terms a certain mode of power relationship 'pastoral care' to indicate its roots in the metaphor, and implied relationship, of a shepherd and the flock. In this relationship the power of the shepherd is based within the activities involved in ordering the flock; through knowing each member and providing for them and their needs. The shepherd's 'role is constantly to ensure, sustain, and improve the lives of each and everyone' (Foucault 1988: 67). A prominent feature of pastoral care is the way each member of the herd is individualised.

> Everything the shepherd does is geared to the good of his flock . . . The shepherd's power implies individual attention paid to each member of the flock (Foucault 1988, 62–3).

Therefore, pastoral care is a technique of power explained by the extended shepherd/flock metaphor. Order is created through kindness, nurturance and knowledge. It is the shepherd who is in command but the methods of control are neither aggressive nor malicious, and appear to be in the best interests of the individual animal and the flock.

Although Foucault discusses pastoral care in relation to leaders and the led, he also implies a tendency for many contemporary forms of social relationship to be formed around this mode of power. This mode of control can be applied to the analysis of caring. In residential care homes the idea that care is carried out in the best interests of residents still exists: each resident is known; files and notes are kept; their likes and dislikes are noted and attended to; their temperaments assessed and reassessed through messages in communication books and oral reports. The carers' remit is to create the environment for the resident both on a physical and emotional level, this work is often referred to as 'total care'. Furthermore, care tends to be delivered through the careful surveillance of, and provision for, individual needs. Lack of privacy and an open policy of staff surveillance (of both public and privates spaces) operate to make home life the continual subject of the gaze of staff.

Foucault's (1977, 1980) notion of surveillance is compatible with a pastoral conceptualisation of care. Self-surveillance by residents is still very important for the maintenance of social control in the residential home. In this chapter I present an interpretation of life in one home and highlight the ways that residents were controlled via the emotion work of staff. Through this, and the emotion incentives provided for those who exhibited the 'correct' behaviour, residents were encouraged to regulate their own emotions and behaviour.

The emotional nature of the residential home setting

Emotion work can be perceived as having a highly interactive, emergent nature in many settings. The residential home presents a clear illustration of how pivotal emotions can be in the context of the small organisation. Residential and institutional living evoke ideas about the types of emotional relationships expected between staff and residents. On the one hand there are ideas about institutions as devoid of emotional facilitation – as epitomised in Goffman's Asylums (1961). But there is also the existence of a rhetoric of care, maintained through the professional discourses of, for example, nursing and social work. These maintain that emotions are an integral part of the 'caring' work which goes on in such settings.

Residential home residents are generally younger, fitter and mentally more capable than patients residing in nursing homes. However, residential homes still deal with many emotionally displaced people. During observation at Hazelford Lodge, residents presented emotional problems round issues such as: grief at loss of relatives/families/pets/locality and fears of death and physical or mental disability. It was the assistants' job to manage and balance the emotional environment as much as possible. The type of order the home offered was based on an image of amiable family-type relationships between staff and residents and between the residents themselves. The home's brochure promised a particular type of lifestyle and a certain format for residents. The images used to illustrate home life presented an impression of passive group participation and entertainment, with assistants hovering over residents, offering food or providing physical support. The assistants were depicted as providers, supporters and nurturers. The accompanying text suggested a setting devoid of conflict, of 'family home-style living' and 'caring, competent, conscientious and cheerful staff', 'ready to listen to residents' problems'. The text and images were about the type of older person the institution would produce from the emotionally disordered potential resident.

Residential homes are not expected to order their residents in aggressive ways. At Hazelford Lodge the lucidity and capability of residents, and the belief of the staff that such behaviour was inappropriate in caring work, prevented this. Thus, staff could be said to have an order problem for which the solution must fit the context and the rhetoric of care: non-aggressive, invisible, innocuous. Similar to other residential settings (Paterson 1977), the format used in Hazelford Lodge relied upon notions of emotional ties between staff and residents, mimicking kinship ties. Within this setting control may be evoked by reference to obligation, acceptance, care and nurturance.

The care assistant job and perceptions of emotions at work

Work in Hazelford Lodge was organised on a team basis without a nursing-type hierarchy, and decisions were taken after group discussion between full-time care assistants. Hazelford Lodge functioned as a self-contained unit with little intervention by social services, health professionals or others. The care assistant's job had a number of elements: physical care, emotional care and general management of the setting. There were general chores that were stated in the job description, such as helping with bathing, serving meals, general domestic duties, and also talking to residents. However, physical care in the home was minimal because the residents were highly capable. Interestingly, in the case of emotion work the staff had embellished home life with acts which were not officially defined as part of the job, such as cuddling, kissing, tucking residents in at night and mediating during resident disputes. It was 'providing work', and involved creating a setting in which emotions were balanced.

The components of the work can be perceived as similar to those of women working in the domestic home, identified by Graham (1983). She describes 'providing for health' as the main role of women in the domestic home. This work involved creating a clean physical environment and providing for material needs. It also included providing emotional support to family members through the negotiation of disputes within the domestic home, and the creation of what Graham labels a 'balanced environment'. Women also provide an emotional buffer role, protecting family members from, and mediating with, outside individuals and institutions. Care assistant work was perceived by the workers as an extension of their roles in the family. The orchestration of the home's daily life was the key role of the care assistant, especially in relation to balancing emotions.

Emotions were perceived by the care assistants as in need of balance because of their mercurial nature,

Julie: they [residents] change like the weather, one minute happy, next minute crying.

In addition emotions were also believed to have an infectious quality that needed controlling,

Sally: One'll start getting upset about something and then they'll all do it, then you won't know who's crying wolf.
Carol: You have to keep them busy to stop them dwelling else you could have the whole place wailing.

Lastly, there was the notion that 'like children' older people needed to be monitored emotionally by others because they lacked control over their own emotions.

Sandy: They're like children really, well actually they're worse because they can be really nasty and start upsetting other residents.

Emotions were understood to be very dangerous and in continual need of monitoring and ordering.

The concepts of stress and of emotional contagion were used to explain the need for emotional balance. Many physical problems were perceived to involve an aspect of emotional distress or emotional mismanagement by others, especially relatives, in the past.

Karen: Ethel has this worry about the place burning down, she gets upset and gets headaches. It's because she was on her own outside, her relatives didn't visit her and she became sick with the worry.

The successful organisation of emotion was presented as correct and in the best interest of residents.

All emotion that was out of control was seen as dangerous. For example, while emotions around grieving, sadness and depression were expected, 'over-expressions' of grief or extended periods of upset were treated as negative for the whole home. Residents who caused concern were encouraged to use their rooms more, whilst diversionary tactics were used by staff during interaction with these residents. The case of Alf illustrates this point. He had moved to Hazelford in a depressed state a few months after his wife had died. Unlike most residents, he was not encouraged to come downstairs as he became upset about his wife's death. The prime aim when working in Alf's room seemed to be to placate distress. One morning I observed Judith cleaning his en suite bathroom:

Alf: She was a good wife but now she's gone.
Judith (stops cleaning and puts her head around the door): Yes, but you've got lots of happy memories, haven't you? (continues cleaning).
Alf: Yes I have . . . I wish she could have spoke at the end (cries).
Judith (appears again around the door): But you were there that's the main thing, (she carried on cleaning, occasionally answering Alf's comments. Once finished she held his hand for a few minutes, then she left him alone in his room).

It is important to remember that some residents had to be cajoled into using the public spaces, whereas I observed no evidence that the care assistants tried to do this with Alf. Two days later another assistant, Eileen, discussed Alf's emotions:

Poor man lost his wife and never got over it. But most have lost people here and they can't be seeing it in their front lounge, it's their home. A lot of them would be weepy if they saw that.

Such emotion was seen as ill-befitting to the home because of the effect it had on other residents. Grieving residents were expected to respond to emotion work. Those residents who did not react positively to the usual hug and a cuddle were contained.

'Positive' resident emotions such as over-exuberance and excitability about trips out with relatives, were also considered to be dangerous by the care assistants. Over-excitement was perceived as linked to heart attacks, indigestion, erratic eating patterns and sleeplessness. The appropriate emotional order involved organised, ordered bouts of participation and interest by residents in others or events, with only mild excitement led by the activities of the staff. Both positive and negative emotions were perceived as needing to be controlled and the assistants worked towards maintaining a 'balanced' emotional environment.

The care assistants shared an experience of domestic work and child care, and the basis of the emotional order can be interpreted as an extension of kin relationships from the domestic sphere. This involved obligation on both sides. On the one hand,

Mary: I wouldn't want my mother to be in a state, so I care for them [residents] like my own mother.

On the other hand there was an expectation that residents should behave as if they were 'good' family members: not upset one another, abide by the rules and be good tempered.

Eileen: Nola's real star, lovely she is, always cheerful, always chatty and Stan the little bald man, he's a love.

Rather than being needs-led the emotion work of the care assistants was undertaken in the expectation that residents would respond 'appropriately' and thankfully to it.

Emotion work as an organising feature of care assistant work

Residents' responses to emotion work was one of the main criteria used by assistants to typify them. Typification allows workers to prioritise and order work (Evers 1981, Jeffery 1979). In Hazelford, typifications were based not only on the emotional behaviour of residents but also on their responses to the emotion work of staff. To discuss further the notion of emotion work as a subtle ordering technique, I utilise some typologies constructed by the care assistants. However, the residents themselves had a hierarchy which mimicked the staff one and 'the disliked' tended to be unpopular with their peers. For example, the residents who were disliked by staff were often disliked by other residents, and it was common for the disliked to be openly criticised by other residents. There may have been a strategic component to some residents' behaviours because by choosing to exhibit compliance it was possible to manipulate the staff. This illustrates the complexity of emotion work in Hazelford because resident behaviour could also be interpreted as emotion work. Therefore this account of staff typification of residents should be viewed as a one-sided version of an extremely complex set of emotional relationships.

The Lovelies
The compliant group which made up the majority of residents in the home, were the 'lovelies'. The description of 'lovely' was used in conversations between staff to indicate that a resident possessed a certain set of features. First, lovelies were close to the ideal resident for whom staff enjoyed caring as they allowed complete access to their lives and feelings. For example, they told the assistants about their worries and allowed them into their rooms to talk. They were compliant and responsive to cuddling and cajoling and allowed staff to pat them on the heads, brush their hair and 'tuck them in at night'. The lovelies were verbally supportive to the staff and showed interest in the assistants' lives outside the home. The care assistants adopted individual lovelies who were then provided with bouts of individual attention by 'their' staff member.

Although most of the lovelies were physically highly capable, they allowed the care assistants total surveillance over their lives. This gave the assistants a complete knowledge of the lovelies from their states of mind to the regularity of their bowel movements and 'normal' eating and sleeping patterns. The relationships between care assistants and lovelies were close and often emulated that of parents and children. Similar to the 'dear old grans' identified by Evers (1981, 118–20) in her study of long-term elderly care wards, these patients were infantilised by staff but were accepting of this status.

However, there were positive rewards for the recipient of the typification of 'lovely'. These residents were given longer periods of interaction They were given more emotional support and physical contact (which some residents appeared to enjoy) and were given special treats of food. Lovelies were also given a higher status over other residents at Hazelford. This was symbolised in the granting of responsibility for small domestic tasks, such as collecting the paper or clearing the dinner tables, and over other 'less trustworthy' residents. For example, lovelies were often asked to watch confused residents, to 'keep an eye' on areas whilst the assistants were busy elsewhere (watch the door/lounge/office). These tasks were taken very seriously by lovelies and some took up this work without specifically being asked to do it.

Being typified as a lovely and being allowed to have special responsibilities and rights, however, necessitated their acceptance of the emotion work of staff. The relationships between lovelies and the staff were maintained by a great sense of duty, responsibility and pride on both sides.

Rose: I like to help these girls, they try really hard but they can't be everywhere, they need help to look after them [the confused].

The residents seemed to feel that being chosen was an indication of a close and special relationship with staff. The care assistants also felt there was something 'extra' between themselves and the lovelies, and when a lovely died many openly cried, some wore black arm bands and all available staff would attend the funeral. There was a sense that the lovelies were really 'their' residents, whereas others just lived in the home and were emotionally separate.

The Disliked
In comparison with the lovelies, the disliked residents, though fewer in number, created a sizeable social control problem for the assistants. The disliked could be perceived as similar to the 'awkward Alices' identified by Evers (1981: 122–5). Although male residents were sometimes disliked for being demanding, it was felt that it was more acceptable for them to behave in this way. Evers (1981: 119) found that trained staff in long-stay geriatric wards responded in a similar way to 'difficult' male patients. She suggests that this may be due to staff beliefs that this is a normal part of masculine behaviour, whereas women are expected to be more compliant. The disliked were presented by the care assistants as one-dimensional indi-

viduals and they were always labelled with purely negative emotional traits, 'cold, mean, unkind, cruel, thoughtless, vicious and evil'. Indeed the complaint behaviour of the lovelies was often reinforced by staff through references to the non-compliance and emotional coldness of the disliked.

One of the traits attached to the disliked by the staff was a stalwart refusal to form what they felt was a 'normal' social relationship with staff. Normal relationships, as embodied by the lovelies, allowed a high level of infantilisation and total access. With the disliked, however, in response to pats on the head, the evening 'tucking in', and the baby-talk that the assistants exhibited with them, the disliked became rude or ignored staff. In response staff denied such residents any form of emotional support.

> Eileen: I wouldn't even try to comfort Mary, she'd reject you.
> GL-T: Have you tried going up and talking with her:
> Eileen: No point, she'd reject you.

There was little recognition that residents might prefer, and have a right to a different form of emotional support, less or none. The emotional hardness of the disliked was seen as cancelling out any emotional needs.

An example of the way staff perceived the disliked to be emotionally hard can be seen in the case of Dotty [resident] who needed an operation on a painful lump on her head. At the same time Lily a 'lovely old granny' (Eileen) needed podiatric treatment. Whereas Lily evoked the concern and emotional support of staff, the response to Dotty was quite different.

> Julie: I wouldn't worry about her, old bat, she'd do the operation
> herself and wouldn't feel a thing her skin's so thick.

Dotty's emotions about the operation were not seen as relevant to how she would cope with the treatment. Similarly, a disliked resident who was found crying in her room during a bout of illness, evoked an unsympathetic response from the staff.

> Eileen: She's not really upset, she'll be off on her broomstick next.

Once typified as disliked, it was very hard for residents to change their categorisation as positive emotional behaviours were perceived as suspicious.

> Kath: Oh she [disliked resident] can be nice all right, but there's always
> something behind it. If I see her smiling I think, what does she want?

The disliked were presented, and treated, as if operating within a range of either false, aggressive or unkind emotions. Displays of emotions, such as fear, sadness, kindness or concern were perceived as short-lived, unreal, and/or manipulative rather than as genuine exhibitions of emotion.

Although disliked residents were negatively typified, their refusal to comply with the emotion work of staff gave them power. They rejected the emotional order of the home and through this reinstated the 'real' nature of their residence; that they were paying, that they were adults and that they reserved the right to complain. The disliked exhibited the opposite emotional behaviour to that expected in the home by getting angry, refusing to comply, and refusing to be positive. The behaviour of the disliked reduced the care assistant's role to that of housekeeper or maid and this disallowed the type of 'total care' relationships that ideal worker/ resident relationships were based upon. The epitome of disliked residents behaviour was expressed in the term, 'treating the home like a hotel' (Jenny). Without the usual 'familial' basis of relationships, held together by emotion work, order was breached and care assistant power was diminished. As a result the disliked residents got swifter service than most residents but received less interaction and emotional support from staff.

The Confused

The importance of emotional order to the boundaries of residenthood can be seen in the case of residents who were typified as confused. The care assistants defined residents as confused when they exhibited certain behaviours, such as talking about things in a way the assistants could not understand, walking around at times deemed inappropriate and losing things. Evers (1981: 121) uses the concept of 'poor old Nellie' to indicate female patients on long-stay wards who were categorised by staff as highly confused. 'Poor old Nellies' evoked sympathy from staff because they were so confused they could not interact fully with their environment. In contrast, Hazelford's confused were more able than the Nellies to take care of themselves. The activities of these residents were often labelled by the care assistants as sweet, cute or comical and they made the work more lively.

As long as the confused continued to exhibit amiable character traits the assistants were happy to have them within the home. The confused were generally easy to order through continuous emotion work by staff, such as cajoling, cuddling and kind words. However, once a resident could not be ordered through emotional means, their status changed to 'nursing home material' (NHM); a term used in staff conversation but never written upon documents. To the assistants NHM was a subsection of the confused category, as they recognised that confused residents were likely, at some stage, to reach this level of confusion. Once in this state, the confused could be moved on to nursing home care relatively easily.

One example is that of Hilary, a resident who from admission was considered to be confused. Her behaviour included anorexia, wandering and forgetting where she was. But it was only when her behaviour could not be disciplined with soft words that the assistants confided that they were, 'At the end of our tethers' (Sandy). Eventually Hilary moved to nursing home care. In the assistants' oral accounts of the progression from residential to nursing care a gradual downhill movement was described which involved the accumulation of unmanageable symptoms. However, those who were moved on to nursing homes were unresponsive to the care assistants' attempts to discipline them. In Hilary's case, her wandering could usually be stopped with a 'kiss and a cuddle' but later she became unresponsive to this and was agitated. One night I observed a care assistant dealing with Hilary.

Teresa: Get back to bed, for Christ's sake how many times?
Hilary responded by turning towards her room, later Teresa spoke to me. 'I don't shout usually but she's going to have to go'.

Hilary was beyond the methods available within the home to discipline residents. The assistants' accounts of why residents were moved on did not place significance upon the ways that NHM disrupted the power balance between resident and worker.

Despite workers' claims that NHM had 'lost it' or 'gone' there was very little difference between these residents and the confused, except that they no longer responded appropriately to emotional ordering. Also, other residents who fulfiled the criteria for nursing care, such as the sick and dying, would be kept if they were emotionally controllable, regardless of their physical symptoms. The emotional labels applied to residents by the care assistants became more important than others applied by the 'outside' or other professional discourses. So, although in theory there were official boundaries which defined the type of resident Hazelford would care for, it also catered for people outside those boundaries. Those who were moved on to other forms of care often could no longer be controlled by emotional means.

Discussion: towards an understanding of emotion as power

In Hazelford Lodge the care staff harnessed their emotional skills to create order. The staff's remit was to care but they exhibited a high degree of independent emotional work. They defined the nature of the emotional order within the home and also typified and responded to residents in relation to it. Although this chapter emphasises the staff's work in creating and maintaining the emotional arena of the home, it is important to note that many of the residents also played an important part in its continuation; by accepting the power of the staff, ostracising the difficult and keeping the confused in check. The research focused upon the staff work and a different emphasis upon the residents' world would have added another dimension. For example, certain patterns of emotion behaviour could (potentially) be used by residents as a strategy for 'getting by' in the home. Therefore, emotion work in the home was extremely complex and this applies to many settings.

Much of the emotion work of the assistants in Hazelford Lodge was self generated. Tolich (1993) asserts that there is a basic level of management-defined emotional behaviour in many forms of work but that some of the emotion work undertaken in the process of many jobs is autonomous. Tolich found that autonomous emotion work was important in checkout clerk work and especially the creation of a special 'my customer' emotional relationship between check out clerks and certain customers. The workers gained a sense of personal fulfilment through maintaining warm relationships with customers. This was emotion work extra to that expected by their employers. Similarly, the care assistants also created a sense of belonging in their relationships with particular residents and each worker had favourites; particularly lovelies who they enjoyed working with and supporting. This was autonomous emotion work, undertaken from choice by the worker, yet at the same time it ordered individuals towards compliance and smoothed over worker/resident differences. Emotion work in this setting operates to provide order for both residents and care assistants.

The care assistants' work deviated from traditional sociological notions of emotional labour in two ways. First, the use of emotion work had a pattern or set of patterns and these were used by the assistants to define, organise and react to resident behaviour. Residents who breached the emotional order were negatively typified by both staff and other residents as a matter of course. Secondly, emotion work appeared to be a strategy which empowered the women workers as it provided an effective means of ordering the residents. The routine of the home relied on somehow getting residents to move around the home and engage with home life. In the absence of the acceptability of more physically manipulative strategies, the assistants utilised emotional bonds to evoke the idea that the 'good' resident should do what the assistants demanded. Through emotion work the assistants had created an effective means of controlling the home.

In Hazelford Lodge the care assistants were left to run the home as a team with little support from outside and with little formal training. They strove for control in their work place through methods derived from the resources and skills they had. These workers were not powerful in one sense, but in another sense they had tremendous power over the lives of the residents. Lorentzon's (1989) notion of 'nurturant power' can be usefully applied in this context. She highlights the important point that nurturant power has been misconstrued within sociology as more acceptable and weaker than male power, despite the long-term effects that such relationships may have on recipients. Hockey and James (1993: 45) argue that dependency is a power relationship which incorporates a social metaphor about child-likeness and maternal care. It is ideas such as these that acknowledge the existence of female power within health care which could provide a base for the development of more dynamic views of emotion in health and care work.

Conclusions

In this chapter I argue that emotional skills are not necessarily commodities used by management against the best interests of workers. Emotion work in care assistant labour is presented as a dynamic means of creating social order which is also attractive to lay ideas of caring as maternal and nurturing and in the best interests of the recipients. Foucault's notion of pastoral care is useful to my analysis as it offers term which combined nurturance and caring with the concepts of order and control. Furthermore, he perceived pastoral care as a modern form of power which, through its innocuousness is not necessarily recognised. Although Foucault (1988) does not discuss the emotional content of pastoral care in great detail, the development of his ideas can provide us with new ways of understanding power and care. Sociology should consider the concept of emotion ordering as a credible form of social control and this may be particularly useful within the study of caring and health labour.

Care assistant work at Hazelford Lodge illustrates the close links between emotion work, power and the need to create order. The care assistants' work load was eased by encouraging residents to order and monitor their own behaviour through emotional skills similar to those they may have used in their domestic homes. For women workers, emotion can be seen as a key frame of reference and cultural resource from which to derive methods of ordering others. But emotion work may be difficult to identify and understand without an insider view of the meanings involved in such work. The ethnographic approach of my work allowed a detailed analysis of care practices and beliefs which are not generally scrutinised in everyday life. It may be that similar approaches will be essential in providing intimate understandings of emotion work within other health settings.

Note

All names – those of the care assistants and residents, and Hazelford Lodge – used in this chapter are pseudonyms.

Acknowledgments

I would like to thank Angus Erskine, Stephanie Linkogle, David Stopforth and the anonymous referees whose constructive comments have helped me develop the ideas in this paper.

References

Barrett, M. (1980) *Women's Oppression Today: Problems in Marxist Feminist Analysis*. London: NBL.

Bloor, M.J. (1986) Social control in the therapeutic community: re-examination of a critical case, *Sociology of Health and Illness*, 8, 4. 305–324.

Challis, L. and Bartlett, H. (1986) The paying patient: customer or commodity. In Phillipson, C., Bernard, M., Strang, P. (eds) *Dependency and Interdependency in Old Age*. London: Croom Helm.

Curtis, P.A. (1991) *Midwives in Hospital: Work, Emotion and the Labour Process*. Unpublished PhD thesis, University of Manchester.

Evers, H. (1981) 'Care or custody? The experiences of women patients in long stay geriatric wards', In Hutter, B. and Williams, G. (Eds) *Controlling Women*. London: Croom Helm.

Foucault, M. (1977) *Discipline and Punish*. London: Penguin.

Foucault, M. (1980) 'The eye of power'. In Gordon, C. (ed) *Power Knowledge. Selected Interviews and Other Writings*. Brighton: Harvester Wheatsheaf.

Foucault, M. (1988) Politics and reason. In Kritzman, L.D. (ed) *Politics, Philosophy, Culture*. London: Routledge.

Goffman, E. (1961) *Asylums*. London: Penguin.

Graham, H. (1983) Caring: a labour of love. In Finch, J. and Groves, D. (eds) *A Labour of Love. Women, Work and Caring*. London: Routledge.

Hochschild, A. (1983) *The Managed Heart: the Commercialisation of Human Feeling*. Berkeley: University of California Press.

Hockey, J. and James, A. (1993) *Growing Up and Growing Old*. Milton Keynes Open University.

James, N. (1989) Emotional labour: skill and work in the social regulation of feelings, *Sociological Review* 37, 1, 15–42.

Jeffery, R. (1979) Normal rubbish: deviant patients in casualty departments *Sociology of Health and Illness*, 1, 1, 90–108.

Kings, R., Raynes, N. and Tizzard, J. (1971) *Patterns of Residential Care*. London: Routledge.

Lee Treweek, G. (1994) *Discourse, Care and Control: An Ethnography of Nursing and Residential Elder Care Work*. Unpublished PhD thesis, University of Plymouth.

Lorentzon, M. (1989) *Professional Status and Managerial Tasks*. Paper given to the BSA Annual Conference 1989.

Paterson, E. (1977) *Care Work: The Social Organisation of Old People's Homes*. PhD Thesis, Institute of Medial Sociology, University of Aberdeen.

Rowbotham, S. (1972) *Women's Resistance and Revolution*. New York: Random House.

Tolich, M. (1993) Alienating and liberating emotions at work, *Journal of Contemporary Ethnography*, October, 361–81.

Wharton, A.S. (1993) The affective consequences of service work, managing emotions on the job, *Work and Occupations*, 20, May, 205–32.

Willcocks, D. (1987) Residential care. In Phillipson, C. and Walker, A. *Ageing and Social Policy, A Critical Reassessment*. Aldershot: Gower.

6. Maternal–baby unbonding: rituals for undoing nature. Professional conceptions of maternal emotion and the relinquishment of babies for adoption

Sally Ruane

Introduction

The objective of this chapter is to analyse the techniques employed by professionals to separate or 'unbond' the mother from her newborn infant in certain prescribed social circumstances. The analysis is based upon an examination of data collected whilst researching the experiences of single women intending to relinquish newborn babies for adoption. The material presented here is drawn from professionals engaged in the adoption process: principally social workers and, to a lesser extent, midwives and nurses. The paper focuses on the postpartum confinement period and argues that the 'emotion talk' of nursing, midwifery and social work professionals suggests subscription to a theory of mother–infant bonding. This is evident not only in the expectations professionals have of postpartum maternal emotion but also in their undertaking of techniques and rituals designed to manage this emotion in the process of mother–child separation. Here, I shall be examining professional conceptualisations of 'typical' or 'normal' maternal emotion and professional practices designed to manage this emotion in what can be termed a 'ritual of unbonding'. The management of women who do not display 'typical' emotion is not considered in this paper because this would entail discussion of professional dilemas of a largely distinct nature

The remainder of this section examines literature relating to maternal–baby bonding and the sociology of emotions whilst the next section outlines various methodological considerations. I then explore professional conceptions of maternal emotion, how professionals construe the relationship between this emotion and a placement decision and how these professional beliefs give rise to practice dilemmas during the confinement period. The techniques and procedures used by professionals to manage the unbonding process during confinement are examined in the penultimate section and the chapter concludes with a discussion of issues raised by unbonding in relation to the nature of maternal attachment.

A number of observers have drawn attention to the emotional component of certain social roles (*e.g.* Hochschild 1983, on flight attendants;

James 1989, and Smith 1992, on nurses). It is a significant feature of the social role of motherhood that observable behaviours vis-a-vis the child are at least matched in importance by the feelings the mother has towards her child. Additionally, 'inappropriate' maternal behaviour is often taken to infer inappropriate maternal emotion. Arguably, the significance attached to feeling distinguishes the role of mother from many other social roles, *e.g.* bus conductor, cleaner, conference organiser (and see Everingham's (1994) discussion of motherly love as unsocialised). I shall be examining beliefs about maternal emotion in relation to a body of work claiming to establish the existence of a process known as 'bonding'. However, it is worth exploring first some themes within the sociology of emotions which have particular pertinence to the subject under investigation here.

Various theoretical perspectives differ on what makes emotion 'social' (Hochschild 1979, 1983, Kemper 1981, Wiley 1990). Hochschild (1979) contrasts 'organismic' and 'interactive' accounts. She is critical of those who conceptualise emotion most narrowly as physiological impulse or instinct, reducing the role of the social to that of stimulation or outward expression. She endeavours to demonstrate that feelings are not irrational or unpredictable but regulated and orderly and argues that emotions are social because they are a prerequisite for conduct and interaction (Hochschild 1979, 1983).

This suggests the appropriateness of certain feelings in certain interactional settings and Hochschild develops her arguments in what she terms 'a conceptual arena "between" the Goffmanesque focus on consciously designed appearances. . . . and the Freudian focus on unconscious intrapsychic events' (Hochschild 1979: 555). Hochschild notes that Goffman acknowledges that participants hold in check certain psychological states but claims he does not demonstrate by what techniques this is achieved. While Freud's analysis focuses on anxiety and the unconscious, involuntary means of avoiding pain, Hochschild broadens her perspective to encompass a wide range of feelings and also deliberate, conscious efforts to shape these feelings. She extends Goffman's conception of 'surface acting' to the manipulation of emotion – its evocation and suppression – through emotion work and deep acting. Feelings are managed according to feeling rules which govern the extent, direction and duration of emotion in given situations. Cultural display rules govern the means of their expression.

Wiley describes Hochschild's position as a 'modified version of the existential view' since the very act of managing emotion can be seen as part of what the emotion becomes (Wiley 1990: 128). Wiley rejects Hochschild's account as insufficiently social and argues that both inner sensation and external display are socially constructed objects. Within this view,

Just as reality and the self are constructed through an unending process of interaction and self-indication, so is feeling (Wiley, 1990: 129).

Whether one subscribes to a view that feelings are primal but made social through regulation, or to the view that the social is prior to both inner sensation and external display, it is difficult to escape the subjection of emotion to the moral order.

James (1989, 1992), Wiley (1990) and O'Brien (1994) have demonstrated that much emotion management is not intrapsychic but that certain groups – often occupational groups – undertake the management of others' feelings as part of their routine work practices (hospice nurses, 'therapists' and nurses engaged in health promotion, respectively). In drawing attention to the labour involved in dealing with other people's feelings, James (1989) highlights the centrality of feelings to social processes. These studies also point to the potential role of organisations in the scripting of emotions for their members (Wiley 1990) and to the role of emotional labour in social control (O'Brien 1994).

The literature relating to bonding provides an interesting illustration of a conceptualisation of feelings located at the 'organismic' end of Hochschild's continuum since it emphasises the biological and physiological, confining the social context to the status of a trigger. Research in this area occurred against a background of first, studies investigating the impact of maternal deprivation on child development (see Bowlby 1951, Ainsworth 1969, Yarrow 1961, Rutter 1972, Schaffer 1977); and second, 'popular' baby care manuals. These, notably those of Dick-Read (1942) and Spock (1945), asserted the importance of mother–baby contact following delivery to some extent contrary to previous advice (see King 1913). Whilst the latter had stressed hygiene and regularity, the former shifted the emphasis to the psychological and emotional aspects of mothering. Indeed, the focus upon 'getting to know the baby' progressed to the idea that early mother–baby contact provided the necessary foundation for a healthy developing mother–child relationship (Sluckin et al. 1983).

Such thinking developed significantly during the 1970s, for instance, in the work of Leifer et al. 1972, Kennell et al. 1974, Ringler et al. 1975. Klauss and Kennell (1976) claimed that mother–infant contact during a 'sensitive period' engendered innate behaviours which, they believed, imply close contact such as cuddling, fondling, smiling, kissing, vocalisations, face presentations and prolonged gazing. Following these claims, a number of studies were carried out to examine whether certain early contact experiences were more likely to produce affectionate attachments or bonds to infants than contact experiences at any other time (e.g. Hales et al. 1977, Collingwood et al. 1979). It was suggested that when this bonding process was interrupted, the child's development would proceed impaired, and various aberrant forms of parental behaviour would ensue (Herbert et al. 1982, Lamb 1983). This view that, immediately after the birth of a baby, the mother must be made to hold and fondle it in order to become emotionally tied to it, is referred to by Sluckin et al. (1983) as the 'critical period bonding view of maternal attachment' or the 'bonding doctrine'.

These research 'findings' appeared rapidly to influence professional practice as 'sensible' advice shifted towards prescriptive dogma and the doctrinaire (Valman 1980). For instance, where mother and newborn baby are separated,

> . . . there will of course be enormous difficulties in establishing contact between mother and child, with the result that she may feel alienated towards it and a normal bonding cannot develop (Vesterdal 1976, cited in Sluckin *et al.* 1983: 18).

Controversy surrounding the significance of neonatal bonding has centred upon a number of issues, including the presence of a sensitive period, whether such a period is 'optimal' or 'critical', and the actual mechanisms involved. These are analytically difficult to separate from serious methodological doubts, as well as presenting difficulties with the conceptualisation of bonding itself. There are a number of problems which lie in the concept of bonding. Studies of bonding have tended to assume it to be unidimensional and unidirectional. Reification and reductivism have left bonding mechanical, the sum of physical contacts over a defined period of time:

> the working of a kind of affectional superglue which will only 'take' if applied at the appropriate time in the appropriate manner. If successful, the mother . . . is 'tied' or 'stuck' figuratively to her offspring (Sluckin *et al.* 1983: 27).

This has been compounded by the close relationship the theorising of maternal emotion has borne to 'attachment' theory. The influence of ethological approaches in the latter has reinforced a biocentric tendency in the former (Herbert *et al.* 1982). Bonding has been seen as species specific and biologically based, where previous biographical experiences and cultural meaning are devoid of significance. (For a powerful exposition of the cultural basis of mothering, see Badinter 1981; and see MacFadyen 1994 for an analysis of different theoretical perspectives on parent–child relationships.)

The events or mechanisms operating in bonding have not been precisely specified, but hormonal events accompanying pregnancy and childbirth are believed to 'prime' a mother biologically to 'behave maternally' following delivery. (This might in part account for the absence of an analysis of paternal attachment. Sluckin *et al.* 1983 observe that the role of father is consistently subordinated to the mother–child relationship.) Additionally, contact through all sensory modes was also believed to elicit attachment behaviour in the mother, 'through a cascade of reciprocal interactions' (Klauss and Kennell 1976). This belief, in turn, was based upon hormonal determinants of maternal behaviour in rodents and ungulates, seen, for instance, in Kennell *et al.'s* (1974) explicit comparison with animal behaviour. Lorenz's ethological studies of geese also contributed to the extension of the concept of 'attachment' – the young's tie to the mother – to human experience. The extrapolation of such animal findings to human maternal behaviour has been criticised by several observers and on various grounds (Arney 1980, Lamb 1983, Scarr and Dunn 1984). In fact, closer and more critical examination of the relevant studies reveals substantial methodological flaws and their findings are at the very best inconclusive. For instance, there are problems of operationalisation where mother–infant attachment as an internal state is inferred from observable externals (Lamb 1983). Lamb connects the work of Klauss and Kennell with the criticisms made by both mothers and nurses, who objected to birthing practices which separated babies from their mothers following delivery. He suggests their 'findings' lent scientific credibility to demands for changed hospital neonatal procedures in the face of opposition from some medical staff.

Here, the significance of the dispute lies in evidence that professionals interviewed in the current study appear to assume the existence of a sensitive period, and proceed in their practice on the basis of this assumption. As Sluckin and colleagues suggest, ideas about maternal love, maternal attachment, maternal instinct and bonding are 'floating about' in various day-to-day settings (1983: 5). Bonding is considered as an attachment which is specific and discriminating and which ties the mother to the child in space and over enduring periods of time. It is considered to encompass love for the child, a sense of responsibility for the child and a sense of mutual belonging. However, my aim here is not so much to examine bonding *per se* as its inverse: the rituals in certain circumstances which surround the *unbonding* of mother and baby. The circumstances set out here concern cases where the mother is planning to place her newborn infant for adoption. As Mathieu (1979) has pointed out, in advanced Western society, we tend to overlook the fact that the coinciding of biological and social maternity is not inevitable or transhistorical but is a cultural accomplishment. Adoption represents one socially organised practice in which social and biological motherhood are separated. We shall be examining the social, physical and emotional techniques adopted by professionals to disengage a mother from her baby.

Methodology

The material presented in this chapter was drawn from interviews with social workers, in the main, and nurses and midwives, to a lesser extent. The material was collected in the late 1980s whilst researching for a PhD

(Ruane 1991). Professionals were invited for interview on the basis of their contact with women in the adoption process: they were based in four adoption agencies and seven hospitals in the North of England.

Twenty-five social workers were interviewed. Fifteen worked for an adoption agency. They possessed not simply information about legal and bureaucratic procedures and about their own role in adoption, but also about the mothers/clients they encountered. They had experienced a range of different client situations and often a range of institutional settings and procedures. These factors placed adoption workers in a good position to compare across case, time and setting. Other social workers were hospital based. They were likely to encounter mothers considering adoption at two points in the process: where she was referred for assistance from the ante-natal clinic and where she came into hospital to deliver the baby, for whom special care arrangements were often made. These workers varied in the extent of their involvement with the adoption process ranging from minimal to very considerable. This appeared to flow from the individual's interests and personal approach. Where the hospital based worker defined for herself a more encompassing role, the boundary between her own role and that of the agency based worker became blurred.

In addition to this boundary blurring, there were other reasons for not distinguishing the contribution of hospital based and agency based workers. One concerned the broader issue of social relations amongst social workers in a particular geographical area. Adoption and hospital workers tended to know each other and had, over time, developed formal and informal ways of working together. Indeed, there was degree of overlap in personnel, with one worker moving from hospital to agency during the course of the research. Additionally, although the hospital social worker's task tended to be briefer and broader, the focus upon providing information, evaluating alternatives, identifying obstacles and decision-making was shared. Midwives and nurses who worked with special care babies had a much less significant role in the adoption process. However, they did have some limited contact with mothers during confinement and a small number of interviews (six) were arranged, generally following introductions by social workers.

These professionals were selected strategically in a sample which comprised both judgement and opportunistic elements (Honigmann 1973, Tremblay 1957). Contact was made with adoption agencies and hospitals within a geographically convenient area. Initial contacts led to further introductions. Professionals were selected for interview on the basis of a number of factors: their role in the adoption process; their willingness to participate; and social and organisational processes within the relevant institutions (for instance, organisational hierarchies and levels of workloads were influential). The interviews were semi-structured, recorded on tape and usually, thought not always, conducted on a one-to-one basis.

Most were quite lengthy, reflecting professionals' willingness to talk, and lasted between 30 minutes and two-and-a-half hours in length. Interviews were designed to gain information about birth mothers' experiences of the adoption process, and of the role of professionals in that process. At the same time, interviewees were able to raise matters which they considered of relevance and to present information in a way they considered appropriate. Information presented spontaneously is likely to differ in significance from that given in response to a directive question, and its value should not be underestimated (see, for instance, Becker and Geer 1957, Miles and Huberman 1994).

The small sample size and the rich qualitative data collected facilitated a detailed analysis of a limited number of cases, focusing upon what occurred, in what context, with what implications and with what relationship to other features of the situation (Honigmann 1973). Taped interviews were transcribed in full and analysis proceeded through initial coding in broad categories, followed by more detailed coding of selected material around significant themes. Some of these themes had been identified earlier through an analysis of relevant literature; others emerged during the course of data analysis. Whilst maternal emotion was a category derived from earlier literature, the preoccupation of professionals with practice dilemmas which arose in response to maternal emotion was unanticipated. In this respect, the design of the interview process to accommodate themes and topics raised by the interviewees themselves, proved particularly fruitful. The data presented here have been selected from interviews with all categories of respondent mentioned above, for the light they shed on the relationship between practice dilemmas and the unbonding of the mother from her baby.

The question remains of the representativeness of the organisations and individuals selected where various social processes have operated to modify the researcher's control over informant selection (see Sinclair and Brady 1987, Binns 1987). Jenkins (1987) claims that both the degree of internal consistency among respondents and the broad agreement of the researcher's findings with an existing body of knowledge suggest that a sample is not unrepresentative. Although the doctoral research under consideration did not quite reproduce any previous study, its findings did 'fit in' broadly with other related areas (*e.g.* concerning the operation of situation-specific feeling rules and the problematic nature of motherhood outside marriage). Furthermore, whilst, within categories of respondent, opinions and perspectives expressed were not identical in each case, there was consistency regarding what the issues were and lines of debate or 'schools' of thought could be discerned.

The relationships social workers developed with women considering adoption extended over a longer period of time and were usually qualitatively richer than those between the mothers and nursing/midwifery staff.

This is evident in the reflections of the two professional groups upon the experiences of mothers during confinement. Social workers spoke at greater length and in greater detail about the nature of maternal emotion as well as implications for professional practice. Nursing and midwifery beliefs and assumptions about maternal feeling were more implicit in their accounts of post-delivery practice. Reflecting this, the material presented in the early sections of this chapter are derived in the main from social workers.

Professional conceptions of maternal emotion

Social workers were asked how mothers went about making or confirming decisions for adoption after the birth of their babies. The responses of social workers reflected a significant preoccupation with postpartum maternal emotion. There were two types of response relating to emotion. The first was characterised by a marked reluctance to make generalisations or draw anything more than tentative conclusions about what 'normal' women feel. The second type of response presented the post-delivery period as an emotional crisis. These may be conceptualised as distinct but associated repertoires used by professionals in accounting for maternal emotion; that is, a professional might draw on both repertoires during the course of an interview. In the first repertoire, emotion talk reflected an ambivalence about what normal postpartum feelings are, and about what inferences can be made about felt emotion from expressed emotion. This, to some extent, contrasts with Macintyre's (1976) analysis of the imputation of 'instincts' according to marital status. However, and more in keeping with Macintyre, it was the second, more prescriptive, repertoire which predominated.

Within the first repertoire of responses, any generalisations were usually accompanied by qualifying remarks. Thus, although there seemed to be fairly general agreement amongst social workers that the feelings of mother towards her newly delivered child are *usually* strong and positive, there was a certain ambivalence regarding the universality of these feelings:

> It is difficult to imagine how strong emotional feelings can be. . . . I mean they're not always. . . . (SW1)

> A lot of mothers don't bond with their babies immediately. . . . (SW2)

Within the second type of account or repertoire, however, the postpartum period was perceived as constituting a veritable emotional crisis. This was partly due to physical exhaustion and hormonal alterations imputed to most newly delivered women, and partly due to the special circumstances of the mother planning to relinquish her baby for adoption. In particular, social workers referred to certain features of maternal emotion which created a crisis for the mother planning adoption: these were primarily, love/desire, grief and guilt. They stressed the overpoweringly strong nature of the emotion and its unanticipated character.

> This emotional reaction to having a baby – I also warn the first-time mothers about this. Because they can be very confident that adoption is going ahead, and they have no idea of the emotional reaction that they are going to have when the baby is born. It's something which you can't appreciate until it's happened to you. . . . (SW3)

This implies a relationship between the likelihood of adoption and the strength and nature of maternal emotion, which is something which 'happens to you', almost inevitably. One social worker linked the 'instinctive' with the 'physical', whilst others echoed this with explicit references to hormonal changes:

> It's a very difficult time. I think the whole body. . . . you know, it's a physical thing, an instinctive, physical thing really. Your whole body is crying out to protect this baby. (SW4)

> It's a tiring and emotional kind of thing that's happening to her. . . . within the first couple of days, there's a lot of changes – emotional changes, hormonal changes – which cause a lot of inner conflict. . . . (SW3)

This perceived connection between the delivery of the child, hormonal changes and emotional conflict emphasises the exhausting and destabilising impact of childbirth. A related feature of the emotional crisis is grief. 'Typical' mothers are expected to experience grief when they face the loss of their children. The centrality of this expectation for definitions of maternal respectability can be appreciated by considering references to women who express no such emotion as 'callous' and 'without a lot of emotional depth'. One social worker compared loss through adoption to death:

> They said: That girl doesn't want to part from her baby: she's been crying all morning. And I say: Yes she's been crying. How would you feel if you had experienced a bereavement or death? (SW5)

But in fact, social workers talked less about grief *per se* and more about guilt:

> I don't think one can possibly give up one's baby without there being some element of guilt. (SW6)

> I always tend not to say 'giving away'. It sounds harsh to them. It makes the guilt stronger. You can say the wrong thing to a girl to

reinforce guilt and anxiety. You try to be gentle and not give her any reason for feeling worse. (SW7)

This is linked to the notion of adoption as abandonment:

They have this need to feel they have given something. I think there's a very big fear that if they don't, they are just abandoning the baby (SW4)

Outlined above, then, are the feelings which, professionals claim, mothers intending relinquishment are forced to deal with once they have given birth. Such powerful feelings may pose problems for women who face the prospect of separation from their babies, and for the professionals whose task it is to support them in their decision. In order to examine the implications of maternal emotion for professional practices, it is necessary to explore the meaning conferred upon emotion in the context of intended adoption.

The relationship of maternal emotion to the placement decision

The meaning of maternal emotion may be considered by examining how professionals believed this emotion influenced the making of the placement decision. Again, two types of account emerged. First, a small minority of social workers perceived maternal emotion as a source of strength and a key to the 'truth' about the woman, about what she wanted, about what was right for her. Here, emotion was an essential ingredient in the decision-making process and the reversal of a placement decision following 'the emotional upheaval' of delivery could be seen as positive. They referred to the 'true' decision:

I don't think decisions are ever made before the baby is born. Not truly. I think people can pay lip-service to it. Perhaps on some very rare occasion a girl makes that decision and sees it through, but I think the true decision is made after the birth. (SW8)

However, most social workers evaluated a change of plan following birth negatively. In this second account of emotion in decision-making, despite the insistence of social workers that either keeping or surrendering could be the 'right' decision in different circumstances, there was a tendency for social workers to associate the reversal of firm or tentative plans for adoption birth with emotional weakness. For example:

They need this strong will to be able to think ahead and perhaps it's some of the more soft or sentimental mothers who give in. (SW4)

It appears that susceptibility to the bonding process is taken as failure. Most adoption workers viewed the confinement following delivery as a critical period in the formulation of plans for the mother's and baby's future. They believed women were overcome by powerful emotion following birth and that such emotion had two effects. First, there was a dramatic and qualitative shift in the mother's feeling and desire for the baby. Second, this 'maternal love and protectiveness' rendered the woman vulnerable to pressures around her (environmental and interpersonal, generally seen by professionals as undesirable). This suggests that any management of the bonding process is going to involve the management of her environment.

The women's 'emotional state' after delivery was understood by several social workers to make a sound decision through 'reason' difficult to achieve.

> If they're in such an emotional state, it is very difficult to be able to reason. (SW10)

> I think this is such a strong, instinctive need, that it's not something that you are at all practical or realistic about. (SW4)

> The wave of emotion has just wiped everything out, completely out of her mind. (SW6)

This appears to draw on a rationalist morality. Here, feelings are considered inferior since they are associated with base instinct and closeness to nature. They are thought subjective and capricious and so cannot be the basis of morality. Rationalist ethics present goodness as the triumph of reason over inclination or feelings. This follows from a view of the nature of moral difficulty constituted of a tension between doing what we want and what we ought (MacMillan 1982, Mestrovic 1989). Love, therefore, can be no guide to judgement and knowledge.

Thus, there is a strong contrast between the naturalness and desirability of the bonding process normally and the danger of 'emotionalism' in cases of adoption. Here, bonding is seen as hazardous, fogging the 'real issues', a source of self-deception, a trap to be avoided through careful manipulation. It is considered liable to jeopardise the 'right' resolution to the question of adoption. This is linked to the idea that the strength of emotional feeling weakens the woman with respect to pressures and influences around her in favour of keeping the child:

> It is such an emotional time for the women that these pressures can have much more effect than they would do at other times. (SW3)

So within this mode of reasoning, it is clear that the 'real' decision or the 'true' decision is the decision made by the woman, uncontaminated by what is claimed to be 'her instinctive need' for her child. The mother experiencing a powerful emotional bond with her child cannot be trusted to make the 'right' decision.

Concomitantly, the decision to place tends to be associated with ideas of emotional strength:

> I think some can be very level-headed and strong-willed. And I think they need a very strong will to get through it. (SW8)

> I think people who aren't tough and resilient – it's much harder for those people to go through with adoption. (SW1)

Thus, the 'good' mother is the mother who can resist her own maternalism. This should not be taken to suggest that relinquishing mothers were exempted from the usual expectations of maternal love, but rather it reflects a certain ambiguity in the 'feeling rules' (Hochschild 1983) surrounding the role of the mother who plans adoption. Since 'normal' mothers experienced powerful maternal emotion, relinquishing mothers were also required to convey their feeling for the child for the purposes of respectability. Thus, mothers had to present their adoption plans as resulting from their love of the child, but at the same time hold this 'love' in check. They were required to demonstrate a capacity to bond but a simultaneous capacity to 'unbond'.

Conflicting objectives during the confinement period

It is clear from the foregoing, therefore, that management of the bonding process could be expected in cases of baby adoption first, because the feelings concerned were powerful and might constitute a crisis for the mother and, second, because emotion was considered an inappropriate guide to sound decision-making. However, this management, during the confinement period, of what becomes an unbonding process, was further complicated by a conflict between two objectives. First, the need successfully to implement the adoption decision required a careful check on feelings of love and desire whilst, second, healthy grieving in anticipation of the loss of the child was considered by social workers to require a degree of 'knowledge' of the child, with the associated risk of nurturing that love and desire.

Much emotion work was carried out with the purpose of rendering operable a decision for adoption. The fear that certain feelings might intensify (and ultimately become 'unmanageable') was linked to a fear that powerful emotion obliterated 'reason', making the 'right' decision hard to reach, as we have seen. The careful management of emotion could earn the woman vital 'space' in which to consider all possibilities 'realistically', safely outside what has been referred to as the 'tender trap' (see Gough 1971).

A conflicting objective, however, was that of preparing the mother for a smooth and successful 'grieving process'. Where the woman had committed herself to adoption, the central task was to gauge how much contact with the baby and others she could tolerate, which would enable her to satisfy her longing for the child and reassure herself about its physical health, without jeopardising her placement decision. As we have seen, several social workers believed their clients could be helped to cope with the loss of the baby, if they had had some knowledge of the child, had been able to reassure themselves as to the welfare of the child and were able to feel they had given something to the child.

These objectives conflict, since the first prescribes avoiding emotion while the second demands accepting it. In fact, professionals envisage an emotion management strategy which does not depend exclusively upon the successful management of the mother's access to the child, but upon the practice of a broader range of techniques and it is to these I now turn.

Emotion management and hospital practices

In this section, I shall consider the techniques and procedures deployed by professionals in the management of this unbonding process during the confinement period. Unbonding occurs through first, the manipulation of contact with the baby; second, counselling; third, the restriction of others' access to the baby; and fourth, the mother's restricted exposure to the 'culture of maternity' (by which I mean the social world of talk and practices related to babies, breast-feeding, sleeplessness and so forth). Unbonding has been to some extent crystallised into a routine set of practices and procedures within hospital maternity units.

There are minor variations amongst hospitals but, typically, the newly delivered mother is asked if she wishes to see her baby, and possibly if she wishes to know its sex. She will be informed that she can see the baby whenever she wishes, but that there will be no pressure on her or expectation that she should. The baby will almost certainly be removed to another, separate nursery, often a special care nursery. If there is one available, the mother will be placed in a single room, unless she specifically requests otherwise. She may be advised that, if she wishes, she can tell other mothers her child is in special care due to illness. She may be informed that she can leave the hospital after 48 hours or even sooner. These are what Lovell, in another context, has termed the 'informal rituals' which mark her off as socially distinct and separate from other mothers (Lovell 1983: 758–9).

The location of the baby after birth in the special care nursery was usually justified in terms of its distance from the post-natal ward. This was important, suggested the staff, in a number of respects: it meant that if the mother wished to see her baby, she would have to make a positive decision to do so; a woman would not be tormented by wondering whether any and every baby's cry belonged to her own baby. As mentioned, one worker suggested the arrangement enabled the mother to present herself to the other patients in a different role: as the mother of a sick baby (though, arguably, the fabrication involved in sustaining such a role might itself have been stressful to these mothers). Some added that this practice was also beneficial because of the high staff:patient ratio in special care which afforded more attention to the baby.

If we look at this more closely, we can identify an unbonding strategy comprising a range of *techniques* or tactics:

1. Information concerning basic details about the baby is withheld.
2. The child is physically removed and a physical distance is created between mother and infant.
3. The mother is enabled to exercise choice about the nature and extent of her interaction with the baby, including eye contact, tactile contact and aural contact.
4. The mother is physically separated from other mothers and she can choose the extent and nature of contact with other mothers.
5. The mother is able to fabricate a false account of her motherhood career ('passing' in Goffman's (1963) terms, with the associated assumption of a different social role as the mother of a sick infant).
6. There is a premature termination of rite of passage and early exit from this institutionalised culture of motherhood.

Likewise, we can identify certain *conditions* necessary for the exercise of this management strategy as well as constitutive of its precise form:

1. The architectural design of the hospital maternity services is appropriate (*e.g.* location of the special care unit relative to the post-natal ward; the presence and number of single rooms).
2. The extent and nature of other material resources are adequate (*e.g.* staffing levels; size of special care unit relative to number of needy sick infants). Here, the dramatic decline of adoption as an outcome of extramarital pregnancy is important since there are fewer relinquished babies who make a claim on such resources.
3. The 'philosophy' or ethos of the hospital is conducive. (A multi-disciplinary approach appears to foster greater co-ordination amongst departments and greater involvement by social workers.)
4. Connected to this, the beliefs and initiative of 'key' workers in the hospital in bringing about these practices may be decisive (*e.g.* Consultant, Director of Midwifery Services who have institutionalised changed practices).

Social workers and midwives defended flexibility on the grounds that each woman's needs were different. Implicit here is the belief that she had needs and that these needs should be respected and met (where possible). Moreover, the needs appealed to are emotional rather than material or medical, and it appears that, where adoption is intended, the confinement period is conceptualised by all concerned as a major operation in emotion work. Indeed, what marks these women off from others passing through the maternity unit is that their 'passage', certainly after the birth, itself is constructed primarily as an emotional rather than medical event (see Van Gennep 1960 for an analysis of rites of passage). This contrasts sharply with the analyses of, for instance, Rich (1976) and Oakley (1980, 1984) which argue that medical power, coupled with technological advances, has led during the course of the twentieth century to the redefinition of childbirth as a medical event. Given a level of material provision and adequate staff–patient ratios, practices regarding baby care, location of the mother and length of stay are determined by emotional considerations, except where there are medical complications. As one social worker said:

> Obviously, if they are ill or they have a caesarian, it's a medical thing rather than an emotional thing. (SW11)

One of the consequences of this management strategy is that the woman planning adoption articulates with the hospital system in a way different from other mothers. Different expectations exist with regard to her role, her interaction with other patients, control over her movements. Most significant, perhaps, she is more autonomous. Typically, nursing staff in a hospital setting are expected to maintain order and routine, offer advice and take charge (Breen 1978, Oakley 1979). Compliance is also expected. This professional role, however, is transformed where the newly delivered mother plans for adoption: routine is relaxed, advice is strictly not offered and control is loosened. A special care nurse remarked:

> The Ward staff tell them where the baby is and they know they can come and look at him anytime they want to. Sometimes they just want to look through the window. It's entirely up to the mother. Nobody pressurises. (N1)

Thus, the woman's role is subject to less regulation through normative expectations (Gibbs 1965). Lovell (1983) provides an account of the comparable experiences of women whose babies die perinatally or through miscarriage or stillbirth. Nursing and midwifery staff adhere strongly to the notion that the placement decision must be the mother's and mother's alone (in contrast to adoption social workers who have a much stronger grasp of the social constraints upon 'individual free choice'). For nurses and midwives, this belief was reflected in their willingness, upon request, to restrict access to the baby by the mother's family and friends (including the baby's father). One midwife ventured:

> Often the guys come. It depends on what the mother wants to do. We always ask her, we always find out. We never just let them look. It's her right; it's her baby. (M1)

A nurse suggested that the mother, rather than a relative, partner or professional, possessed the necessary knowledge to make the right decision:

I don't think anyone has the right to make them change their minds. They know what their life is and what they've got to look forward to. (N2)

Nurses and midwives attach importance to the mother's 'right' to make 'her own' decision. This evaluation of maternal choice relative to the constraints of routine necessity suggests that, perhaps ironically, an ideology of maternal rights, even the sanctity of the maternal bond, if not a condition of this unbonding strategy, is certainly perceived as providing an acceptable vocabulary in its justification. This, of course, contrasts with the position of other patients who are much more strongly subject to staff control. This mother appears released from medical control and from membership of a maternity culture as it is sustained through the conversations, activities and rituals of maternity staff and mothers. The 'deconstruction' as a mother entails simultaneously her deconstruction as a patient.

Whilst midwifery staff withdraw to some extent from the mother who plans adoption, social workers, attached both to the hospital and to adoption agencies, assume a more prominent role, further weakening the medical nature of the event. Although in all hospitals investigated, social workers had reached broad agreements with midwives and doctors concerning the handling of mothers anticipating adoption, conflict did sometimes arise over the meaning of evident maternal distress. This stemmed not so much from the comparatively individualistic perspective of midwives and nurses, but from different conceptions of the grieving process. One social worker commented of nursing and midwifery staff:

In a society like ours, it's very hard to accept grief so they see grief as an unnatural thing, although it's a very natural thing. They see grief as something to avoid. (SW5)

This may explain the emphasis by nursing and midwifery staff upon early discharge, though this was interpreted by them as humanitarian:

It's much more humane now to separate mother and baby and to get the mother home as quickly as possible and then proceed with the adoption of the baby. I would discharge them the same day if the conditions were conducive. (M2)

Whilst nursing and midwifery staff emphasised the mother's right to make her own decisions and order her own priorities in the management of immediate maternal pain primarily through avoidance, social worker accounts differed to some extent. Social workers had a much stronger grasp of a structure of social constraints and opportunities within which mothers make their placement decisions. They also addressed, in addition to immediate pain, actual or potential maternal guilt and the possible or imagined consequences of maternal action or inaction during confinement for longer-term mental health. The principal medium through which social workers addressed these issues was that of counselling. This was used to 'work through' the difficulties the mother was facing and particularly was tied to decisions the mother had to make immediately about her contact with the baby. One social worker expressed her preferences:

> I always say that many people feel it's better to actually see the baby to reassure themselves that they really have a perfect baby. That's a very significant worry to a lot of people. And also, they will have some memory, not just a complete blank. (SW12)

Generally, however, social workers claimed that they avoided giving directive advice and resolved dilemmas resulting from the conflicting objectives outlined earlier through appeal to the principle of self-determination. For instance:

> It's the person's decision what they feel they want to do. And it is part of my job to be sure that she has thought this through. (SW2)

Finally, then, we can see that the unbonding strategy employed has a number of *consequences*:

1. The woman engages differently with and is even released from bureaucratic and medical considerations and enjoys relative autonomy from staff control.

2. Nurses and midwives surrender their usual control, authority and responsibility, offering information in what they believe is a strictly neutral way, defining themselves now as non-experts and avoiding advice giving.

3. The woman's deconstruction as a mother results in her deconstruction as a patient.

4. The mother's passage through confinement is managed by a different set of professionals: social workers become more prominent relative to midwifery and medical staff. This is a crucial part of the redefinition of the confinement period as non-medical.

It could be argued that there is an apparent paradox between on the one hand, the autonomy and self-determination offered to the mothers and, on the other, the regularity of techniques and rituals utilised by social workers in relation to them. That is, the mother appears able to make choices but nonetheless these choices have been to some extent institutionalised. Generally, the details of the mother's care after giving birth to her child are decided in advance in consultation with a social worker and are then communicated to midwifery staff through her hospital notes.

However, individual staff attitudes and 'ward ideology' (Strauss *et al.* 1985) are necessary conditions in the exercise of this unbonding strategy. It is true that the open-ended nature of the role of the mother who intended adoption could allow for considerable self-determination on the part of the woman, as 'official' accounts of policy suggest (*i.e.* there is no obvious 'script' for the woman who rejects social mothering in this way). On the other hand, it could be precisely the vague and ambiguous nature of social expectations regarding this role which endows the interaction process itself with a certain capacity to determine the mother role in a given case. This would be to favour an interactive over a normative account of this particular social role; that is, the role is *made*, not taken (Turner 1962).

Another approach to this apparent paradox is to recall that 'feeling rules' do obtain. The techniques and practices outlined are not random because, despite the language of individual needs, social expectations do exist in relation to these needs. The overall increase in the availability of facilities and services for mothers in the delicate position of surrendering their babies seems, paradoxically to have set in motion a certain moral claim upon these mothers in a way which could be seen to militate against flexibility. Both the hospital social worker and the midwife in one hospital commented disapprovingly upon relinquishing mothers who preferred to remain on a ward with other mothers, rather than take an available side room, with its attendant 'boredom'.

In brief, the data collected suggest that the 'rites de passage' symbolise by the confinement period are differentially constructed according to the expected outcome. Where this period does not embody a transition to social maternity, the hospital experience represents the breaking of the maternal bond, the rupturing of what is possibly society's most sacred relationship. Here, the medical character of the event pales to a lesser significance. The passage is now constructed around beliefs about 'normal' maternal feeling, maternal rights and self-determination. It is worth remembering that developments since data collection – for instance, in relation to greater patient choice (Flint 1995) – might have reduced the differences between relinquishing and other mothers by increasing self-determination for all newly delivered mothers. Further empirical work would be required to clarify this. The rite of passage is also differentially constructed by nurses and midwives on the one hand, and social workers on the other and I shall return to this point in the discussion.

Discussion

I have explored in this chapter the evidence of a certain subscription to the 'bonding doctrine' amongst professionals in a particular social setting and its influence upon professional practices and policies. Whilst previous studies have investigated its possible practical implications in other areas of policy making, this chapter has focused upon its impact on professional practices vis-a-vis the natural mother in the adoption process. Where previous studies have tended to focus upon implications for subsequent child development and parenting behaviour, this analysis examines implications for the disengaging mother and her professional carers.

This subscription to a theory of bonding can be seen in professional beliefs about the implications postpartum emotion has for the adoption decision and in the practices and techniques they utilise in order to manage this emotion. These techniques together can be conceptualised as comprising a more or less ritualised process through which mothers are unbonded from their babies, or are prevented from completing or fulfilling their bonding potential, thereby facilitating separation. The professionals who participated in this study did, on the whole, expect bonding to be automatic, as something which happens to the parturient mother, even when she does not anticipate it. In addition, though, they shared in common with previous researchers a sense of the precariousness of the bonding process, or at least its susceptibility to disruption.

However, the concept of the bonding process implicitly drawn on by these professionals appears broader than that suggested in many previous studies. Whilst previous studies associate bonding with physical exposure, particularly skin-to-skin contact between mother and child, the professionals in this study subscribe to a broader notion of bonding. This is evident in the range of unbonding techniques used and considered available. Professionals here do believe that strong emotion results from childbirth and that this pre-disposes the woman towards attaching to her infant, but the techniques discussed go far beyond the management of baby handling. They can encompass removing the baby from visual and aural contact; preventing others from seeing or handling the baby; emotion work through counselling; isolating the woman from other mothers; and freeing her from the usual routines with which most parturient mothers engage (what we have called the 'culture of maternity').

This suggests, first, that the concept of bonding used by these professionals does not echo the biocentric focus of many prior observers and, second, that the unbonding process extends beyond the management of emotion which was our starting point. Rather, the data indicate that, where the interaction of significant others with the baby can be restricted and where the mother herself can be removed not only from the baby but also from the cultural world of mothers and babies, the definition of the woman as a mother can be countered. Let us look more closely at this.

It is throughout the daily round of the post-natal ward, through routine events and interactions that the woman is most likely to find her situation defined as comparable to that of other mothers and her self defined as a mother like them. Baby relinquishment is so rare that it is improbable others will spontaneously anticipate adoption. Thus, she is likely to find herself defined as a woman whose confinement represents the passage to social maternity. The availability of an alternative social role – as the mother of a sick infant – suggests sensitivity to issues of stigma and respectability and merely reinforces the definitional as opposed to emotional processes at work. Likewise, her release from the usual bureaucratic routines and medical concerns marks her off as different. The controlling of access to the baby by others also serves a definitional function by avoiding settings in which the father or grandparents might claim the infant as a member of the family – as 'one of ours'. Similarly, counselling constitutes an interactive process through which the social worker and woman together negotiate reality, make sense of and give meaning to events, circumstances, feelings and the actions of others.

Thus, the management of unbonding involves blocking the process by which the woman comes to be socially defined as a mother and by which she might reconceptualise her own identity to encompass social motherhood (Breakwell 1983, 1986). This, then, is not merely a biological but a social and cultural process at work. This process constitutes not merely the frustration of 'instinctive' or 'biological' or 'hormonal' triggers, but the management of social and self definition.

Whilst the point has been made that the process of unbonding extends beyond the management of emotion, we should not overlook the role of emotion management in the broader social and cultural process of identity management. Mothers intending adoption must manage emotion and make decisions about its social display in ways which are socially consequential: the maintenance of respectability (Ball 1970) as well as the defence of one's own sense of self, depend upon the successful resolution of dilemmas concerning contact with the child, expectations regarding maternal emotion and its appropriate social display. However, emotion work is not merely a matter of impression management through the application of certain feeling rules or cultural display rules. The management of emotion for these women in this setting is part of and constitutive of a broader social process of identity construction. This would suggest a more radically social constructionist account of emotions than Hochschild's interactive approach offers and appears to correspond more closely to Wiley's position. Furthermore, emotion work here is not merely an intrapsychic event. Emotion work during the confinement period is actively entered into by, and depends to a considerable extent upon the emotional labour of, others as James 1989, Wiley 1990 and O'Brien 1994 have suggested in other contexts.

One further comment should be made in relation to different conceptualisations of the confinement period where adoption is intended. Social workers, nurses and midwives assume both that the separation of a mother and baby is intensely difficult and painful and also that mother–baby contact in the postpartum period has 'bonding' potential. However, there are some differences. Nurses and midwives adopt a more individualistic and less social stance in their understanding of the woman's placement decision. This does not, in my view, equate with more 'organismic' conceptualisation of emotion but could be accounted for in terms of the nature of their contact with the mother. These professionals tend to encounter the mother solely in a hospital setting. An additional explanation could be the training of nurses and midwives which paid, at that time, scant attention to social scientific concepts and theories which might 'socialise' their professional world view. Moreover, nurses and midwives conceptualise the rite of passage which confinement constitutes as a **termination** rite in cases of adoption. Social workers, by contrast, in appealing to a notion of long-term mental health (grief and bereavement) and by distinguishing short-term from long-term emotional considerations, reflect a conceptualisation of the confinement period as a rite, ironically, of **initiation**. The woman may be unbonding herself from the baby in terms of a specific tie which endures in space, with responsibility for care, but in fact this is not an absolute psychological disengagement. This, again, suggests that the concept of bonding these social workers implicitly draw upon is more sophisticated than the 'all or nothing', uni-dimensional and uni-directional concept of bonding for which previous researchers have been criticised.

Acknowledgments

I am grateful to David Armstrong for his comments on an earlier draft of this paper.

References

Ainsworth, M. (1969) Object relations dependency and attachment: a theoretical review of the infant–mother relationship, *Child Development*, 40, 969–1025.

Arney, W. (1980) Maternal–infant bonding: the politics of falling in love with your child, *Feminist Studies*, 6, 3, 547–57.

Badinter, E. (1981) *The Myth of Motherhood*. London: Souvenier Press.

Ball, D. (1970) The problematics of respectability. In Douglas, J. (ed) *Deviance and Respectability: The Social Construction of Moral Meanings*. London: Basic Books.

Becker, H. and Geer, B. (1957) Participant observation and interviewing: a comparison, *Human Organisation*, 16, 28–32.

Biddle, B. (1979) *Role Theory: Expectations, Identities and Behaviours*. London: Academic Press.

Binns, C. (1987) The study of Soviet and Eastern European elites. In Moyser, R. and Wagstaffe, M. (eds) *Research Methods for Elite Studies*. London: Allen and Unwin.

Bowlby, J. (1951) *Maternal Care and Mental Health*. Geneva: WHO.

Breakwell, G. (1983) Identities and conflicts. In Breakwell, G. (ed) *Threatened Identities*. London: John Wiley and Sons.

Breakwell, G. (1986) *Coping with Threatened Identities*. London: Methuen.

Breen, D. (1978) The mother and the hospital. In Lipshitz, S. (ed) *Tearing the Veil: Essays in Femininity*. London: Routledge Kegan Paul.

Collingwood, J. and Alberman, E. (1979) Separation at birth and the mother–child relationship, *Developmental Medicine and Child Neurology*, 21, 608–18.

Dick-Read, J. (1942) *Childbirth Without Fear*. London: Pan Paper.

Everingham, C. (1994) *Motherhood and Modernity*. Buckingham: Open University Press.

Flint, C. (1995) *Communicating Midwifery: Twenty Years of Experience*. Hale: Books for Midwives.

Gibbs, J. (1965) Norm: the problem of definition and classification, *American Journal of Sociology*, 70, 586–94.

Goffman, E. (1963) *Stigma: Notes on the Management of Spoiled Identity*. Harmondsworth: Penguin.

Gough, D. (1971) Adoption and the unmarried mother. In Tod, R. (ed) *Social Work and Adoption*. London: Longman.

Hales, D., Lozoff, B., Sosa, R. and Kennell, J. (1977) Defining the limits of the maternal sensitive period, *Developmental Medicine and Child Neurology*, 19, 454–61.

Herbert, M., Sluckin, W. and Sluckin, A. (1982) Mother-to-infant bonding, *The Journal of Child Psychology and Child Psychiatry*, 23, 3, 205–24.

Hochschild, A. (1979) Emotion work, feeling rules and social structure, *American Journal of Sociology*, 85, 3, 551–75.

Hochschild, A. (1983) *The Managed Heart: Commercialisation of Human Feeling*. Berkeley, C.A. University of California Press.

Honigmann, J. (1973) Sampling in ethnographic fieldwork. In Naroll, R. and Cohen, R. (eds) *A Handbook of Methods in Cultural Anthropology*. New York: Columbia University Press.

James, N. (1989) Emotional labour: skills and work in the social regulation of feelings, *Sociological Review*, 37, 1, 5–42.

James, N. (1992) Care = organisation + physical labour + emotional labour, *Sociology of Health and Illness*, 14, 4, 487–509.

Jenkins, R. (1987) Doing research into discrimination: problems of method, interpretation and ethics. In Wenger, C. (ed) *The Research Relationship*. London: Allen and Unwin.

Kemper, T. (1981) Social constructionist and positivist approaches to the sociology of emotions, *American Journal of Sociology*, 87, 2, 336–62.

Kennell, J., Jerauld, R., Wolfe, H., Chester, D., Kereger, N., McAlpine, W., Steffa, M. and Klauss, M. (1974) Maternal behaviour one year after early and extended post-partum contact, *Developmental Medicine and Child Neurology*, 16, 172–9.

King, F.T. (1913) *Feeding and Care of Baby*. London: Macmillan.

Klauss, M. and Kennell, H. (1976) *Maternal–Infant Bonding: The Impact of Early Separation or Loss on Family Development*. St Louis: Mosby.

Lamb, M. (1983) Early mother–neonate contact and the mother–child relationship, *Journal of Child Psychiatry*, 24, 3, 487–94.

Leifer, A., Leiderman, H., Barnett, C. and Williams, J. (1972) Effects of mother–infant separation on maternal attachment behaviour, *Child Development*, 43, 1203–18.

Lovell, A. (1983) Some questions of identity: late miscarriage, stillbirth and perinatal loss, *Social Science and Medicine*, 17, 11, 755–61.

MacFadyen, A. (1994) *Special Care Babies and their Developing Relationships*. London: Routledge.

Macintyre, S. (1976) 'Who wants babies?' The social construction of 'instincts'. In Barker, D. and Allen, S. (eds) *Sexual Divisions in Society: Process and Change*. London: Tavistock.

MacMillan, C. (1982) *Women, Reason and Nature: Some Philosophical Problems with Feminism*. Oxford: Blackwell.

Mathieu, N.C. (1979) Biological paternity, social maternity on abortion and infanticide as unrecognised indicators of the cultural character of maternity. In Harris, C. (ed) *The Family*. Sociological Review Monograph No. 28, University of Keele.

Mestrovic, S. (1989) Moral theory based on the 'heart' versus the 'mind': Schopenhauer's and Durkeim's critiques of Kantian ethics, *The Sociological Review*, 37, 431–57.

Miles, M. and Huberman, A. (1994) *Qualitative Data Analysis*. London: Sage.

Oakley, A. (1979) *From Here to Maternity: Becoming a Mother*. Harmondsworth: Penguin.

Oakley, A. (1980) *Women Confined: Towards a Sociology of Childbirth*. Oxford: Martin Robertson.

Oakley, A. (1984) *The Captured Womb: A History of the Medical Care of Pregnant Women*. Oxford: Basil Blackwell.

O'Brien, M. (1994) The managed heart revisited: health and social control, *The Sociological Review*, 42, 393–413.

Phoenix, M. and Woollett, A. (1994) Introduction. In Phoenix, A., Woollett, A. and Lloyd, E. *Motherhood: Meanings, Practices and Ideologies*. London: Sage.

Ringler, N., Kennell, J., Jarvella, R., Novojoskly, B. and Klauss, M. (1975) Mother-to-child speech at two years – effects of early postnatal contacts, *Behavioural Paediatrian*, 86, 141–4.

Rich, A. (1976) *Of Woman Born: Motherhood as Experience and Institution*. New York: WW Norton and Co. Inc.

Ruane, S. (1991) *Adoption Talk and the Social Construction of Motherhood*. Unpublished PhD thesis, University of Durham.

Rutter, M. (1972) Parent–child separation – effects on the children, *Journal of Child Psychology and Child Psychiatry*, 6, 71–83.

Scarr, S. and Dunn, J. (1984) *Mother Care/Other Care*. Harmondsworth: Penguin.

Schaffer, H. (ed) (1977) *Studies in Mother–Infant Interaction*. London: Academic Press.

Sinclair, B. and Brady, D (1987) Studying members of the United States Congress. In Moyser, G. and Wagstaffe, M. (eds) *Research Methods for Elite Studies*. London: Allen and Unwin.

Sluckin, W., Herbert, M. and Sluckin, A. (1983) *Maternal Bonding*. Oxford: Blackwell.

Smith, P. (1992) *The Emotional Labour of Nursing*. Basingstoke, Macmillan.

Spock, B. (1945) *Baby and Child Care*. New York: Pocket Books Inc.

Strauss, A., Fagerhaugh, S., Suczek, B. and Wiener, C. (1985) *Social Organisation of Medical Work*. Chicago: University of Chicago Press.

Tremblay, M-A. (1957) The key informant technique: a non-ethnographic application, *American Anthropologist*, 59, 4, 688–701.

Turner, R. (1962) Role-taking: process versus conformity. In Rose, A. (ed) *Human Behaviour and Social Processes: An Interactionist Approach*. London: Routledge and Kegan Paul.

Valman, H. (1980) The first years of life: mother–infant bonding, *British Medical Journal*, 280, 6210, 308–10.

Van Gennep, S. (1960) *The Rites of Passage*. Chicago: University of Chicago Press.

Vesterdal, J. (1986) Psychological mechanisms in child abusing parents. In Cook, J.V. and Bowles, R.T. (eds) *Child Abuse: Commission and Omission*. Toronto: Butterworth.

Wiley, J. (1990) The dramatisation of emotions in practice and theory: emotion work and emotion roles in a therapeutic community, *Sociology of Health and Illness*, 12, 2, 127–50.

Yarrow, L. (1961) Maternal deprivation: towards an empirical and conceptual re-evaluation, *Psychological Bulletin*, 53, 6, 459–90.

7. Your life in their hands: trust in the medical encounter

Deborah Lupton

Introduction

Over the past two decades suggestions have been made that the dominance of the medical profession has been diminished by its loss of prestige and patients' trust, related in part to an improvement in lay people's understandings and knowledge of medical matters and their increased willingness to challenge doctors' authority (see, for example, Haug 1976, 1988, McKinlay and Stoeckle 1988). Patient advocacy groups have made calls for the doctor–patient relationship to be 'democratised', arguing that in their own interests lay people should adopt a consumerist approach to seeking and evaluating health care (for example, Australian Consumers Association 1988). The consumerist discourse has also become increasingly evident in policy forums relating to health care in western countries (Lupton *et al.* 1991, Nettleton and Harding 1994, Grace 1994).

In its emphasis on patients *qua* consumers 'taking control', the consumerist discourse largely fails to acknowledge the emotional dimension of the patient–doctor relationship, If this dimension *is* acknowledged, it is often discounted as peripheral to or even undermining of other factors considered more important, such as lay people's clear-headed evaluation of doctors' services. Consumerism in the context of the medical encounter relies upon the modernist notion of individualism, of each person looking out for and asserting her or his 'rights' and resisting a situation of dependency upon another. As a 'consumer' the individual is questioning and assertive, ready to challenge doctors' opinions in the medical encounter. This approach assumes that individuals are 'willing and able to exercise choices about their doctors in the same way as they do about restaurants, hairdressers, or supermarkets' (Leavy *et al.* 1989: 737). Consumerism is therefore characterised by mutual distrust, including an emphasis on the doctor's legal accountability and the practice of defensive medicine (Beisecker and Beisecker 1993). Previous commentators have suggested, however, that this model of consumerism simply does not operate as expected in relation to the medical encounter (Elston 1991, Calnan and Gabe 1991; Lupton *et al.* 1991). While it is clear that at least some patients are capable of consumerist behaviour at least some of the time – particularly if they are well-educated and members of the middle-class

(Lupton *et al.* 1991) – there are many occasions on which people simply do not wish to adopt consumerist approaches to health care.

Recent writings in the sociology of health, illness and medicine, while sometimes acknowledging the emotional dimensions of the doctor–patient relationship, have not often been supported by indepth empirical research with members of the lay population. Further, while writings on the sociology of emotions are generally enlightening in theorising the socio-cultural aspects of the emotions, they have tended not to devote much attention to studying the emotions inherent in the patient–doctor relationship or the experience of illness. In this chapter I attempt to bring empirical research and theorising on the emotions together by drawing upon an interview-based study on the medical encounter, that elicited the views of both lay people and doctors living in Sydney carried out between late 1994 and mid 1995. The present discussion focuses, in particular, upon trust as it is phrased through discourses on communication, uncertainty and dependency as central features of the medical encounter, drawing here only upon the comments made by lay people.

The study

The study involved semi-structured one-to-one interviews with 60 lay people (30 women and 30 men).[1] The participants were asked to talk about their experiences with medical practitioners over their lifetime, their strongest memories of doctors, the ways in which doctors are portrayed in the mass media, their notions of 'good' and 'bad' doctors and their opinions on whether the medical profession had lost some of its status in recent times.[2] They were recruited making use of a variety of social networks and limited snowball sampling, with attempts made to maximise heterogeneity.

The participants were from a wide range of occupations, eduction level and ethnic backgrounds, ranging from socio-economically privileged people with high levels of formal education to blue-collar workers, the unemployed and those who had left school early. Their ages ranged from 16 to 81 years: 23 per cent of the participants were aged 30 or younger, 40 per cent were in the 31 to 49 years age group and 37 per cent were 50 years or older. Thirty-seven were Australian born of Anglo-Celtic ethnicity, 13 were of non-English-speaking European ethnicity (either born in continental Europe or first-generation Australian-born with European parents), four participants were of Chinese ethnicity, three were British-born, two had one parent who was of European origin and the other an Anglo-Celtic Australian, and one participant was of half-Aboriginal and half-Scottish descent.

The interviews, lasting an average of 45 minutes to one hour in length, were audio-taped and transcribed in full. The transcripts were analysed adopting a poststructuralist phenomenological approach, in which an interest in people's lived experiences was combined with the recognition that the participants' accounts were 'situated narratives' shaped by the interview context itself, and dependent on the ways that they chose to present themselves and their experiences at that particular time. The transcripts were scanned for recurring discourses, or patterned ways of articulating points of view and conveying meaning, under which individuals' accounts of their experiences and opinions could be grouped. A particular focus was placed on identifying the ways in which the participants expressed their views on specific doctors they had seen, on the medical profession and medical knowledge as a whole and on the role of the mass media in portraying medicine and doctors (this latter issue is not taken up in the present discussion).

Trust and 'talking things over'

How are the emotional features of the medical encounter expressed in the ways in which people talk about their experiences with doctors? One major finding of the interviews with Sydney patients was that 'communication' was a central concept when the participants were discussing notions of the 'good' or 'bad' doctor. The majority of participants considered the interpersonal features of doctors most important, over and above their medical knowledge or expertise, particularly their ability to 'listen' and 'communicate' and their willingness to 'spend time with you' and 'talk things over'. The notion of the 'good doctor' rests very strongly on a notion of trust, of feeling able to share one's intimate feelings and allow another person to touch one's body. For Paul, a 'good' doctor was: 'Somebody that you could talk to without a problem, you know, and they'd have a laugh. They'd tell you, explain it not in big words, like explain it like, basic, that you understand'. Similarly, Valerie described a 'good' doctor thus: 'Oh, well, of course, caring. But listening to the patient, taking all of their fears and concerns and thoughts, analysing them, talking to them over and over again, getting clear what they want and what happens to them'.

According to the participants, trust is built largely on communication, on a doctor having the ability to 'draw out' a patient as well as the interest to go beyond the symptoms to the patient's emotions and personal relationships:

> . . . people ought to be able to go to a GP if, for instance, they are ill and their illness is probably due to being run down, being overstressed and the doctor then should be able to identify what is actually causing the illness . . . I think the doctor ought to be able to look behind the

symptoms and say perhaps, 'You ought to see a counsellor because your marriage is causing a lot of stress'. You know, they ought to be able to delve a little bit more into a person's life rather than just prescribe for the illness that is presented. (Carol)

It is clear that most people still expect a high level of compassion, empathy and comfort from their doctors and not just adequate medical knowledge and expertise. The notion that one should 'feel comfortable' with one's doctor as well as being comforted was mentioned by most participants. Tracy, for instance, described two doctors she had consulted when she was pregnant, comparing one unfavourably with the other. The GP she consulted she found to be very good, because he showed a personal interest in her and alleviated her fears:

He was very concerned and very comforting and there was a couple of times where I was very, very sick and he made a point of ringing me up after hours off his own accord, just to make sure that I was okay. Just a quick phone call just to see I was okay. So he was excellent, you could not have asked for a better doctor. Brilliant doctor.

She compared this doctor with the gynaecologist she also consulted around this time, who appeared to be uncaring:

I found him to be too old, and he should have been retired and that was the way I thought about, that was the way I perceived him. Not caring enough, not a lot of enthusiasm, just basically doing what he had to do there and booting you out – 'See you later!'

She consulted a third doctor, this time a woman, for back pain soon after she had had her child. Tracy found her to be very reassuring, particularly in relation to her empathetic skills:

Tracy: I remember walking in so tired and drained and worn out and sitting in a chair crying and her putting her arm around me, telling me, 'Don't worry, you will be all right, you are just tired and overworked'.
Interviewer: Feeling very comforted?
Tracy: Yes, feeling very comforted and cared about, you know. It is very easy to give a script or, you know, open your mouth and have a look in it, but for somebody to actually take a personal concern is a nice feeling and reassuring feeling.

A 'bad' doctor, in contrast, was typically described as someone who treats patients as if they were on a 'production line', who 'doesn't spend time with you', who hurries and does not listen to the patient's concerns or questions. Marcus described one doctor he had consulted as 'a very cruel doctor, just a business doctor. In out, in out, away you go', while Fred said, 'Well, I regard a bad doctor as someone who races you in, runs around you in about 30 seconds, gives you a script, and out the bloody door'.

While such criticisms may originate from a belief that a 'good' doctor should be thorough in his or her dealing with patients, there is also the suggestion that people resent doctors who do not treat them as 'real people' with feelings, as individuals rather than part of a mass of anonymous patients. Further, while this emphasis on 'good communication' may incorporate elements of the consumerist approach to the medical encounter, it goes beyond this to a recognition of the emotional dependence patients invest in doctors. The participants tended to respond highly emotively to instances where doctors appeared to abrogate the trust that their patients invested in them, or failed to demonstrate enough care for their patients. Rochelle, for example, recounted with revulsion the item she had seen on the television news of a doctor who had sexually harassed his female patients: 'I thought, "*You arsehole!*"'. It just made me just sick'. Diane told a story of how her father, who was very ill with emphysema, was in his doctor's surgery when the doctor took a call from a colleague about another patient. During this telephone conversation, her father's doctor made the following observation about the other patient to his colleague; 'Well, I wouldn't worry too much, he's ratshit anyway.' Diane recounted how highly upset her father became after overhearing this remark, because it made him realise that his doctor could have a similar uncaring attitude to him. Her father had said, 'He could've been saying that about me, that could've been me.'

This insistence upon the importance of the interpersonal dimension of the medical encounter, incorporating the understanding that the doctor should be able to 'communicate' and 'listen', discuss the patient's problems 'over and over again' and recognise the deeper emotional needs of the patient, fits into a broader assumption in western societies that intimate relationships should involve intensive 'talking over' and negotiating problems and emotional states. There has been a growing emphasis over the past few decades upon the need for 'communication' in all intimate human relationships. This is part of the 'confessing society' described by Foucault in volume one of his *History of Sexuality*, where he observes that 'the confession has spread its effects far and wide. It plays a part in justice, medicine, eduction, family relationships, and love relations, in the most ordinary affairs of everyday life, and in the most solemn rites' (1978: 59). In the 'confessing society', there is an 'obligation to confess': it is generally accepted that people should discuss their problems and emotional states in detail with significant others, inciting talk rather than 'bottling things up'. Trust in others, it is believed, is generated through such 'openness' and mutual disclosure. The inability to communicate is viewed as a problem, something that requires working on.

Trust and the uncertainties of abstract knowledge

A different source of uncertainty is that emerging from debates over the accuracy and efficacy of contemporary medical treatment and advice. Uncertainty is a central feature of medical care, given that the object of treatment is the capricious human body, for which known therapies may have unpredictable effects. The more experienced doctors become, the more they are aware of uncertainty in their practice, and that choices among alternatives for treatment are always present. Medical judgement is, therefore, the management of uncertainty (Katz 1984, Cassell 1991: 229–30). While 'the facts' around a medical condition may be mastered by a lay person, it is the knowledge engendered by the 'art' of practising medicine that they cannot access: 'Often implicit, ineffable, and tacit, clinical knowledge is less open to public scrutiny and outside surveillance: it cannot be reduced to rules and supports a hierarchy based on expertise' (Gordon 1988 260). Such knowledge is often not exercised at the level of calculation, but is embodied knowledge, the type of knowledge that some might describe as 'intuitive' or a 'gut feeling' (Gordon 1988: 269).

It is apparent from several sociological studies that members of the lay public are highly aware that medical knowledge is subject to dispute; for example, in relation to the controversy around the health benefits of controlling dietary cholesterol and fats (Lupton and Chapman 1995). Such awareness was evident among the participants in the present study, who mentioned several examples, drawn either from their own experience, that of friends or family members or reports in the news media, of cases of medical negligence or medicine failing to have an effect. One particular condition, that of breast cancer, was brought up in stories of differing medical opinion and uncertainty told by several participants. In one story, Marcus recounted how his friend's mother had been told she had a lump in her breast by her doctor, who then sent her to a specialist for further investigation. The specialist told the woman that the breast must be removed and that she should enter hospital the following week for the operation. The woman sought another opinion, only to be told that the lump was just fatty tissue and did not require surgery. Alan told a similar story relating to his wife discovering a breast lump, except this time the first doctor told her it was 'just a fatty cyst' and needed no further treatment. His wife was still worried, and eventually consulted another doctor who sent her to a specialist. The specialist decided that the lump should be operated on, and it was removed and found to be a small malignant cancer.

Even when people acknowledge the uncertainties around medical treatment and the possibility of negligence on the part of doctors, many are still reluctant to relinquish their faith or trust in medicine (*cf.* Calnan and

Williams 1992). For example, it was acknowledged by the above participants that breast cancer is one of those conditions that is difficult to diag-
nose and treat effectively, where different doctors may dispute each
other's opinions and where it may not necessarily be a doctor's 'fault' that
a diagnosis is incorrect. Most of the participants said that they continued
to respect medical knowledge, citing 'breakthroughs' or technological
wonders such as organ transplants and penicillin as examples of how contemporary medicine can 'work'. In their accounts, the words 'trust' and
'faith' recurred. Joel, for instance, said he believed that medical knowledge and medical practitioners should be respected for their extraordinary
achievements:

> I think you've got to be able to trust it. The medical system has done
> some wonderful and marvellous things. Only years ago you would have
> only dreamt about it and they're now doing it – I mean, it's amazing
> some of the things they can do now. So I mean you've got to put some
> trust in the doctors.

Valerie similarly said of doctors:

> I don't really lose faith because I know it's hard work and they've got
> to – you've got to give things the test of time before it can work. You
> can't really lose faith, because what have you got left then? If you lose
> faith in everything? Because we all rely on it at one stage or another.

As these comments suggest, while there may be an increasing sense of dis-
illusionment on the part of many individuals towards the promises offered
by medical science, there is a continuing need to maintain some sort of
faith in medicine. This is particularly the case in a context in which individuals are required to make choices themselves about what types of
treatment they want. Patricia commented that doctors as a whole command respect because:

> . . . a doctor, well he's taking your life in his hands and you respect
> him for that. You know, and he's studied a lot and, you know, he
> knows what he's doing, or supposed to. You hope to think that's what
> they do, know what they are. You know, they are a doctor. And you
> hope to think that they know what they're doing, you know. And you
> try to put trust in them. And that's the way I think of doctors.

The phrase used by Patricia, 'he's taking your life in his hands' was one
that was repeated by several participants in the study. This metaphor
raises a central feature of the status of doctors; that they are responsible
for human life, they hold the power of life and death when dealing with
patients, and that therefore they must be regarded with respect. We must
trust doctors' expertise because there is no alternative. As Eva argued,
most people respect doctors because 'there is something about a doctor

which normal people, I mean normal humans do respect – that they are healers, that they can help you if you are sick'. These comments point to Weber's notion of charismatic authority, or that authority bestowed upon individuals or groups by virtue of certain qualities by which they are treated as extraordinary or exceptional. As Hillier notes, the apparently 'irrational' belief and trust invested in doctors is based upon this charismatic authority as well as upon economic and political factors. Faith in medicine is bolstered by the charismatic authority invested in those people who sometimes 'take your life in their hands' (1987: 204–5).

Most people, particularly those who are very ill, must eventually deal with uncertainty by investing their trust in their doctor, allowing her or him to take on the responsibility for managing uncertainty by virtue of their greater medical knowledge and expertise. Patients *want* to believe that the doctor will 'do his or her best' by them – indeed often they have little other alternative but to trust him or her. In relation to the medical encounter, Cassell has observed that

> Uncertainty is intolerable at all times but more so in the ill because
> their existence seems threatened, yet they are required to make decisions
> about themselves . . . Trust in others is one of the central human
> solutions to the paralysis of unbearable uncertainty . . . Sick persons,
> then, are people who are forced to trust. (1991: 75–6)

Indeed, trust in the face of uncertainty is pivotal to the construction of 'doctor' and 'patient'; if patients do not invest their trust in doctors, then the role and function of doctors are altered. The provision of faith and hope is a central feature of doctors' position; they are therefore 'powerful therapeutic agents in their own right' (Katz 1984: 40). Too great an acknowledgment of uncertainty, on the part of either doctor or patient, damages this.

Trust and dependency

Some lay people may seek to 'take control' of uncertainty by engaging in consumerist behaviour such as reading up about their illness, consulting several different doctors or asking other patients for recommendations. As noted above, however, this is mostly a middle-class phenomenon, and tends to be expressed in situations where people are not actually 'ill', such as assisted reproduction services, or where biomedical treatment has little to offer, for example, people with chronic illness, or where rapid technological development has aroused concern, such as in prenatal screening (Elston 1991). In the present study it was largely younger rather than older people, and those with higher levels of education who tended to articulate archetypal consumerist attitudes to the medical encounter. Nonetheless, even these individuals also expressed their willingness to invest their trust in medical practitioners, often moving back and forth in their interviews from adopting a consumerist discourse to acknowledging their dependence on doctors (see Lupton in press).

The bodily and sensual dimensions of the doctor–patient encounter are integral to the emotional nature of the relationship. No other professionals have the same access to the body as do doctors and other health care workers. The examination and touching of the patient's body by these professionals is a central feature of the medical encounter. Doctors and other health care workers touch patients' bodies in ways that are not reciprocated by patients; they have the power to listen to the patient's body and to look inside it via such technologies as the stethoscope, X-rays, ultrasound and surgery in ways that patients cannot of either their own bodies or those of others. In western societies, touching and looking at parts of the body, particularly those that are generally kept hidden from others, are actions that are fraught with emotion. Allowing another to see and touch the naked body, and particularly the genitalia, involves an investment of trust that often contributes to feelings of vulnerability as well as those of love and closeness.

Because we understand our bodies as reflecting our selves, and because certain parts of the body are invested with secrecy and shame, the relationship between carer and the person cared for differs from other relationships. To care for someone in that way is to express a love and acceptance of sorts, but is also to exert a certain degree of power over the person who is cared for. Caring may be understood as a gift, an action that requires something in return from the person who is cared for, thereby establishing an imbalance of power (see Fox 1993, 1995 for an elaboration of the notion of the gift in relation to health care). In the familial caring relationship, the efforts exerted by the carer may be expected to be rewarded with gratitude, love and affection but never by monetary rewards. In the medical encounter, caring is mediated overtly through professional duty and the exchange of money rather than through the love of an intimate relationship, but the patient's gratitude, docility and compliance are also expected. The doctor–patient or nurse–patient relationship is therefore based on reciprocality and exchange (Cassell 1991: 72–3, Fox 1993: 93–5). Trust is required on both sides:

> Patients trust staff not to hurt them unduly, to treat them with compassion and as fellow humans, not to exploit them for sexual fantasy or actual use, not to breach confidentiality. Staff trust patients to cooperate and submit to the technologies and competences claimed by the discipline. Both parties may invest the other with a degree of responsibility. Patients, we might expect, would invest staff with caring and curing capabilities, or with more general human attributes as comforters or advisers. (Fox 1993: 42)

While the consumerist approach is insistent upon the need for members of the lay public to approach the medical encounter in a 'rational', calculating and dispassionate manner, the experience of illness, physical dependency and vulnerability goes beyond conscious rationality to a situation of semi-conscious or unconscious needs, desires and emotional states. Graham's experiences with doctors serve to illustrate this point. Graham remembers visiting his family doctor as an adolescent recently diagnosed with muscular dystrophy. He was going through emotional turmoil at the time and he found that he could not trust this doctor enough to seek his help, even though he had known him all his life:

> Graham: Whenever I would see him about something he would say, we would finish with the business of the consultation and he would say, sort of 'off the cuff', 'Oh, anything on your mind, anything you want to talk about?' And I used to sort of think to myself, 'Well if I have, I certainly wouldn't fucking well tell you!'.
> Interviewer: Right. And the reason you wouldn't tell him is why?
> Graham: I didn't trust him.
> Interviewer: And you didn't trust him because?
> Graham: I didn't have confidence in him with that sort of trust. Not that I thought that he would betray me – with that sort of mistrust it was just that I thought I had no confidence in him, I didn't feel prepared to yield myself forward, to treat him as a confessor. I just didn't think he was a warm person.

Graham contrasts his response to this doctor with a psychiatrist he saw after having a nervous breakdown at the age of 23:

> As soon as he saw me I said, 'Look, I am in a great deal of pain, I am in agony, you are my last hope'. And he shook me very warmly by the hand, looked me straight in the eyes and said, 'I will do what I can for you, Graham,' and in such a way I knew I was going to be okay . . .
> Once I went to see him and I was in a hell of a lot of psychogenic pain, I was just weeping and very distressed. I went to see him – and I think I was seeing him twice a week at that stage – and he could see I was really, really upset and in pain, and he said to me, 'Look Graham', he said, 'tell me to keep my distance but actions speak louder than words'. And he just came across to me and he just put his arm around me and sat next to me for about ten minutes. And I thought that was extraordinary and I was very moved by it.

As Graham's narrative suggests, not only the personal demeanour of the doctor but also the type of illness or condition for which an individual seeks medical care influence the emotional nature of the interaction. When an individual seeks help for a serious and perhaps life-threatening illness, is suffering depression, anxiety or other psychological disturbances or needs a doctor's advice on a matter that is complex, issues of vulnerability, dependency and emotionality are often uppermost. De Swaan (1990) provides the example of people receiving treatment for cancer in hospital. In such a situation the patient's social network contracts and is reduced to almost total dependency on medical and other health care staff. As de Swaan notes, the increasing dependency upon others on the part of such ill people is accompanied by loss of status: 'sick people become the lesser, the asking party, who need more from others while having less to offer them' (1990: 28).

Discussion: the emotional ambivalences of the medical encounter

I have argued that trust relations in the doctor–patient relationship are always characterised by ambivalence, uncertainty, anxiety and a sense of risk because this relationship characteristically involves a high level of vulnerability and dependency. Allowing oneself to be cared for evokes the emotions of comfort and reassurance, but also generates emotions of dependence and anxiety. The bodily care required when someone is ill, sometimes involving the viewing or touching of the genitals (as in washing or assistance with excretion), requires an extraordinary investment of trust and the related risks of vulnerability, humiliation, embarrassment and anxiety. It is not only the body that is revealed to doctors and other health care workers in quite exclusive ways. As noted above, they are also privy to patients' confessions of private thoughts and feelings which patients may never reveal to others.

The contemporary subject is highly aware of the dangers of investing trust in others, given the unpredictability and fickleness of human relations (Giddens 1990, 1992, Beck and Beck-Gernhsheim 1995). Giddens (1990: 35) argues that there is a symbiotic relationship between trust and risk, for trust serves to minimise the dangers to which particular types of activity are subject. While trust always carries the connotation of reliability in the face of contingent outcomes, it is also always ambivalent. This is because trust is required in the face of reliance upon others, which itself demands caution: 'To trust the other is also to gamble upon the capability of the individual actually to be able to act with integrity' (Giddens 1992: 138). The 'opening up' of oneself to another which is part of trust relations is therefore characterised by ambivalence and anxiety: 'Torment and frustration interweave themselves with the need to trust in the other as the provider of care and support' (Giddens 1990: 144). In intimate relationships, people must struggle with positioning themselves as autonomous individuals and as dependent beings bound up with and reliant upon others. 'Talking things over' offers a means of ordering this uncertainty, of formulating generalisations and of getting to 'know' the other person, of 'working through' the contradictions and tensions between individuals' need for both autonomy and dependency.

While these observations have hitherto been generally related to romantic, marital and familial relationships, their implications for the doctor–patient relationship are clear. As is evident from the ways that people describe 'good' and 'bad' doctors, individuals express the desire for doctors to understand them as individuals. This 'understanding' helps them to negotiate a situation in which they must invest considerable trust in another person. Indeed, this emphasis on feelings signals the ways that the medical (and other allied medical) encounter differs from most other services offered from a 'provider' to a 'client'. For example, we do not usually expect lawyers or accountants or even dentists to make special efforts to know our innermost feelings, for we tend not to see them as having an intimate relationship with us.

However, there are also aspects of the doctor–patient relationship that do not conform so readily to the above analysis of trust in personal relationships. Giddens (1990) argues that trust in intimate relationships involves mutual self-disclosure, the 'opening up' of each individual to the other. As I have noted above, in the context of the medical encounter, while the patient is encouraged to speak, to reveal his or her thoughts and feelings as well as to describe bodily symptoms and signs, this disclosure is rarely reciprocated. As in other professional encounters (such as counselling and social work), the expectation of medical professionals is that while they should incite the disclosure of the patient they should not reveal their own personal thoughts and feelings. It may be argued, therefore, that in such professional–client relationships personal disclosure is potentially even more fraught with uncertainty than in relationships in which both parties 'confess' to each other. The person to whom an individual confesses, as Foucault (1978) points out, generally has power over the confessor, both in inciting the confession and prescribing what to do about the details that are revealed.

Because of the high degree of potential emotional expression in the medical relationship, strategies are often employed to deflect too much investment of the self on the part of both carer and the cared for. The use of the terms 'clients', 'consumers' and 'patients' is one such strategy used by health care workers, as is the impersonal manner adopted by many doctors and nurses in dealing with their patients. Patients themselves also sometimes attempt to engage in this deflecting process. When individuals are not actually seriously ill, as is the case with perhaps the majority of the members of consumerist movements, they are able to engage in the projection upon doctors of their vague anxieties about illness and their resentments of domineering, authoritative figures. At either a conscious or an unconscious level, doctors may be constructed as 'other', as alien from the self, the repository of bad or disturbing feelings and thoughts (de

Swaan 1990: 52–3). Indeed the consumerist movement itself could arguably be interpreted as an attempt to deal with uncertainty and anxiety by evoking rationalist anti-authoritarianism against an 'other' (in this case members of the medical profession) defined as controlling.

When, however, individuals *are* seriously ill or disabled, perhaps hospitalised or bedridden, their fears become more specific and are devolved into emotional dependency. It is not simply ontological security patients seek, but assistance to retain their bodily integrity: to avoid or alleviate physical disorder and pain. In this context the doctor as authoritarian figure may no longer be considered threatening or controlling, but rather is reassuring. The doctor with whom one is dealing is no longer constructed as the 'other', but becomes allied with the 'self' in the mutual project of 'becoming well'. In this psychic scenario, it is the disease that is split from the self and becomes the 'other', a foreign entity lurking within one's own body that must be attacked by the doctor and medical science (see Figlio 1989: 94). It is here that the battle imagery so common in the medical context is used by both doctor and patient to refer to the disease as the 'enemy' which must be 'fought' using the 'weapons' of drugs or surgery (Lupton 1994: 61–4). Patient and doctor are allied together in this fight against the invader. To attempt to construct one's attending doctor as 'other' in this situation is to diminish the necessary trust one requires in the doctor's capabilities and care. While patients in this situation might consciously be aware of the consumerist discourse, and even subscribe to it, their subconscious or unconscious desires and idealised phantasies of the protective, patriarchal doctor/parent figure may well prove overwhelming, even while they may simultaneously produce resentment: 'what so many people really blame the doctors for is that they need them' (de Swaan 1990: 56).

I am not arguing here for a return to an appraisal of the medical encounter that is naively consensual, ignoring the ways in which doctors, either as individuals or as part of organised medical lobby groups, may set out deliberately to exploit their patients (or do so unconsciously), promote their professional interests to the detriment of patients' welfare or cover over cases of malpractice, sexual harassment or assault of patients or negligence. These events clearly do happen and should be resented and challenged by patients and consumer advocacy groups. Rather, I am arguing that calls for patients to behave consumeristically often go to the other extreme, and fail to acknowledge the deeply-felt and often ambivalent emotional needs of many patients, both conscious and unconscious. While the consumerist approach tends to represent people as autonomous individuals who are self-reliant, we need to acknowledge the emotional ties that bind people to each other in ways of which they are often not fully aware. There are times in which people derive reassurance and comfort from allowing themselves to become dependent upon others: the experience of acute pain or serious illness is often one of these times.

Rather than alleviating the inevitable vulnerability and anxiety accompanying this dependence, the continuing emphasis upon autonomy, individualism and distrust in consumerist discourses may only serve to generate further uncertainty and vulnerability.

Notes

1 Demographic details of the interviewees referred to in this chapter are as follows (all names are pseudonyms):

Paul: 19 years old, Italian–Anglo, storeman, single, no children.

Carol: 41 years old, Anglo–Celtic, part-time counsellor and Master of Arts student, separated, one adolescent son.

Valerie: 33 years old, Anglo–Celtic, graphic designer, single, no children.

Marcus: 73 years old, Polish, businessman and local counsellor, de facto relationship, four adult children.

Fred: 71 years old, Anglo–Celtic, retired painter, married, no children (one son died in adulthood).

Rochelle: 23 years old, Anglo–Celtic, unemployed, de facto relationship, no children.

Diane: 42 years old, Anglo–Celtic, secretary/telephonist, de facto relationship, two adult children (a third died in infancy).

Tracy: 23 years old, Anglo–Celtic, interior designer, de facto relationship, one young daughter.

Alan: 71 years old, Anglo–Celtic, retired fitter and machinist, widowed, three adult children.

Joel: 26 years old, Anglo–Celtic, handyman, single, no children.

Patricia: 53 years old, Anglo–Celtic, secretary, married, three adult children.

Eva: 67 years old, Czechoslovakian, retired, married, one adult daughter.

Graham: 41 years old, Anglo–Celtic, unemployed (on sickness benefits), single, no children.

2 To provide a context for the study, it should be noted that the Australian national health insurance scheme, entitled Medicare, provides subsidised medical care to all citizens which is funded by a compulsory levy upon those with taxable incomes. The scheme reimburses patients up to the full cost of consultation fees charged by general practitioners and specialists as well as medical care in public hospitals. Several private health insurance schemes operate simultaneously to provide cover for services that do not fall under Medicare, such as treatment in private hospitals and dental care. Under the health care system, patients are free to choose their own general practitioners and to change to another whenever they like.

Acknowledgements

I am grateful to the Australian Research Council for funding this research by awarding a large grant for 1994–95. Thanks are also due to the project's research assistant, Jane McLean, for her expertise in arranging and carrying out the interviews, and to the participants themselves.

References

Australian Consumers Association (1988) *Your Health Rights.* Sydney: Australasian Publishing.

Beck, U. and Beck-Gernhsheim, E. (1995) *The Normal Chaos of Love.* Cambridge: Polity Press.

Beisecker, A. and Beisecker, T. (1993) Using metaphors to characterize doctor– patient relationships: paternalism versus consumerism, *Health Communication*, 5, 1, 41–58.

Calnan, M. and Gabe, J. (1991) Recent developments in general practice: a sociological analysis. In Gabe, J., Calnan, M. and Bury, M. (eds) *The Sociology of the Health Service.* London: Routledge.

Calnan, M. and Williams, S. (1992) Images of scientific medicine, *Sociology of Health and Illness*, 14, 2, 233–54.

Cassell, E. (1991) *The Nature of Suffering and the Goals of Medicine.* New York: Oxford University Press.

De Swaan, A. (1990) *The Management of Normality: Critical Essays in Health and Welfare.* London: Routledge.

Elston, M.-A. (1991) The politics of professional power: medicine in a changing health service. In Gabe, J., Calnan, M. and Bury, M. (eds) *The Sociology of the Health Service.* London: Routledge.

Figlio, K. (1989) Unconscious aspects of health and the public sphere. In Richards, B. (ed) *Crises of the Self: Further Essays on Psychoanalysis and Politics.* London: Free Association Books.

Foucault, M. (1978) *The History of Sexuality. Volume 1: An Introduction.* London: Penguin.

Fox, N. (1993) *Postmodernism, Sociology and Health.* Buckingham: Open University Press.

Fox, N. (1995) Postmodern perspectives on care: the vigil and the gift, *Critical Social Policy*, 15, 44/45, 107–25.

Giddens, A. (1990) *The Consequences of Modernity.* Cambridge: Polity Press.

Giddens, A. (1992) *The Transformation of Intimacy: Sexuality, Love and Eroticism in Modern Societies.* Cambridge: Polity Press.

Gordon, D. (1988) Tenacious assumptions in western medicine. In Lock, M. and Gordon, D. (eds) *Biomedicine Examined.* Dordrecht: Kluwer.

Grace, V. (1994) What is a health consumer? In Waddell, C. and Petersen, A. (eds) *Just Health: Inequality in Illness, Care and Prevention.* Melbourne: Churchill Livingstone.

Haug, M. (1976) The erosion of professional authority: a cross-cultural enquiry in the case of the physician, *Milbank Memorial Fund Quarterly*, 54, 83–106.

Haug, M. (1988) A are-examination of the hypothesis of physician deprofessionalization, *Milbank Quarterly*, 66, supp. 2, 48–56.

Hillier, S. (1987) Rationalism, bureaucracy, and the organization of the health services: Max Weber's contribution to understanding modern health care systems.

In Scambler, G. (ed) *Sociological Theory and Medical Sociology*. London: Tavistock Publications.

Katz, J. (1984) Why doctors don't disclose uncertainty, *The Hastings Center Report*, February, 35–44.

Leavy, R., Wilkin, D. and Metcalfe, D. (1989) Consumerism and general practice, *British Medical Journal*, 298, 737–9.

Lupton, D. (in press) Consumerism, reflexivity and the medical encounter, *Social Science and Medicine*.

Lupton, D. (1994) *Medicine as Culture: Illness, Disease and the Body in Western Societies*. London: Sage.

Lupton, D., Donaldson, C. and Lloyd, P. (1991) Caveat emptor or blissful ignorance? Patients ad the consumerist ethos, *Social Science and Medicine*, 33, 5, 559–68.

Lupton, D. and Chapman, S. (1995) 'A healthy lifestyle might be the death of you': discourses on diet, cholesterol control and heart disease in the press and among the lay public, *Sociology of Health and Illness*, 17, 4, 477–94.

McKinlay, J. and Stoeckle, J. (1988) Corporatization and the social transformation of doctoring, *International Journal of Health Services*, 18, 2, 191–205.

Nettleton, S. and Harding, G. (1994) Protesting patients: a study of complaints submitted to a Family Health Service Authority, *Sociology of Health and Illness*, 16, 1, 38–61.

8. Emotional expression during medical encounters: social dis-ease and the medical gaze

Patricia S. Baker, William C. Yoels and Jeffrey M. Clair

Introduction

The sociology of emotions has become an increasingly popular area of inquiry although, as Fineman (1993: 20) recently noted, little is known about the interplay between emotions and organisational life in general; about how '[e]motions, as social currency, vary in their rates of exchange and validity. The relative status of participants, their work role, sex, type of job and previous familiarity, all make a difference'. In a related vein, Thoits (1989: 221) in her 'state of the field' literature review on emotions, stressed the need for data on how emotions are distributed across organisational positions. Given the considerable power and status differentials between doctors and patients, the medical encounter is an ideal arena for examining the organisational structuring of emotional expressivity. While much has been written about the importance of physicians attending to patients' emotional expressions (see, for example, Hendrie and Lloyd 1990), there are few empirical analyses of emotions actually occurring during the various phases of medical encounters.

Within medicine some still argue for an emphasis on the biomedical model with its technical focus on patient care. Spitzer (1987), for example, claims:

> that indices can be designed so that clinicians can score the quality of life or health status after observing or examining a patient even without eliciting information from the patient about how he or she feels at a given point in time (Quoted in James 1992: 504).

Other physicians have long acknowledged they bring more than just their technical skills to the examination room, while eloquently noting that patients bring more than just their bodies and diseases (see especially, Blackwell [1902] 1972, Engel 1977, Kleinman 1988). European medical educators and physicians also have a well-established tradition in this regard, as reflected, for example, in the works of Michael Balint and his colleagues (see Balint 1957, 1971, Balint *et al.* 1969). Contemporary health researchers increasingly advocate a patient-centered, holistic approach encompassing the patient's lifeworld and subjective experiences as essential aspects of medical practice (see, for example, More and Milligan 1994, Clair and Allman 1993).

In this chapter we explore the range of emotions in medical encounters, who expresses them, and where they occur. We should note at the outset that our sample is North American-based and thus generalisations may be limited. To set the context for examining this problem, we first review the literature relevant to our topic, namely: 1. studies of medical students' and residents' socialisation, bearing on how they deal with feelings; and 2. studies empirically reporting on the role of specific emotions in medical practice.

Learning to master emotions

Medical schools typically recruit from a self-selecting pool of applicants who have pursued a rather narrow, natural science-based, undergraduate pre-medical curriculum. In addition, the image of North American medical education as a highly competitive, 'cut-throat' endeavour, 'may actually dissuade students with more reflective and contemplative orientations from seeking a medical career' (Conrad 1986: 158). In regard to medical students' training, studies all point towards one continually documented theme: how medical school socialises students to view emotions – both their own and patients' – as obstacles to the practice of medicine (see especially Smith and Kleinman 1989, Good 1994). Through classroom, laboratory, and ward experiences students quickly learn that 'real' medicine applies a biomedical model to physically-based diseases while ignoring the extraneous psychosocial 'wrapping' in which the diseased body presents itself. This is not to deny, however, that medical school is an emotionally powerful, anxiety-provoking experience (Fox 1990).

Developing a 'cloack of competence' is perhaps the key task facing medical students, as Haas and Shaffir's (1977, 1987) studies of Canadian students indicate. Appearing skilled and expert in front of one's peers and medical school faculty is an ongoing concern, especially in view of the many situations wherein students can easily be embarrassed or humiliated by their medical superiors for not quickly providing the correct answer. Students soon learn that appearing knowledgeable is paramount, even if one does not really know the answer to the question being posed. They adopt a strategy to 'mask their uncertainty and anxiety with an image of self-confidence. Image making becomes recognised as being as important as technical competence' (Haas and Shaffir 1977: 83). Such experiences are not limited to North American medical schools, as Atkinson's work (1984) on medical education in Great Britain indicates. While students may experience feelings of inadequacy, this 'does not necessarily shake their faith in the sort of knowledge they are expected to acquire: one may be perplexed by a problem or puzzle, but that does not always lead one to doubt whether there is a solution awaiting discovery . . .' (1984: 952). What is critical here is that early in their careers medical students are taught *to overcome or master their emotions rather than talk about or examine them in detail* as important aspects of medical practice. Efforts to appear knowledgeable and in control may also carry over later into their actual practices when physicians exhibit an emotional stance of 'detached concern' (Fox 1963) in dealing with patients.

The seductive allure of the biomedical model in creating a 'medical gaze' (Foucault 1973), which bifurcates patients into physical bodies and socio-emotional selves, may be a way of managing emotions. Novice students, especially, can transform their anxieties about physical contacts with both cadavers and live persons by defining such contacts as:

> a part of scientific medicine [which] makes the students feel safe. They are familiar with and confident about science, they feel supported by its cultural and curricular legitimacy, and they enjoy rewards for demonstrating their scientific know-how. In effect, *science itself is an emotion management strategy*. By competing for years for the highest grades, these students have learned to separate their feelings from the substance of their classes and to concentrate on the impersonal facts of the subject matter. In medical school they use these 'educational skills' not only for academic success but also for emotion management (Smith and Kleinman 1989: 61, emphasis added).

Confronted with structural arrangements which give them little power over the curriculum and working conditions, medical students, as Smith and Kleinman (1989: 60–5) have noted, develop numerous strategies for handling their emotions: by generating good feelings in themselves, for example, through seeing body contact as an opportunity to do 'real medicine', by managing their own discomfort through empathetically 'shifting their awareness away from their own feelings and to the patient's' (1989: 63); by laughter and joking about patients and work conditions; and occasionally by deferring examinations when they feel anxious about examining patients' sexual parts, or by covering such parts and thereby removing 'disturbing sites and protecting [themselves] from their feelings' (1989: 64).

In medical school, students are taught new ways of seeing, speaking, and writing. They become active participants in the socio-cultural process by which 'medicine constructs its objects' (Good 1994: 65). Through exposure to clinical training in their last two years, students learn they must master the art of correctly 'writing up' patients. Such a write up is especially significant for the issue of emotional expression because here again students learn that patients' subjective experiences, their stories, that is, are superfluous and time consuming. A third-year Harvard Medical

School student, interviewed by Good as part of a four-year ethnographic and interview-based study of medical students, cogently notes:

> You're not there to just talk with people and learn about their lives and nurture them. You're not there for that. You're a professional and you're trained in interpreting phenomenological descriptions of behavior into physiologic and pathophysiological processes. So there's the sense that if you tried to tell the people [his medical colleagues and superiors] really the story of someone, they'd be angry; they'd be annoyed at you because you're missing the point. That's indulgence, sort of. You can have that if you want it when you're in the room with the patient. But don't present that to me. What you need to present to me is the stuff we're going to work on (1994: 78).

Most of the studies cited above deal with North American medical schools. We should note that medical educators in the United Kingdom have expressed concern about students' communication skills for quite some time. Research on actual medical practices, however, documents a similar hegemony of the biomedical model and its slighting of the psychosocial domain (see, for example, Silverman 1987, Thompson 1984). In addition, Kelly (1990) has argued that social science materials used in United Kingdom medical schools reflect the content of *undergraduate* sociology and psychology programmes. Incorporating such materials into the medical curriculum presents serious problems, especially relating them to other parts of the curriculum; moreover, 'how these ideas are to be "used" in practice by doctors remains unclear' (1990: 272). Responding to concerns about medical practice, the British General Medical Council in 1993 directed medical schools to revise their curricula with an increased emphasis on communication skills.

As students graduate and begin a variety of lengthy residency programmes, their training focuses on making case presentations of patients to medical superiors, that is, attending physicians. Here again, they further refine their skills in 'properly' speaking and writing about patients for an audience of medical professionals. In this regard, it is important to recall that 'the central speech acts in medical practice are *not interviewing patients, but presenting patients*' (Good 1994: 78, emphasis added). In other words, far more attention is paid to how one communicates with and presents oneself to medical colleagues and superiors than to patients! As James Thompson (1984) notes concerning British medical practice, this is especially ironic, given that the medical interview 'is the one thing which distinguishes medicine from veterinary [medicine]. Despite being the cornerstone of medical practice, it is often seen as a tiresome interface between the doctor and the disease' (1984: 87).

Structural conditions of residency work involve enormous responsibilities and workloads (typically 70–100 hours per week), accompanied by little control over work schedules. Such conditions approximate to Goffman's (1961) notion of a 'total institution', wherein the inmates' total 24-hour-day is dictated by the schedules established by the institution. Faced with such conditions, residents become centrally concerned with carving out niches of autonomy and free time that they control, rather than are controlled by (see Mizrahi 1986, Yoels and Clair 1994). The emotional experience of feeling continually pressured, sleep-deprived, and fatigued leads to a mentality in which residents may express happiness over outpatient clinic 'no shows' – that is, patients who fail to appear for scheduled appointments. Efforts to control scarce time lead to strategies for controlling the time spent actually examining patients. As a second year resident in internal medicine interviewed by Yoels and Clair stated:

If you let patients and families, they will talk your ear off. A lot of times you just don't want to spend the time, I mean you don't really have the time or the time could be spent more efficiently, so you have to cut the conversation down. Especially during an admit, I've learned only to get what's important. I know that I have to be sensitive and be objective enough to make sure I don't overlook something critical, but for the most part, a lot of what they have to say is irrelevant (1994: 207).

Through humour residents also make an effort to manage their frustrations about being unable to control time. Such back-stage, off-limits joking also promotes a sense of collective solidarity and 'we-ness' among residents while simultaneously distancing themselves emotionally from patients who appear as 'others'. Beginning residents learn from higher-ranking ones the most effective procedures for controlling the workflow. As we have noted elsewhere in our ethnography of outpatient clinic humour:

Two interns [first year residents] are talking about an Attending [supervising physician] who has a reputation for keeping the wards full, which is why one of them is so tired and busy. A PGY-2 [Post Graduate Year 2 of the residency program] joins the conversation and they talk about being MOD – Medical Officer of the Day. The PGY-2 says that he writes the whole time while the patient is talking and then when the patient is done, he looks up and says 'Sorry, I didn't hear what you were saying. I was writing. Here's your prescription'. Everyone laughs. Another PGY-2, mentioned as someone who is an artist at GROP tactics [Getting Rid of Patients], stops by and adds that, 'If you let the patients talk, you'll be there the whole day' (Yoels and Clair 1995: 46).

Such humour distances residents from having to deal with a much more disturbing issue, namely, their failure to allow patients the opportunity to participate in their own health care treatment. Joking of this kind also places residents in opposition to the humanistic patient-care standards often espoused by official medical agencies and educators. More significantly, the structure of the medical workplace and the subtle features of the medical subculture – with its focus on controlling scarce time and talking to patients rather than listening to them – may help explain why efforts to 'humanise' medical training have met with such little success (see Fox 1990).

On concluding this section we might suggest that by the time medical students in the USA have graduated and completed residencies, it is debatable as to how many will want to listen to patients' stories when they are in the examining room. When doctors begin their own practices they will have been exposed to almost seven years or so of socialisation. Such training powerfully communicates to them that listening to patients' stories may be a nice thing to do, but is really an 'extra', to be indulged in only after the real work of medicine is accomplished.

Having described how their training prepares, or rather poorly prepares, physicians for dealing with emotional matters, let us briefly examine the literature on doctor–patient communications. While much is known about patients' information-seeking and physicians' information-giving behaviours (see especially Roter and Hall 1992, Beisecker 1990), less is known about the dynamics of emotional expression during medical encounters. This is particularly surprising in view of the fact that between 60 and 90 per cent of general ambulatory patients fail to display any 'serious physical disorder' (Barsky 1981: 492); moreover, about 30 per cent of patients seen in primary care come to the doctor with significant psychosocial problems worthy of physician attention (Bertakis et al. 1991), and as many as 85 per cent have some degree of psychological distress (Starfield et al. 1981). There are many 'hidden reasons' for patients seeking medical help related to emotional issues such as life stress, psychiatric problems, and social isolation (Barsky 1981).

Positive emotional expressiveness by physicians, such as friendliness, displaying interest and empathy, contributes to the 'social climate' of the medical examination (Roter and Hall 1992: 136). Numerous studies indicate that such a climate strongly predicts patients' satisfaction with medical care (see Hall et al. 1993, Hall et al. 1988, Like and Zyzanski 1987).

In contrast, however, follow-up studies of *patients' actual health conditions after the baseline medical encounter*, report that negative emotional expression by physicians, such as tension, frustration, and impatience, predicted better health at follow-up, using indicators such as blood pressure or blood sugar, days lost from work, and number of health problems (see Kaplan et al. 1989, Hall et al. 1981). These findings suggest physicians are seen as caring when they display frustration with patients' progress or health regimens. Patients 'may attribute more concern and sincerity to a physician who is emotionally engaged than one who appears emotionally neutral' (Roter and Hall 1992: 148).

Given the well-documented desire of patients for physicians' approval and their reluctance to challenge physicians directly (see Beisecker 1990, Taylor 1979), physicians must take the lead in inviting patients to talk about their fears and concerns; moreover, Heath's (1992: 262–3) analysis of British patients suggests they are hesitant to question medical diagnoses because challenging physicians' expertise may undermine patients' reasons for seeking such professional help in the first place. Patients' ambivalence about discussing their anxieties may result in covert forms of expressing it. Data from gynaecological examinations in Holland, however, indicate physicians' willingness to explore patients' concerns *always* led to patients overtly expressing their anxiety (Weijts *et al.* 1991: 160).

Finally, the issue of emotional expressiveness in medical examinations is of much more than just academic concern. More importantly, it has real-life consequences for health outcomes. Anxiety, for example, has been found to result in longer patient hospital stays (Devine and Cook 1983); dissatisfied patients are more likely to drop out of health plans (Davies *et al.* 1986), change doctors (Lo *et al.* 1994), and fail to follow medical recommendations (Roter 1977). In regard to more dramatic illnesses, such as breast cancer, for example, physicians' own emotional discomfort about communicating a diagnosis may significantly influence what they disclose to patients (Clair 1990, James 1993). Failure to communicate openly may prevent patients from actively participating in their own medical care (Mosconi *et al.* 1991: 279).

The sample

The 39 encounters used in this study are part of a larger research project of doctor–patient communication. Recordings were collected from two outpatient clinics of an urban university's medical centre. To rule out the effect of any prior medical record, we focused on patients new to the clinic. We attended approximately half of the clinics scheduled during the 15-month phase of this project. Sampling patients from the clinic's new appointments list was not practical since lists were often changed at the last minute, and patients often failed to appear for scheduled appointments. As a result, we tried to approximate a random sampling design by selecting the first new patient to arrive for an appointment during the morning or afternoon clinic sessions covered. New patient visits were scheduled for one hour.

In terms of race and gender, these patients are representative of the combined clinic populations, being 51 per cent male and 72 per cent African-American. The sample mean age of 47 years (standard deviation of 17 years) is younger than the clinic population. Patients are predominately low income, with a median annual family income of approximately $7,800.

Physicians from the university's Division of General Medicine covered both clinics. Our data set incudes 30 resident physicians (87 per cent male), all of whom were white. Approximately half of the encounters were with first year residents. Most of the physicians (84 per cent) were between 26 and 30 years of age. The breakdown of interactions resulted in 19 male physician/female patient encounters; 15 male physician/male patient encounters; and 5 female physician/male patient encounters.

Methods

Transcripts were analysed by a coding system, VEXIS, the Verbal Exchange Initiation System (Baker 1993, Baker and Clair 1995). This system combines techniques of discourse analysis (Jefferson 1978) with an adaptation of the interaction exchange system developed by Sinclair and Coulthard (1975). Initiatory, response, and follow-up speech acts were classified into sequences called exchanges. Using the concept of adjacency pairs introduced by Sacks (1967, cited in Coulthard 1985), conversation can be analysed as complementary pairs of utterances. These pairs can be classified by function, with the nature of the first utterance predicting the type of verbalisation that follows (see Appendices I–II).

As suggested by Sinclair and Coulthard (1975), an *exchange* is the minimal interaction in communication, from which sequences develop. Speech turns are separated into the components of individual exchange sequences. For example, the following segment is one speech turn, but it can be analysed as having three elements: (a) acknowledgement of a preceding question; (b) a summary of information given; and (c) a question that in turn elicits another response:

D: Okay. These were given to you by Doctor L. Was that in the emergency room?

Particular expressions of emotion are located and identified within this structure as initiating, response or follow-up segments of conversation.[1]

Structural features of conventional medical interviews predict a patterned sequence within typical medical encounters (Fletcher 1980a; 1980b, Pendleton and Hasler 1983, Waitzkin 1991). In this study, portions of the medical encounter were specified as follows: Phase 1 – Opening and determination of presenting symptoms; Phase 2 – Medical and social histories; Phase 3 – Physical examination; Phase 4 – Diagnosis and treatment plan; and Phase 5 – Conclusion. Although the first three phases were present in all encounters, physicians sometimes skipped or combined the concluding portions. If an attending physician was consulted and conducted a portion of the encounter, as often happened with the first year residents, this portion was identified separately. Since we were interested in the primary physician–patient relationship, we excluded those portions involving patient–attending physician interactions. The length of the encounters included here range from 12 to 59 minutes with a mean time of approximately 32 minutes (S.D. of 10.6 minutes). The total time covered for the 39 encounters is 21 hours.

Whether emotions should, or can be, quantified is an important issue. Schegloff (1993: 114), for example, has argued that 'quantification is no substitute for analysis' (also see Drew and Heritage (1992: 3–65). Efforts to quantify may be 'premature' if investigators do not know 'what the phenomena are, how they are organised, and how they are related to each other . . .' (1193: 114). Quantitatively grounded observations, however, may be beneficial when they lead to:

> a return to the data – to singular episodes of interaction – to track in the details of single occurrences the phenomenon . . . that had come to light through other modalities . . . (1993: 117).

In this study, we have quantified emotional expressions by counting their occurrences in order to identify their distributions in the transcript data. These distributions led us to a more detailed analysis of specific emotional occurrences, which we have conceptualised as 'anxiety-scenarios' and 'nervous laughter'. In that sense, then, our study is an effort to integrate, or rather, to move back and forth, between a quantitative and a more qualitative, contextual treatment of specific emotions. As Glenn (1989: 148, footnote 7) has noted in his study of shared laughter, while '[p]eople do not organise talk by statistical trends . . Nevertheless, the numbers are there; something is going on.'

Coding of emotions

Transcripts used were coded in the VEXIS format, making it possible to identify expressions of emotion as initiations or responses. For instance, patients' anxiety might be followed by physicians' empathy or reassurance. To focus specifically on communications of emotion, we borrowed from Davitz (1969) and Gottschalk *et al.* (1969). First, we used the word list developed by Davitz (1969) and added words and terms likely to occur in medical encounters. Basic paralinguistic cues identified and marked on the transcribed audio-tapes, including crying, laughter, and exclamations were added to the word search list (see Appendix III). Second, following Gottschalk *et al.*, we used minimal or unique root-stems, such as *anx* (for anxiety, anxious) or *worr* (for worry, worrisome) to locate all grammatical forms of a particular word. In addition, contextual expressions of emotion not captured by any of the vocabulary words were identified by reading printed transcriptions.

The search feature of the *Word Perfect* computer software program was used with each of the root stems to locate potential emotional expressions and create a data base. Each item was coded for the following: (a) the discourse number; (b) the phase of the encounter; (c) who was expressing the emotion; (d) whether it was expressed as an initiating, response or follow-up move; (e) the nature of the emotion; and finally (f) whether the expression was followed by an emotional response. This method of quantification enables us to locate specific emotional expressions occurring anywhere in the approximately 1,200 pages of transcript data analysed here.

For each portion of the 39 discourses, as well as for the encounter in its entirety, summary measures of the expression of emotion were calculated. SPSS was used to organise and analyse the data. We did not correlate the number of emotional expressions with the length of encounter because of the problematic nature of timing the durations of particular expressions. For example, humourous exchanges would take much longer than approval spoken by a single word. Likewise, laughter can be expressed over seconds or last only a tenth of a second.

The word search list was used only to locate potential instances of emotional expression, not to categorise the expression. For example, in these discourses, anxiety was never expressed by the patient saying 'I feel anxious' but rather by words such as worry or stress; and reassurance was expressed by the doctor saying such things as 'There is no reason to think that this is anything serious' rather than 'I want to reassure you that . . .' There were a number of located words that were unclear contextually. These were coded as uncertain emotions. All other emotional expressions were categorised positive or negative as explained below:

Positive emotional expressions:

1. Approval: any expression indicating positive re-inforcement (more than umm humm or okay) – 'That's great'. 'Good'.

2. Caring: any expression indicating personal interest, or a query of an emotional state – 'I want you to be aware of things'. 'How's your mood been?'

3. Etiquette: Expressions of politeness and civility – 'Good to meet you'; 'We're glad you came to our clinic'. 'Thank you'.

4. Empathy: any expression involving the taking the role of the other – 'That's been hard for you.'

5. Humour: a joke, accompanied or unaccompanied by laughter, or laughter in obvious response to a joke or humourous statement.

6. Reassurance: any expression indicating comfort or encouragement – 'Your EKG is perfectly normal'. 'We'll take care of that'.

7. Other positive emotions: items obviously positive in affect but occurring infrequently.

Negative emotions:

1. Anxiety: any expression communicating worry, stress or tension.

2. Disapproval.

3. Nervous laughter: laughter accompanying disclosure of potentially stigmatising, embarrassing or discomforting information, such as alcohol, drugs, or physical conditions.

4. Other negative emotions: items obviously negative in affect but infrequent.

We should note here that if there is any bias to our coding procedures, it may entail an overly generous definition of positive physician utterances such as 'approvals'. We do not have any data on how patients interpret physician responses such as 'that's good'. Patients may view such phrases, however, as communicating positive feeling on the part of physicians.

Emotion work in medical encounters

Table 1 presents aggregated results for all 39 encounters. Physicians and patients dramatically differ in their expressiveness, with 90 per cent of physicians' responses clearly positive compared with only 33 per cent of patients' responses. While not indicated in Table 1, the overwhelming majority of patients' negative responses (71 per cent) are instances of anxiety and nervous laughter. Clearly, the medical encounter, which is probably a routine situation for physicians, is a much more discomforting experience for patients. While patients' expressions were more difficult to classify than those of physicians, for both, however, most of what was coded as 'uncertain' comprised instances of laughter which were neither clearly humourous nor what we described earlier as 'nervous laughter'.

Although not presented in Table 1, further analysis revealed an interaction between gender and patient's age, with males significantly older. While females were twice as likely to express etiquette and one and one-half times more likely to express negative emotions, given the small sample it is unclear whether such findings are associated with gender or age.

Table 1. *Distribution of expressions of emotion*

	Speaker			
	Physician		Patient	
	n	%	*n*	%
Positive expressions	817	90	226	33
Negative expressions	30	3	344	50
Uncertain	58	6	115	17
Total	905	99*	685	100

*Total does not sum to 100% due to rounding.

Tables 2 and 3 present data on patients' and physicians' expressions of specific emotions, by encounter and phase of the encounter. Anxiety was only expressed by patients; caring and reassurance were only used by physicians. Because empathy and approval were so rarely expressed by patients they are excluded.

Overall results from Table 2 indicate patients engage in humour in 56 per cent of the encounters and such humour is most likely during the physical examination, Phase 3. Etiquette is present in 67 per cent of the encounters and occurs mostly in the conclusion.

Nearly 75 per cent of the encounters have instances of patients' anxiety and nervous laughter; both of these are most likely in Phase 2, the phase of the encounter when doctors elicit patients' social and medical histories. Such emotions typically occur 3–4 times during that phase. Phase 2 also is likely to impinge on psychosocial and life-style issues. Patients clearly show discomfort here – perhaps 'dis-ease' with the uncertain border line between medically relevant data on personal habits and physicians' possible moral judgements about such habits.

Since negative expressions were so rare, Table 3 focuses on physicians' positive expressions which range from instances of humour in 46 per cent of the encounters, to approval in 97 per cent. When physicians verbally express approval it is most likely during the physical examination, with 87 per cent of encounters showing this pattern. There are typically 5–6 expressions of approval during this phase. More importantly, 78 per cent of these approvals consist of a short, benign utterance such as 'Good' or 'That's good' following patients' compliance with directives given as part of the physical examination. Physicians' expressions of caring peak in Phases 2 and 4. Such expressions typically occur 5–6 times during Phase 2. Reassurance is most likely to be expressed during the physical examination or diagnosis. In about one-third (36 per cent) of the encounters, physicians terminate the encounter with an expression of pleasure at having met the patient.

In comparing Tables 2 and 3, humour by both physicians and patients is most likely during the physical examination with patients and physicians joking with each other. This may be a way for both doctors and patients to manage or perhaps 'lubricate' the uncomfortable 'tenseness' of the situation by allowing interaction to flow smoothly. It appears that the diagnosis phase is a very serious one for both participants, with only three per cent of the encounters reflecting humour by physicians and nine per cent by patients. The end of the encounter is a way, perhaps, for physicians and patients to re-establish the social bond – with Phase 5 showing the highest percentages of etiquette. For physicians this may be a way to re-acknowledge the self's presence in the body/self dialectic of medical practice. Here we also see patients expressing politeness and physicians' appreciation for patients' using the clinic.

Table 2. *Patients' expressions of emotion by encounter and phase*

	Percentage of encounters with positive emotion expressions					
				Phase		
Emotion	% Encounters with any	1	2	3	4	5
Humour	56	10	31	33*	9	19
Etiquette	67	18	5*	10	18	61
	Percentage of encounters with negative emotional expressions					
Anxiety	74	18	51*	33	15	14
Dissatisfaction	28	3	13	10	6	—
Nervous laughter	72	5	41*	38	24	6

*Average number of expressions is 3–4.
Phase 1 – Opening and determination of presenting symptoms
Phase 2 – Medical and social history
Phase 3 – Physical examination
Phase 4 – Diagnosis and treatment plan
Phase 5 – Conclusion
Note: Unless otherwise indicated by an asterisk, the average number of expressions is 1–2 per phase per encounter.

Table 3. *Physicians' expressions of emotion by encounter and phase*

	Percentage of encounters with positive emotion expressions					
				Phase		
Emotion	% Encounters with any	1	2	3	4	5
Approval	97	13	41*	87**	24	6
Caring	92	23	62**	44	61	22**
Empathy	85	10	41	51	39	11
Humour	46	8	23	31*	3	11
Etiquette	67	26	—	18	21	36
Reassurance	72	13	18*	36	42	17

*Average number of expressions is 3–4.
**Average number of expressions is 5–6.
Phase 1 – Opening and determination of presenting symptoms
Phase 2 – Medical and social history
Phase 3 – Physical examination
Phase 4 – Diagnosis and treatment plan
Phase 5 – Conclusion
Note: Unless otherwise indicated by an asterisk, the average number of expressions is 1–2 per phase per encounter.

While at first glance it may appear that patients' anxieties are directly followed by physicians' expressions of caring, the situation is in fact far more complicated. As Table 4 indicates, of 127 instances of patients' expressions of anxiety, 92 were initiated by patients' themselves, independent of any physician prompting. Of these 92, only 18 (about 20 per cent), were immediately responded to by physicians with expressions of empathy, caring, or reassurance.

Table 4. *Patient anxiety scenarios*

	Physician Speech Following Patients' Anxiety		
	Immediate emotional expression	No immediate emotional expression	Total number
Patient Speech			
Patient initiated	18	74	92
Direct response to physician inquiry	1	34	35
Total number	19	108	127

Emotions in context

Having described the broad quantitative contours of emotional expressiveness in these 39 encounters, we now explore some specific 'emotional scenarios'. In view of its significance in the movement towards a more humane medical practice, we focus on how physicians respond to patients' anxieties. Additionally, given its frequent occurrence in these encounters, we also examine patients' nervous laughter.

Physicians' responses to patients' anxieties
As Table 4 indicated, of 127 instances of patient anxiety (92 of which were initiated by patients without any physician prompting) physicians directly responded to only about 20 per cent with positive emotional expressions. The following excerpts illustrate how brief such physician responses typically are:

Excerpt 1: (African–American male patient, age 62)
P: Well, I wish I could get better. Get to feel back like I used to. (3)
D: Well, we'll work on that.

The patient then goes on to say that he has been coming for eight months, and continues talking about his employment history which has been interrupted by heart attacks. After a 23-second interruption by the nurse, the doctor asks about the heart attacks and finds that the patient has been recently followed elsewhere. The focus switches to whether or not the patient will continue at this clinic and then reverts to the standard medical history taking.

D: Just uh, do you go to the medicine clinic down there? (1)
P: No, (word) I went to the clinic, and they give me a prescription and I got my medicine up here and the drugs, take this drugs. [(words)]
D: [But you go], do you go the medicine at C ((names clinic))?
P: Yes.
D: Are, are you wanting to switch and come up here?
P: Yeah, uh huh, need be, uh huh, I (words) going down there.
D: Oh, you want – okay. I just want to make sure this is not a one-time visit . . .

Excerpt 2: (White male patient, age 28)
P: But uh, I'm just glad to know that my, it isn't any heart thing you know
D: Right.
P: I was – and – and. That really had me scared I was like well, look like I'm about to croak here for something.
D: Right-ha no – But we'll we'll keep getting so – you know a few more tests on the make sure. Ok?

Excerpt 3: (White female patient, age 51)
P: And I hope that (1) you are not gonna hold this on me about what the doc – other doctors (1) won't treat me no more because a black woman told them a bunch of lies (1) about a – I went to a uh home you know, to get me
D: Mmhum.
P: and I left that day because the woman was so mean to me. And so, the other doctors didn't want me no more. They said – they said if you all – you did all this throwed the glasses. I didn't do this other stuff – you know what they all say. And my doctor that I was using too –
D: Umhum.
P: He um, he won't even talk to me. I've called him on the phone and he won't even talk to me.
D: No, I won't hold anything against you.

Finally, we present one instance which is unusual in the length to which the physician deals with the patient's anxiety. This patient is both experiencing and reporting anxiety. After the doctor suggests that the anxiety might be a general medical state, the patient becomes more agitated. The next suggestion, that the patient might have a medical condition of anxiety rather than just apprehension at taking medicines, seems to increase the patient's agitation. At this point the doctor retreats, allowing the patient time to express her feelings (note the four second silence in the patient's speech), perhaps as a way of reducing her anxiety. She says that she can calm herself and the doctor responds to her anxiety by asking if that is how she wants to handle the problem.

Excerpt 4: (White female patient, age 61)
P: I'd like to kn – find out i'd – i'd I want to do something about this, I'm not – (1)
D: Now I understand.
P: Ha, I'm scared (2)
D: That – that's why I was asking also before if you'd ever, sounds like a lot of it is anxiety that you have.
P: ((Voice shaking)) It's anxiety because of the damn medicine (2)
D: But I think the anxiety also is on top of the medicine, not just taking the medicine.
P: Uhh. I didn't have any anxiety when I went to the doctor. ((almost crying)) And then I mean three times, somebody nearly chokes you to death, (1) what are you gonna do? (4) ((calmer)) I can bring my blood pressure down (1) by sitting down and talking to myself and making myself relax I start relaxation, my hands and my feet and I just keep on. And I can get myself calmed down, my blood pressure will go down (1).
D: Would you rather do it that way?
P: Yes.
D: Ok. We'll do that.

Nervous laughter
The issue of nervous laughter involves patients' uneasiness about two broad categories of items: 1. matters that might reflect negatively on their self-worth, social/mental competency, or moral stature; and 2. matters related to their physical conditions and ailments. The former category might best be understood in terms of Goffman's (1961) notion of stigma in which the self 'at-risk' tries to distance itself from the uncomfortable or possibly embarrassing behaviours being probed by the physician (see also Gross and Stone 1964). Such distancing is probably intensified under conditions in which considerable power and status differentials exist – such as here between low income patients and physicians. As we noted earlier, these responses by patients are most likely to occur in that phase of the en-counter where physicians seek information about personal life styles and social/medical histories. Drinking is a frequent topic here, as illustrated below:

Excerpt 5: (African–American male patient, age 35)
D: How much is the most you've ever drank? (1) Say when you were drinking your most – [how much were you] drinking?

P: [(indecipherable words)] I used to be an alcoholic. (Laughs)

Excerpt 6: (African–American male patient, age 55)
D: How, how many packs a day did you smoke?
P: Oh, about one pack. I wasn't no big smoker.
D: (word) (2)
    P: But I was a big drinker. I (indecipherable word) (laughs)
D: How much did you have?
P: (Laughing) o:oh, I was a weekend drinker. I get out then some, it
    was a bunch of guys, we used, probably drink a fifth or two of
    liquor [a bottle or two]. It was probably two-fifths of liquor on the
    weekend.

Excerpt 7: (African–American male patient, age 51)
D: You ever been arrested for drunk driving? (2)
P: Ha, yeah.

With medicine's increasing interest in, and concern about the health-
related risks of smoking, this habit creates uneasiness as well:

Excerpt 8: (White male patient, age 70)
D: Do you smoke cigarettes?
P: Yessir.
D: How much do you smoke?
P: A pack or two a week, a day.
D: Pack or two a day? I'm sure somebody's told you that's bad for
    your lungs, haven't they?
P: Have (laughing) ha ha ha.

Compliance issues also can lead to patients' uneasiness during medical
encounters:

Excerpt 9: (White female patient, age 29)
D: You been – have you been taking your medicines? – excuse me,
    lately?
P: I forgot to take it for the last two days ha.
D: The last [two days?]
P: [Ha ha ha ha.]
D: Ok.

And family relationships can occasion nervous laughter:

Excerpt 10: (African–American female patient, age 45)
D: Why, is your – daughter married?
P: Yes sir, she married. She got a baby.
D: So [that's why – why – why you don't live your your] daughter?
P: [I got – I got one grandbaby] Uh uh, no:o (laughs). I don't wanna
    live with no youngster. (Laughing) I – I have I like to be quiet.

Excerpt 11: (White female patient, age 29)
D: So you gonna – you gonna be with family for Christmas then?
P: Yeah. I guess.
D: You [guess?]
P: [Ha ha.]
D: I hope so.
P: Ha ha.

As such instances indicate, a broad array of personal habits and characteristics may find themselves under the spotlight during the medical encounter; strong testimony indeed, to the power of the medical gaze to range far, wide, and deep in its always-expandable definition of medically-relevant social/personal practices (Foucault 1973, also see Silverman 1987: 192–264).

Finally, those matters more clearly physical in nature also may occasion nervousness, especially when they involve the more 'private' dimensions of bodily functioning:

Excerpt 12: (White male patient, age 76)
D: And have you noticed whether your bowel movements float or do they sink to the bottom whenever you go to the bathroom?
P: That is, when I had them they sank. (Laughs). Lately, of course, that fluid just goes down (laughing). I mean that settles down on the bottom too.

Excerpt 13: (African–American male patient, age 40)
D; So you consider yourself pretty healthy?
P: Other than having those two (laughs) problems.

Excerpt 14: (African–American female patient, age 25)
D: Well, I'll tell you what. I'm going to try something else for the nausea, that's different, that won't let you sleepy (indecipherable word). Okay?
P: Okay. But I like being sleepy (2)
D: You do like getting sleepy?
P: Yeah, (laughs) I do.

Excerpt 15: (White female patient, age 28)
D: Why are you blind in your left eye?
P: Well you can see in if you look in there (1) cause there's scar tissue (2).
D: (word) good.
P: Mmhum. Ha ha ha ha.
D: That's impressive um
P: Can't get it to open, [ha ha ha.]
D: [You didn't] tell me about that.

Conclusions. constraints and dilemmas in medical practice: what's a doctor to do?

As we have shown, physicians' emotional expressions are positive in nature but not lengthy. Approvals, the most frequently used positive expressions, can perhaps be seen as typical to the physical examination, the most biomedically driven portion of the encounter. Through short, benign phrases such as 'Good' following patient compliance with instructions, physicians may keep the examination running smoothly.

By contrast, patients' experiences are more anxiety-laden and discomfort-ridden. In one of the few studies of anxiety-scenarios in medical encounters (Weijts *et al.* 1991), Dutch gynaecological patients expressed anxiety *covertly* rather than *overtly*. When physicians initiated discussions of patients' emotional states, however, anxiety was *always directly expressed*. In our study, by contrast, patients often actively and overtly initiated the expression of anxiety without physicians' prompts. In these encounters, physicians rarely responded directly to patients' overt expressions of anxiety and, when addressing them, responded briefly, with few attempts to elicit further elaborations from patients.

There are few instances here of negative criticism or overt displeasure by doctors, although Roter's and Hall's (1992) work suggests that this type of communication may be an effective way to reach patients. Patients may interpret such criticism as evidence doctors care enough about them to take the time to criticise possibly harmful behaviours.

Current expectations about physicians' emotional responsiveness are perhaps carry-overs from an earlier historical period in which knowledge of the patient as a person was seen as fundamental to the understanding of disease (Rothman 1991). By the early 1900s, however, as

> the physiology laboratory replaced the 'patient' laboratory . . . the patient was treated by a rational system derived from principles discovered in the laboratory. The laboratory data pointed to what was normal in the patient and what processes were deviant. The person was no longer central to the understanding of disease . . . (Borst 1993: 78–9).

During the twentieth century primary care medicine has increasingly moved from the more intimate setting of hearth and bedside to the more impersonal, bureaucratic world of clinics, large-scale hospitals, and health maintenance organisations (HMOs). An essential feature of contemporary medical practice is 'the dislocation of the case from the patient's bedside and indeed from the patient's physical presence' (Atkinson 1995: 149).

Hochschild (1983) has described a broad transformation in the nature of work during the last century, with a shift from work based on producing goods to occupations involving 'emotional work'. The latter now increasingly characterises the main features of work life in an information-based, service economy. The history of American medicine appears to be an exception here in that it now represents a *shift from* an earlier often home-based, person-centered, emotionally-laden form of practice to a technical, procedurally-driven activity; an activity in which only such procedures (not time spent talking to patients) are paid for by health-care insurers.

Medicine finds itself under critical scrutiny, however, in terms of its possible neglect of the emotional service aspects of medical care. The increasing tendency of patients to shop for the best available care, coupled with the proliferation of 'alternative health care' providers, weakens traditional medicine's totalistic claims of expertise.

Contemporary physicians face serious dilemmas in terms of responding to patients' psychosocial concerns. Their socialisation in medical school and residency, as noted earlier, sensitises them to the importance of the biomedical model and its focus on physical causation. As we have argued elsewhere (Yoels and Clair 1994), such a model also maximises physician control over the time agenda by immediately orienting discussion to issues regulated by physicians in their role as technical experts.

Concerns about time pressures may operate against opening up the encounter for a lengthy discussion of patients' psychosocial concerns. Controlling the time agenda may also allow physicians to insulate themselves from the 'emotional-labor' (Hochschild 1983, James 1993) rarely explicitly addressed, yet ever-present in medical practice. As one of their colleagues from medicine told Yoels and Clair (1994: 200): 'You can't ell a patient that they can't have any more of your emotional life. You can say, however, that "I don't have any more time".' Given the time constraints of medical practice (see also Mizrahi 1986) and the large numbers of patients typically seen by a primary care practitioner (with many being seen simultaneously as the physician darts from room to room), an assembly line notion of medical care delivery is not totally inappropriate here. The biomedical model, as noted, also reinforces physician impersonality by its focus on physical causation.

Periodically throughout their careers, however, physicians also hear messages urging them to treat the whole person, to attend to patients' emotional states and life-worlds (see especially Kleinman 1988). As our data suggest, such issues reveal their problematic nature in Phase 2 of the encounter. In their role as physicians it is certainly appropriate, and indeed necessary, to seek information on behaviours such as smoking, drinking, sexual practices, and so on, which may have important health consequences. Such probing, however, also puts physicians in the role of 'moral entrepreneurs' who are custodians and enforcers of mainstream societal moralities. Patients (especially lower-income minority patients) may experience the powerful medical gaze of high-status professionals as morally judgmental as well as therapeutically curative. Thus, the phase of the encounter devoted to these issues is the site laden with patients' anxieties and nervous laughters – intimations, perhaps, of their social dis-ease in the presence of medical 'surveillance'.

In concluding, we should say that this study represents a cautious first step towards mapping the terrain of emotional expressiveness in medical encounters. Our analysis has highlighted the importance of anxiety scenarios in primary-care medicine. We also have delineated the conditions underlying the nervous laughter so pervasive amongst patients – laughter sensitising us to the interconnections between emotionality, self-presentation, and situationally-based power/status differentials. While quantitative data based on actual discourses are a most useful starting point for studying emotions, we must be careful not to mistake the map for the territory. Qualitative, in-depth contextual treatments are essential to a more complete understanding of emotional expressivity.

Acknowledgements

This research was supported in part from grants from the University of Alabama at Birmingham Hospital Continuous Innovations in Patient Care Program (Richard Allman, M.D. and Jeffrey M. Clair, Ph.D., Co-PIs) and the AARP Andrus Gerontology Foundation (Jeffrey M. Clair, PI). We would like to thank Dave Karp and two anonymous reviewers for their comments on this paper.

Notes

1 We should acknowledge that conversational analysts typically begin with detailed micro-level treatments of a few selected transcripts, with a focus on turn-taking and lengthy sequences of interaction (see, for example, Drew and Heritage 1992: 16–19). While such an approach is valuable, we are more concerned with describing what happens throughout entire medical encounters, specifically what and where various emotions occur. We are interested in the generalisability of our findings to the larger population which these transcripts typify. We are not insensitive, however, to questions of sequencing, as our use of Sinclair and Coulthard's (19750 system affirms; moreover the contextual material we focus on – anxiety scenarios and nervous laughters – does involve particular sequences of exchange between patients and doctors.

Appendix I: Transcript conventions

D: P: Speaker, D for doctor, P for patient, other initials as needed
(( ))   Double enclosure 'descriptive', not transcribed utterances
[ ]   Bracket used to indicate overlapping speech

(0)	Silences representing 1.0 second intervals
=	No time elapses between speakers utterances
–	Used when a word or sentence is broken off in the middle
(word)	When a word is heard but remains unclear
(. . .)	Speaking sounds that are unintelligible
:	Used when a word is stretched (as in wel:l)
<u>word</u>	Underlined for marked increase in loudness or emphasis
*	Softness or decreased amplitude
(x)	Hitch or stutter
hh	Alone stands for exhalation
hh.	Followed by period denoted inhalation

Names of persons and places are indicated by number or initial. Titles reflecting patient gender are used, *e.g.* 'Ms.' 'Mr.'

Appendix II: The verbal exchange initiation system

Audiotaped medical encounters were first transcribed according to transcript notation conventions developed by Jefferson (1978) with minimal modifications. The smallest unit of silence times is one second; other pauses and hesitations are indicated by punctuation. The transcript was then divided into exchange cycles as described below.

Exchanges are identified not by grammatical category but by the function of the spoken words. Whereas *utterance* has been used to define everything said within a single speech turn, one utterance can consist of a combination of functional speech units. Using VEXIS, the basic functions of initiatory speech include the transmission of information, the direction of physical behaviour and structuring the conversation. The seven functions of exchanges include those that are *interactive*, predicting sequential moves of participants, and *structuring*. The types of interactive exchanges that comprise the bulk of interviews are: *Eliciting*, a request for information; *Informing*, the transmission of information *Directing*, a request for the listener to perform a physical behaviour in the current time frame that may be accompanied by a verbalisation; and *Prescribing*, direction for future behaviour, such as further treatment or instructions for taking medicines. *Checking* is an exchange that is sequential to informing, directing and prescribing exchanges with the purpose of verifying the compliance or understanding of the listener. *Boundary* and *Aside* exchanges structure the discourse. Boundary exchanges create and mark transitions between exchanges whereas Aside exchanges legitimate temporary withdrawal from an interaction.

Appendix III: Word search list adapted from Davitz

Italicised words were added by the authors. Word search roots are in brackets. Words that never appeared are marked with an *.
contempt [contem]

contentment [cont]
Crying [cry, tear, sob]
Delight [deli]
Depression [depres]
Determination [dete]
Disapproval [disapp]
Discomfort [uncomf]
Disgust [disg]
Dislike [dislik]
*elation [elat]
Embarrassment [embar]
Empathy – Cognitive or *Somatic* [sorry] [understand] [apolog]
Enjoyment [enjo]
Exclamations [God] [goodness] [Lord] [!]
Fear [afra, fear, frig]
Feel, mood [feel] [mood]
Friendliness [frien]
Frustration [frus]
*Gaiety [gai]
Gratitude [grat] [thank] [appreciate]
Grief [grie]
Guilt [guil]
Happiness [happ]
Hard, rough [hard rough]
Hate [hate]
Hope [hop] [wish]
Humour/Joking (contextual)
Impatience [impat]
Incompetence/(contextual)
*Inspiration
Irritation [irrit]
*Jealousy [jeal]
Joy [joy]
Laughter [laug, ha, heh, chuckl]
Like (not used as comparison) [lik]
Loneliness [lone]
Love [lov]
Nervousness, nerves [nerv]
Pain [pain] (not referring to physical symptoms)
Panic [pani, scar]
*Pity [pit]
Pleased, pleasure [pleas] [nice] [glad] [welcome]
Pride [pri] [proud]
Problem [probl] (not referring to physical symptoms)
Psychiatric, psychological [psych] [mental] [crazy]
Reassurance [reas] (also contextual)
Relief [relie] (not physical)
*Remorse [remor]

*Resentment [resent]
*Reverence [rev]
Sadness [sad] [blue]
Satisfied [satis]
Serenity [sere] [calm]
Shame [sham]
Shared laughter
Stress
Suicidal [suic] [kill] [dead] (in relation to patient)
Surprise [!] [wow]
Tension, *intense* [tens]
Terrible [terr]
Upset [ups]
Worry [worr]

References

Atkinson, P. (1984) Training for certainty, *Social Science and Medicine*, 19, 949–56.

Atkinson, P. (1995) *Medical Talk and Medical Work*. Sage: London.

Baker, P.S. (1993) *Patterns and Meanings of Silence during Medical Encounters*. Unpublished Master's thesis, University of Alabama at Birmingham.

Baker, P.S. and Clair, J.M. (1995) *Verbal Exchange Initiation System (VEXIS): Coding Guidebook*. Unpublished manuscript.

Balint, M. (1957) *The Doctor, His Patient, and the Illness*. London: Pitmans Medical Publishing Co.

Balint, M. (1971) The family doctor and patients' secrets, *Psychiatry in Medicine*, 2, 98–107.

Balint, M., Ball, D. and Hare, M. (1969) Training medical students in patient-centered medicine, *Comprehensive Psychiatry*, 10, 249–58.

Barsky, A. (1981) Hidden reasons some patients visit doctors, *Annals of Internal Medicine*, 94, 492–8.

Beisecker, A. (1990) Patient power in doctor–patient communications: what do we know? *Health Communications*, 2, 105–22.

Bertakis, K., Roter, D. and Putnam, S. (1991) The relationship of physician medical interview style to patient satisfaction, *Journal of Family Practice*, 32, 175–81.

Blackwell, E. [1902] (1972) Erroneous method of medical education. In Blackwell, E. (ed) *Essays in Medical Sociology*. New York: Arno Press.

Borst, C. (1993) From bedside to bench: the historical development of the doctor–patient relationship. In Clair, J. and Allman, R. (ed) *Sociomedical Perspectives on Patient Care*. Lexington: University Press of Kentucky.

Clair, J. (1990) Regressive intervention: the discourse of medicine during terminal encounters. *Advances in Medical Sociology Research Annual*, 1, 57–97.

Clair, J. and Allman, R. (eds) (1993) *Sociomedical Perspectives on Patient Care*. Lexington: University Press of Kentucky.

Conrad, P. (1986) The myth of cut-throats among pre-medical students: on the role of stereotypes in justifying failure and success, *Journal of Health and Social Behavior*, 27, 150–60.

Coulthard, M. (1985) *An Introduction to Discourse Analysis*. New York: Longman, Inc.

Davies, A., Ware, J., Brook, R., Peterson, J. and Newhouse, J. (1986) Consumer acceptance of prepaid and fee-for-service medical care, *Health Services Research*, 21, 429–52.

Davitz, J.R. (1969) *The Language of Emotion*. New York: Academic Press.

Devine, E. and Cook, T. (1983) A meta-analysis of effects of psycho-education intervention on length of post-surgical hospital stay, *Nursing Research*, 32, 267–74.

Drew, P. and Heritage, J. (1992) Analyzing talk at work. An introduction. In Drew, P. and Heritage, J. (eds) *Talk at Work: Interaction in Institutional Settings*. New York: Cambridge University Press.

Engel, G. (1977) The need for a new medical model: a challenge for biomedical education, *Science*, 196, 535–44.

Fineman, S. (1993) Organizations as emotional arenas. In Fineman, S. (ed), *Emotion in Organizations*. London: Sage.

Fletcher, C. (1980a) Listening and talking to patients. I. The problem, *British Medical Journal*, 281: 845–7.

Fletcher, C. (1980b) Listening and talking to patients. III. The exposition, *British Medical Journal*, 281: 994–6.

Foucault, M. (1973) *The Birth of the Clinic: An Archeology of Medical Perception*. New York: Vintage.

Fox, R. (1963) Training for 'detached concern' in medical students. In Lief, H., Lief, V. and Lief, M. (eds), *The Psychological Basis of Medical Practice*. New York: Harper and Row.

Fox, R. (1990) Training in caring competence. In Hendrie, H. and Lloyd, C. (eds), *Educating Competent and Humane Physicians*. Bloomington: Indiana University Press.

Glenn, P. (1989) Initiating shared laughter in multi-party conversations, *Western Journal of Speech Communication*, 53, 127–49.

Goffman, E. (1961) *Asylums*. New York: Doubleday.

Good, B. (1994) *Medicine, Rationality, and Experience*. Cambridge: Cambridge University Press.

Gottschalk, L.A., Winget, C.N. and Gleser, G.C. (1969) *Manual of Instructions for Using the Gottschalk-Gleser Content Analysis Scales: Anxiety, Hostility, and Social Alienation-Personal Disorganization*. Berkeley: University of California Press.

Gross, E. and Stone, G. (1964) Embarrassment and the analysis of role requirements. *American Journal of Sociology*, 70, 1–15.

Haas, J. and Shaffir, W. (1977) The professionalization of medical students, *Symbolic Interaction*, 1, 71–88.

Haas, J. and Shaffir, W. (1987) *Becoming Doctors: The Adoption of a Cloak of Competence*. Greenwich: JAI.

Hall, J., Roter, D. and Rand, C. (1981) Communication of affect between patient and physician, *Journal of Health and Social Behavior*, 22, 18–30.

Hall, J., Roter, D. and Katz, N. (1988) Meta-analysis of correlates of provider behavior in medical encounters, *Medical Care*, 25, 399–412.

Hall, J., Epstein, A., DeCiantis, M. and McNeil, B. (1993) Physicians' liking for their patients: more evidence for the role of affect in medical care, *Health Psychology*, 12, 140–6.

Heath, C. (1992) The delivery and reception of diagnosis in the general-practice consultation. In Drew, P. and Heritage, J. (eds) *Talk at Work: Interaction in Institutional Settings*. NY: Cambridge University Press.

Hendrie, H. and Lloyd, C. (eds) (1990) *Educating Competent and Humane Physicians*. Bloomington: Indiana University Press.

Hochschild, A. (1983) *The Managed Heart* Berkeley: University of California Press.

James, N. (1992) Care = organisation + physical labour + emotional labour, *Sociology of Health and Illness*, 14, 488–509.

James, N. (1993) Divisions of emotional labour: disclosure and cancer. In Fineman, S. (ed) *Emotion in Organizations*. London: Sage.

Jefferson, G. (1978) Explanation of transcript notation. In Schenkein, J. (ed) *Studies in the Organization of Conversational Interaction*. New York: Academic Press.

Kaplan, S., Greenfield, S. and Ware, J. (1989) Assessing the effect of physician–patient interaction on the outcomes of chronic disease, *Medical Care*, 27, S110–27.

Kelly, M. (1990) A suitable case for Technik: behavioural science in the postgraduate medical curriculum, *Medical Education*, 24, 271–9.

Kleinman, A. (1988) *The Illness Narratives*. New York: Basic Books.

Like, R. and Zyzanski, S. (1987) Patient satisfaction and the clinical encounter, *Social Science and Medicine*, 24, 351–7.

Lo, A., Hedley, A., Pei, G., Ong, S., Ho, L., Fielding, R., Cheng, K. and Daniel, L. (1994) Doctor-shopping in Hong Kong: implications for quality of care. *International Journal for Quality in Health Care*, 6, 371–81.

Mizrahi, T. (1986) *Getting Rid of Patients*. New Brunswick: Rutgers University Press.

More, E. and Milligan, M. (eds) (1994) *The Empathic Practitioner*. New Brunswick: Rutgers University Press.

Mosconi, P., Meyerowitz, B., Liberati, M. and Liberati, A. (1991) Disclosure of breast cancer diagnosis: patient and physician reports, *Annals of Oncology*, 2, 10–17.

Pendleton, D. and Halser, J. (1983) *Doctor–Patient Communication*. London: Academic Press.

Roter, D. and Hall, J. (1992) *Doctors Talking with Patients/Patients Talking with Doctors*. Westport: Auburn House.

Rothman, D. (1991) *Strangers at the Bedside*. New York: Basic Books.

Sacks, H. (1967) Mimeo lecture notes, quoted in Coulthard (1985).

Schegloff, E. (1993) Reflections on quantification in the study of conversation, *Research on Language and Social Interaction*, 26, 99–128.

Silverman, D. (1987) *Communication and Medical Practice: Social Relations in the Clinic*. London: Sage.

Sinclair, J. McH. and Coulthard, R.M. (1975) *Towards an Analysis of Discourse. The English Used by Teachers and Pupils*. London: Oxford University Press.

Smith, A., and Kleinman, S. (1989) Managing emotions in medical school: students' contacts with the living and the dead, *Social Psychology Quarterly*, 55, 56–69.

Spitzer, W. (1987) State of science 1986: quality of life and functional status as target variables for research, *Journal of Chronic Disease*, 40, 465–71.

Starfield, B., Wray, C., Hess, K., Gross, R., Birk, P. and D'Lugoff, B. (1981) The influence of patient–physician agreement on outcome of care, *American Journal of Public Health*, 71, 127–32.

Taylor, S. (1979) Hospital patient behavior: reactance, helplessness, or control? *Journal of Social Issues*, 35, 156–84.

Thoits, P. (1989) The sociology of emotions. In Scott, W.R. and Blake, J. (eds) *Annual Review of Sociology*. Palo Alto: Annual Reviews Inc.

Thompson, J. (1984) Communicating with patients. In Fitzpatrick, R., Hinton, J., Newman, S., Scambler, G. and Thompson, J. (eds) *The Experience of Illness*. London: Tavistock.

Waitzkin, H. (1991) *The Politics of Medical Encounters: How Patients and Doctors Deal with Social Problems*. New Haven: Yale University Press.

Weijts, W., Widdershoven, G. and Kuk, G. (1991) Anxiety-scenarios in gynecological consultations, *Patient Education and Counseling*, 18, 149–63.

Yoels, W. and Clair, J. (1994) 'Never enough time': how medical residents manage a scarce resource, *Journal of Contemporary Ethnography*, 23, 185–213.

Yoels, W. and Clair, J. (1995) Laughter in the clinic: humor as social organization, *Symbolic Interaction*, 18, 39–58.

Notes on Contributors

Patricia S. Baker is at the University of Alabama-Birmingham's Center for Aging in the United States. Her current research interests are doctor–patient communication and gerontology.

Gillian Bendelow is a lecturer in the Department of Applied Social Studies, University of Warwick, England. Her current research interests include the study of children and health, gender and pain, and the sociology of emotions.

Jeffrey M. Clair is Associate Professor of Sociology and Medicine at the University of Alabama-Birmingham, US, where he is director of the Centre for Aging, Gerontology Education Program. His current interests are medical sociology, gerontology and social psychology.

Andrew Finlay is lecturer in sociology at Trinity College, Dublin, Ireland. He trained in social anthropology. His research interests include conflicting religious and national identities in Northern Ireland, HIV-related risk behaviour, aspects of health service provision, adolescent sexual behaviour and teenage pregnancy.

Jonathan Gabe is Senior Research Fellow in the Department of Social Policy and Social Science, Royal Holloway, University of London, England. He has published in the areas of mental health, health care professions, health policy and the mass media and health. He is co-editor of the journal *Sociology of Health and Illness*.

Veronica James is Professor of Nursing Studies at the University of Nottingham, England. In addition to the sociology of emotions, her research interests include death and dying, citizenship and health pluralism, and women's views of maternity services.

Raymond Lee is Reader in Social Research Methods, Department of Social Policy and Social Science, Royal Holloway, University of London, England. His research interests encompass a number of 'sensitive' topics, including Catholic–Protestant intermarriage in Northern Ireland ánd the politics of the underground economy.

Geraldine Lee Treweek is lecturer in sociology at the University of Stirling, Scotland where she currently teaches units in the sociology of health and illness and the lifecourse. Her research interests include health and care work, complementary therapies, the body and use of qualitative methods.

Deborah Lupton is Associate Professor of Cultural Studies and Cultural Policy and Deputy Director of the Centre for Cultural Risk Research,

School of Social Sciences and Liberal Studies, Charles Sturt University, Bathurst, Australia. Her primary research interests lie in the areas of sociocultural aspects of medicine and public health, the body, sexuality, HIV/AIDS, food and eating, the emotions, the family and the mass media.

Margot Lyon is in the Department of Archaeology and Anthropology of the Faculty of Arts at the Australian National University. She works in the areas of the anthropology of emotion and critical medical anthropology.

Sally Ruane is senior lecturer in the sociology of health and heath policy at De Montfort University, Leicester, England. Her research interests include health policy, infertility treatment, baby adoption and motherhood.

Simon Williams is a Warwick Research Fellow in the Department of Sociology, University of Warwick, England. His current research interests lie in the sociology of the body, pain and emotions, children, health and risk, medical technology, and the lay evaluation of modern medicine.

William Yoels is Professor of Sociology at the University of Alabama-Birmingham, US. His research interests are the social psychology of health and illness and the sociology of rehabilitation.

Elizabeth Young is a Research Officer in the Department of Social Policy and Social Science, Royal Holloway, University of London, England. She has conducted research on the provision of integrated community health and social care services for older people, and is currently working on a project concerned with the role of friendship for women who are dying.

Index